CASTLES
BURNING

ALSO BY MAGDA DENES

In Necessity and Sorrow:
Life and Death in an Abortion Hospital

Iván and Magda, Budapest, 1938

CASTLES
BURNING

A Child's Life in War

MAGDA DENES

W.W. NORTON & COMPANY

NEW YORK/LONDON

For information about permission to reproduce selections
from this book, write to Permissions, W. W. Norton & Company, Inc.,
500 Fifth Avenue, New York, NY 10110.

The text of this book is composed in Galliard
with the display set in Fenice
Composition and manufacturing by the Maple–Vail Book Manufacturing Group.
Book design by Jam Design

Library of Congress Cataloging-in-Publication Data

Denes, Magda, 1934–
Castles burning / by Magda Denes.
p.   cm.
ISBN 13: 978-0-393-33697-9
1. Denes, Magda, 1934——Childhood and youth.   2. Psychoanalysts—
United States—Biography.   3. Women psychoanalysts—Biography.
4. Holocaust, Jewish (1939–1945)—Personal narratives.   I. Title.
BF109.D46A3   1997
150.19′5′092—dc20
[B]   96-16311
CIP

W. W. Norton & Company, Inc., 500 Fifth Avenue, New York, N.Y. 10110
http://web.wwnorton.com

W. W. Norton & Company Ltd., 10 Coptic Street, London WC1A 1PU

1 2 3 4 5 6 7 8 9 0

ACKNOWLEDGMENTS

I want to thank

. . . my mother, without whose help and care I would not have survived to tell the tale.

. . . my friends and colleagues Bertram Slaff, M.D., Julian Barish, M.D., George Naumburg, Jr., M.D., Joel Markowitz, M.D., Robert Porter, M.D., Alan Frisch, M.D., Robert Wortman, M .D., and the late Mortimer Blumenthal, M.D., of the Thursday Group of Adolescent Psychiatry of the Mount Sinai School of Medicine, who, over one long year, were the first to hear this account of my life in a sequential, coherent fashion, and whose empathy, encouragement, and enthusiasm started me writing.

. . . my son Greg Radomisli, J.D., with gratitude for his constant support.

. . . my son Tim Radomisli, M.D., for having been my listener, editor, cheerleader, and fellow weeper at the start and through the progress of this work.

. . . Stephanie Stern, one of my very first American friends, who in emergencies, typed away into the night,

. . . Alane Mason, my editor at W. W. Norton, for being the first to champion this book, and for shepherding it so lovingly.

. . . Gail Hochman, my agent, for her energy and skill, and for believing in me.

And to my brilliant editor and friend Judith Stone, whose shining talent lit my way along the path of this book, I owe profound thanks for her unfailing faith in me, her good humor, enthusiasm and patience, our Thai meals, the fights we had, and all she taught me.

CASTLES
BURNING

ONE

I BEGGED, AND OFTEN MY BROTHER OBLIGED. IN THE DARK when I couldn't sleep, Iván told me fairy tales in a whisper. All the stories began, in the traditional Hungarian manner, "Once there was / where there wasn't / there was once a Castle / that twirled on the foot of a duck." The tales were always intrinsically just. They progressed from peril to joy; they spoke of an orderly, predictable world, where the virtuous were rewarded and the wicked were punished. The prince rescued the princess. Losses were restored, and the near dead revived. Lack of caution was not a fatal error.

Over the years of these whispered fables, I realized that my brother loved to tell them as much as I loved to listen to him. I also realized, with a thorn, that as the years passed, I believed the substance of these stories less and less. And then, less yet.

In 1939, a month after my fifth birthday, my father had left Hungary and me. Iván was twelve. My mother told us that Apuci *had* to go. As the owner and publisher of a newspaper recently seized by the Nazis, as a Jew who had published anti-

Nazi articles, he was now in mortal danger. Nothing was said about the danger to the lives of little girls or their brothers, or their mothers, for that matter. Silence also prevailed regarding Jewish daddies I knew who owned anti-Nazi newspapers and stayed.

Before my father left, our household had included a maid, a butler, a cook, a chauffeur and a governess. As my father put it, we were obviously, hopelessly, outnumbered by the proletariat. We lived in one of the best sections of Budapest, Személynök Utca, in a huge apartment with a view of the Danube. My brother and I went to expensive schools. Private teachers perpetually hovered around the apartment to educate the family in various skills: boxing, fencing, piano, English. My parents' friends were writers, actors, composers, and lyricists. My father was a writer and lyricist himself, with a few successful musicals and some popular songs to his credit. The one *roman à clef* he wrote produced quite a flurry of scandal but not much else. We seemed rich, although cash was forever scarce, since my father always spent more than he earned. F. Scott Fitzgerald was expensive to emulate, particularly if one lacked his talent.

When my father left, he decided that he would need all the money he could lay his hands on. Against everybody's hysterical protests, he moved us—my mother, brother, and me—into my grandparents' two-room apartment, which also served as my grandfather's tailor shop. The Indigs, Zsigmond and Emma, lived in an area that almost qualified as a slum: Teleki Tér 5, floor 5, apartment 5, as I was to eventually memorize it in case I got lost. They were painfully poor. They had no friends. For entertainment they gossiped with the neighbors.

My father sold everything we owned. This enabled him to

pay some but not all of his debts, to secure first-class passage for himself to America, to be outfitted with a wardrobe of forty-five shirts and twelve suits, as befitted his station, and to have enough left over for the necessary bribes to Hungarian officials. We heard later that he also kept a little something extra with which to hit the night spots of Paris while traveling through. This was, after all, his first visit.

Meanwhile, the three of us settled into my grandparents' bedroom. The other room remained occupied by income-producing, and therefore revered, Aunt Rózsi, my mother's younger sister, who had been living with them since her divorce. Rózsi worked as office manager and factotum for a small glass and mirror factory. Her son, my cousin Ervin, was staying with his father in another town.

My mother and I slept next to my grandparents in their adjacent twin beds, I on the crack between mattresses. For my brother we bought a used bed that displaced my grandfather's sewing machine which had to be moved in front of the windows that faced the courtyard corridor. My grandfather claimed that passersby, of whom there must have been three or four a day, distracted him in his work. Still, he behaved as he usually did—with absolute courtesy, from a great distance. Fortunately, his worktable remained in the kitchen where it always had been, a well-constructed beautiful hardwood table of excellent versatility. At mealtimes, it served as the adults' dining table. At night, the servant girl slept on it.

My grandmother was not welcoming; neither was Queen Rózsi. "No matter," my mother would say. "Your father will come through. He will rescue us. He will reinstate our former lives in a better country, in greater splendor. It's just a question of time."

During the wait, to improve our circumstances, my mother sold her few remaining pieces of jewelry and learned to weave raffia. In the absence of clamoring customers, the apartment overflowed with her coasters, placemats, and tea cozies. Next, she took lessons in Esperanto. Her intention was to teach others—for money—this essential, potentially triumphant language of the future. Esperanto, at least, left no debris.

It was, however, followed by mother's homemade perfume. This was the only period in months when food seemed plentiful: No one could eat because of the nauseating stench that pervaded the place. My brother said the neighbors would soon be asking about the corpse we were hiding.

I was my brother's assistant in a variety of vital matters, such as shining his shoes. I did the buffing. When he plaited the leather strap that hung his Boy Scout knife to his belt, my finger pressed the pivotal spot that allowed him to braid. I folded his pocket handkerchiefs to a three-point. He taught me to tie a tie around my own neck, so I could do it around his when he was in a rush to meet other girls. We were comrades-in-arms in our new, deprived, and unfriendly world, a conspiracy of two in the face of outrageous fortune.

From downstairs he could summon me anytime to the corridor of the courtyard by whistling the first four notes of Beethoven's Fifth, our secret code.

Hearing it, I would run, stick my head over the railing and yell, "What is it?"

"Ask Anyu if—"

"No, come up."

"Come on, I can't. Be a good girl. Ask her."

"Please come up. I could go with you then."

"Not today. Hurry up."

Sometimes I rebelled, but mostly I did as I was told. I quizzed my brother on the poems he had to memorize for school. As soon as he knew them he told me that I should now know them equally well. Ha-ha, I did. I graduated to become the first critic of his wondrous poetry. At sixteen, he was published in a major literary journal. (Six months later, presenting another poem to the same editor, he was told, "Come back when times have changed and your race is no longer a handicap. You are a fine young poet.") I was a tough critic. He liked it that way. He told me I was the smartest, shortest person anybody ever had for a junior editor. He picked me up and tossed me about in the air. When he put me down hard, I got hurt. I also got mad and kicked him in the shin. We set upon each other. He was at a disadvantage, acknowledged by both of us: He was bigger, and he was a gentleman.

Occasionally it worked a bit otherwise—he would get really angry over something and twist my arm. I'd clench my teeth. "Cry uncle," he would order me, worried.

"Never!"

"Cry uncle! This is ridiculous. I'll break your arm if we continue. Cry uncle."

"Break my arm."

He would let go. Moral victory, however, was not my most preferred triumph. I'd wait a few hours until the incident left his mind. Then I would whisper, "Lean down, Ivan, I want to tell you a secret." He was twice my size. When we were face to face, I would haul off and deliver a slap worth two arms.

Later he would complain to our mother, who said exactly what I had counted on: "Ivan, are you joking? You are twice her size. Just don't touch her anymore."

My brother was the best part of my life.

Most of the time in the winter, the family would huddle in the kitchen, because it was the only warm room. It had a large coal stove kept afire for purposes of cooking and comfort. Next to it lay the room where we slept, and beyond that was the bathroom. Electricity was expensive; we used lights on a strictly utilitarian basis, very unlike the habits of my real home. At first I was terrified of the dark. Iván was assigned the task of crossing the dark room with me whenever I had to go to the bathroom. He resented it greatly, until we both discovered that the bathroom was our only private realm, the one place where we could exchange secrets. Thereafter, whenever I needed to talk to him, I announced that I had to make peepee. When Iván had something important to say to me, he jerked his head toward the bathroom and signaled me with his eyes. "I have to go to the bathroom," I would declare. Once inside, I sat on top of the closed toilet and rolled myself a pretend cigarette from the hard toilet paper. "Begin!" I'd say.

The first time I did it, Iván said, "You know, you're the smartest kid I know, but you're also very crazy."

"I know," I said, shrugging. "It helps me to think."

"What does? Puffing on a piece of paper? Pretending you're like Rózsi?" I cut this argument short. "Do you have something to tell me?"

"Yes," my brother said with a sigh. "Yes."

I knew, but did not want to know, that I was a last resort. Pitifully for my brother, I was also the first and only resort. I was everything because I was more trustworthy than God, and more silent than any grave. He told me things I had to mediate, and more things I had to forget. If, early in the week, he profligately spent all his meager pocket money, and borrowed mine, then spent that to buy flowers for a girl, I was the one who dropped a hippo-sized hint to our mother about his renewed need for funds. When he was seen at the museum while cutting classes, I kept mum and helped him develop an alibi, in case. I was prepared to do anything for him, sitting on the closed toilet, puffing on my pretend cigarettes, one room removed from the darkness of our lives.

In the summer of 1940, my cousin Ervin came to live with us from Miskolc, a town about 180 kilometers from Budapest. Both my mother and my Aunt Rózsi were born and raised in Miskolc, but Iván and I had never been there. We shared the prejudice of big-city dwellers against smaller towns. Budapest was the Paris of Eastern Europe. What was Miskolc?

Ervin was a dark-eyed, dark-haired, very handsome ten-year-old, of enormous goodwill and crackling vitality. Having been shuffled between divorced parents, at that time a most exceptional life, his primary aim was to please. I thought in this regard he did himself a great disservice.

He wore short pants, in contrast to my brother's knickers; he used short words, in contrast to my brother's multisyllabic speech; he played the violin, which he had with him, in contrast to my brother, who played the piano, which was long gone. Not negligibly, he offered himself as my acolyte, in contrast to my brother, who thought of me, with my full consent, as his.

Because he was not as well read or as educated as my brother, neither of us paid much attention to him at first. The violin helped. I loved to listen to him, and I thought that everything he played was beautiful and sad. "He only closes his eyes to impress you," my brother said, in an attack of peevishness. Dummy. In my open eyes, wanting to impress me was not exactly a black mark on a person's report card.

That summer, Budapest was very hot and very dangerous.

Periodically, the Nazis randomly rounded up groups of citizens. Jews who were caught in the net were arrested and taken away to destinations unknown. Sometimes a letter would come from some forced-labor camp in the provinces. We were confined by parental orders to the apartment.

We played, we quarreled, we dawdled. The boys read. That was a problem. Each morning at eight they would race a block to the lending library, whose policy was half price for books returned by nightfall. The boys raced back home, and they raced through their books. They became uninterruptible. I was due to enter first grade in September. I did not know how to read. I kept pestering them: get me a book, too. Read me a book, read me a book. From time to time they agreed, but still I became desperate and lonely.

One morning Ervin got mad. "Why do you keep nagging? How can you not know how to read?" It had never occurred to me that I didn't have to wait to enter first grade to learn.

"Can you teach me?"

"Do you know the alphabet?"

"Yes, of course."

"Why didn't you say so before? That means you can read."

"Ervin, I cannot read."

"Yes you can; you just don't know it yet. I will show you how."

Hungarian is an entirely phonetic language. If one can sound the letters, one can form the words. One can read. By nightfall, I was fluent. Ervin had changed my life. For the rest of the summer, I, too, was not to be disturbed. I, too, was elsewhere, with almost daily changing families, events, locales, circumstances. I read *Gulliver's Travels, Johnny in America,* and the books of the pseudonymous P. Howard, who never stepped away from his table at the Jappán Coffeehouse in Budapest, but who wrote about the invisible foreign legion, blonde tornadoes, slave traders, lost ocean liners, and other Ferris-wheely, fireworkish, fabulous things.

Writing was a different matter. I learned it in school that fall, laboriously and with reverence. I found the capital letter *A* manageable, but the lowercase *a* eluded my skills. After drawing the circle, I seemed to fall prey to an impish form of gravity that pulled the stem downward, well below the limiting lines of my notebook.

My mother, seeing the difficulty I was having, decided to practice with me. She showed me how to do it. I could not. She showed me again. I failed. Thereafter, in exuberant Pavlovian spirit, she slapped my hand each time I slipped. I slipped, she slapped. She slapped, I slipped. Once, when I glanced behind me, I saw both boys sitting with their hands plastered to their ears. It never occurred to me to protest. With the infinite acceptance and goodwill of little children, I assumed this was the best way to learn. When my hand turned the color of poppies, we quit.

In the interest of fairness, I want to note here two things. One, I did learn how to write. Two, I was the only little girl I knew who never, ever had reason to weep because her mother pulled her hair while combing it, or braided her pigtails too tight.

With seven of us crowded into the tiny apartment, we were constantly flaring up, bickering, fighting. The household mood was nearly always gunpowdery. Divisional lines of loyalty developed—on the horizontal axis, separating children and adults; vertically, separating the three families, although often Rózsi and Ervin joined my grandparents as one family against ours. Whenever that happened, my cousin apologized in secret to Iván and me, even though all three of us knew it was "their" doing, not his.

Once, after a fight with Rózsi, Ervin, the lonesome, incautious fool, told our mother, "I wish I were *your* son." My mother's competitive heart instantly melted. In secret she confided this staggering confession to Iván, swearing him to silence. Then, separately, she confided it to me, making me also swear not to tell. When Iván and I shared the gossip in the bathroom, he said, "Poor Ervin. He means he wants to be our brother. Let's let him."

"Fine with me," I said, grinning. Iván gave me a fake rabbit punch in the arm. "Time to go," he said.

"Iván, I know a riddle. You're the world's biggest balloon. Do you want to know why?"

"No. Definitely not. It will be one of your dumb jokes, and then you'll laugh hysterically by yourself. Come on, let's go." He extended his right arm, with which he could hoist me and swing me onto his back if I, too, executed the correct maneuver according to the Boy Scout rules he had taught me. "We'll play horsey," he said, neighing as he ran toward the kitchen at a gallop, traversing at top speed the intervening dark room. His neck was right in front of my mouth, so I kissed it for the duration of the ride.

Research topics came up among the three of us. If you want something very, very much, is it better to believe that you will get it, or better to bet that you won't? My brother thought it was better to bet that you won't. That way you avoid disappointment and could be pleasantly surprised. I disagreed. I thought a state of "maybe" was more exciting. "And anyway," I said, "If you don't get what you want, you'll be sad no matter what you pretend."

In a gathering, if you absolutely had to pass gas (it was inconceivable to mention the word "fart"), would you rather do it noisily without a smell, or silently with a stink? I opted for the latter, trusting myself to shift attention elsewhere. My brother chose the former. "You could always apologize," he said, "and not offend anyone."

"You'll never make it in this world," I said.

If you could kill Grandma, would you do it with a hammer or a bullet? Me: Hammer. Ivan: Bullet. Ervin abstained.

"The old hen," a daring children's insult in Hungary in those days, was what the three of us secretly called our grandmother. She was a practiced soul-skinner, the queen torquer of Torquemada.

"Look at Ági," my grandmother might say, referring to my friend across the hall, two years younger and not very bright. "Look at the intellect and kindness that shine off her face. One just knows she will grow up to be brilliant."

"Grandma, Ági is stupid. Everyone knows it."

"Says who? The Mr. Publisher's daughter? The one who eats if I feed her and who otherwise would starve? Where is Mr. Publisher? Where is the money I am owed for what you eat?"

"Grandma, we started with Ági."

"What about Ági? Ági is a wonderful girl. We are talking about you. Tell me, what do you think you are worth? Tell me exactly, what qualifies you to be a worthwhile human being?"

"I don't know, Grandma."

"Ha. Ha! There you have it. Neither do I. But you do eat. You do put food in your mouth. Who do you think pays for that? The absent Mr. Publisher? When was the last time that an envelope came from your father, with his love and money from Amerika, from glorious, wonderful, exalted Amerika? Well, when was it?"

"I don't know."

"The bastard quit when the going got rough. And you look just like him."

Iván came home from school in time to hear the last exchange. "How can she look just like him? She's a kid and a girl, and besides, she's not responsible."

Oh, God, I thought. He should never come to my rescue. I can take care of myself. I'm a kid and a girl and I can sink slowly under the table unharmed. But he was ornery.

He stood there, drawn to full height. "Well?"

Grandmother's voice was sarcastic and sharp, her face contorted with rage. " 'Well?' Did you say 'well' to me? How dare you say 'well' to me, mister? No more chauffeur, mister. No more German governess. No more airs, rich boy. No more fancy butler. I am the butler. Look at the butler." She performed a maniacal imitation of a bowing butler serving food.

My brother would not stop. "You're being ridiculous," he said. "The point is, I'm warning you. Don't pick on my sister."

I thought my grandmother would explode. Her face got red and she started gesticulating in front of his nose. "You are warning me? You? Who are you to warn me? You beggar, you pauper, you bum?"

I came out from under the table and stepped between them. Turning to my brother, I said, "I like her picking on me. I love it. I want her to pick on me. Go for a walk, you fool." Grandmother grinned.

Iván glared at me. "You have no character," he said.

"I know it, but I have savings. A full pengö, in one piece." I took the coin out of my pocket. "At fifteen percent a week you can have it for about a month," I said. My brother's face slowly relaxed and expanded into a secret smile. His slightest smile could quiet my heart, transmute a room and make it glow.

"You have no character," he said, as he took the money. "No character. Zero."

"Oh well." I loved the sound of that slammed door.

MY GRANDFATHER LET his anger at his wife show by the way he ate his portion of raspberries. Let us say that these raspberries, sprinkled with sugar, doled into a bowl by my grandmother, whom he did not love, were served to him at the twilight of an almost summer Sunday, after a fight between them, during which he had remained silent.

Picture him, sitting at his sewing machine. He would ignore the bowl and stitch a little further on the sleeve of a coat he was sewing before he turned, three-quarters profile, under the green glare of the gambler's lamp he used to illuminate his blinding work. With his right hand, he would push the fixture slightly upward—the pulley made a noise like mice squeaking—causing the lamp to spread a wider angle of light.

Then, with a teaspoon, he would put a small portion of berries into his mouth, thereby bestowing upon them an existence of their own. He sucked, swirled, smacked, reswirled, chewed, and swallowed with the flair and control of an acrobat. Oh, those berries. What magnificence they acquired in my grandfather's mouth. What marvelous answers they became to all sorts of hunger, to frustration, to rage. How I wished I could learn his art, how I wished I could send my messages to the world through berries. I merely ate berries. He was transfigured through them.

Putting his spoon down, wiping his mustache, and turning

his head another quarter, he would, without raising his eyes, say toward my grandmother, "Not enough sugar."

NEARLY THREE YEARS had passed since my father's escape, and my mother was at the end of everything—ideas, hope, pawnable objects, her tether. Even at the end of the expensive antique lace pillowcases she had been selling one by one at the Sunday flea market. Something had to happen if we were to go on living.

Rózsi suggested my mother get a job. This was problematic. My mother qualified for nothing, other than to construct crossword puzzles, which she had done every week for my father's newspaper. Also, there were new laws limiting the employment of Jews. Nevertheless, Rózsi maneuvered a job for her in the glass and mirror factory, owned by the Fischer brothers. Thus the former mistress of five servants, the Mrs. Publisher Lady who in the past would occasionally favor the Fischers with house seats for her husband's musicals, the elegant Madame Margit Dénes who in rare encounters with these brother-owners had been greeted by deep bows and heartfelt I-kiss-your-hands—naturally without the temerity of matching action to words—now became their government-permit petitioner and general fixer. Her many duties included sometimes sweeping the office and occasionally helping people put on their coats.

In the evenings, at home, she would reenact, to our general hilarity, the day's servility, curtsy included.

At the time, I had no idea that this was painful for her. She presented the situation as funny, and I believed her. Mommy the Servant. Ha-ha.

In time the pantomime and laughter stopped. She worked

from dawn to late evening during the week, and I hardly saw her. On weekends she mostly slept. She became irritable, withdrawn, alienated. I missed her.

When I was nearly eight years old, my best friend, after my brother and Ervin, was my grandparents' servant girl, Kati. She was twenty, a poor farm girl from the northern part of Hungary who had come to the big city to flee starvation and find her fortune. What she found, as did the other unschooled, untrained peasant girls like her, was sixteen hours a day of hard work, a place to sleep in the kitchen, three small meals, a lot of abuse, and a little money. Kati, unlike the others, did not even look for a husband on Sundays. Being a Seventh-Day Adventist, she preferred her free day to be Saturday, and she spent it at home.

She loved me and I loved her. Like my brother, she wrote poetry, although not of his high literary standard. To this day I can recite one of her quatrains about the war, never printed, never even written, I think, spoken to me:

Mikor lesz vége
Mikor lesz béke
Mikor lesz elég a vér
Lesz e ki visszatér

"When will it end? When will there be peace? When will the bloodshed be enough? Will anyone return?"

She taught me many things on Saturday afternoons, when she was off by virtue of her religion, and I was alone by virtue of mine. Unlike my parents, who had observed no rituals or holidays, my grandparents were religious. My grandmother kept a kosher house and lit Friday-night candles, and on Saturday, everyone dressed in his best clothes—I, too, even though I just stayed home with Kati. My grandparents went to temple, although my grandfather sometimes sneaked away to visit friends. The rest of the family were off, too, in all directions. My mother and Rózsi were at the Jappán meeting their friends. The boys went to the flea-ridden moviehouse around the corner, which we referred to as "the Little Dirty," where they watched old romance and adventure movies.

Kati taught me three of her many duties. One, to make a coal fire; two, to make tea; three, to scramble eggs. For glory, she taught me to tell time. This has proved to be an invaluable asset over the years.

We hugged a lot, and kissed, and ate pilfered jam with the same spoon. She had a bad cough. No one thought anything of it. When the sputum turned bloody, I tried to help her hide the evidence. We were caught; she was dismissed. Then and there, in the kitchen.

A short while later, I developed a cold. It seemed to linger. My mother noticed that both my shins had big red blotches on them. I suggested that perhaps I kept hitting them climbing in and out of bed. The cold continued. My mother decided that despite the expense, I really should be taken to our old family pediatrician, Dr. Lukács.

When my mother and I arrived on Podmanicky Utca, it was a cold late-October dusk. I did not feel well, and I still had a slight fever, so that each little gust of wind made me shiver and yearn for my old home, where at this time of year and at this hour of the day, every room had an open fire and all the chandeliers were extravagantly lit.

On the corner near the tram stop stood a chestnut vendor. Against my better judgment, I asked my mother if we could buy some. She looked very sad when she said, "No. We cannot afford it." Had my brother been there, I could have explained to him that what I really wanted was not the chestnuts but the flickering light cast on them by the vendor's burning coals. As it was, I just said, "That's all right. Really, Anyu, it is all right."

Dr. Lukács saw me, took a chest X-ray, tickled me as usual, and talked to my mother in private. When we came downstairs, it was dark, and she offered to buy me chestnuts. I knew I was done for.

In less than a week, I found myself in a sanatorium, flat on my back with infectious tuberculosis. I was almost eight. At first, in my confusion, I thought that my family would move in with me at the Szani, as it was nicknamed. When my mother left after settling me in, it became evident that I had been imprisoned and abandoned.

The Szani, a former resort, was a familiar, well-hated place to me. My parents, Iván, and the governess, called Fräulein, Fräuli for short, had started summering there before I was born. Iván always liked it, but all my memories were bad. By the time I was around, my father would often phone from the city to say he would be late. Many nights he just didn't show. My mother cried, Fräuli was irritable, and I vomited. Without comparative experiences I could not be absolutely sure, but I strongly suspected that this was not what people meant when they said, "We are having a fabulous summer."

My father spent a great deal of money at the Szani. We had rooms for five, all meals, and occasionally dinner for twenty when my father capriciously did arrive and brought with him a flock of friends. Iván and I had every available optional instruction, which cost additional fees. And the Mr. Publisher Dénes was an all-around big tipper.

I imagine the owners, the very decent Mr. and Mrs. Rabow-sky—professionally, she was Dr. Révész—must have felt sorry for my mother long before she arrived one fall morning in 1942, hat in hand, looking pale and poor. Of course they remembered her and the Mr. Publisher.

"In Amerika? Really? How interesting! Magduska is dying of tuberculosis? That is tragic. We must not permit it."

They agreed at once to a drastically reduced fee. There was just one thing. As they remembered, Magduska had lots of opinions and was not reticent about expressing them. It would be better if the Jewish question did not come up. My mother assured them in all sincerity that the intervening years had had a highly positive effect on my sense of discretion.

My mother visited as often as she could, my brother once a week, Ervin never. Rózsi didn't allow it because she feared that he would be infected.

Medical opinion in those years maintained that body fat acted as an antidote to tuberculosis. Consequently my mother, by extraordinary efforts and sacrifice, obtained additional black-market food for me, which she brought each week to the sanatorium and handed over to Nurse Dóra. Through threats, humiliation, and disciplinary measures, I was force-fed eggs, butter, and bacon like a goose being prepared for slaughter. Dóra néni would yell at me in front of the other kids—about my starving family, their abject poverty and sacrifice, my ingratitude. I was not allowed to leave the table until I had finished everything served me, which was about twice as much as I could possibly eat. When I said I would throw up, Dóra néni assured me that was all right, I'd just have to eat my vomit. Looking at her face, I believed her.

For a while, I would spend the entire afternoon trying to finish lunch. Then I hit on a partial solution. I carried paper bags in my pocket. Left alone in the dining room, I would scoop the food into a bag and return it to my pocket. It was a delicate maneuver, because I had to work very fast. Once my plate was empty, I was dismissed from the table and allowed to return to my room. I would promptly throw the bag on top of my armoire. It was winter and the building wasn't too well heated, so I got away with the stunt for about three months. After that, the stink of the rotting food seeped into the corridor, and I was caught.

At dinner, where only the adults were allowed to speak to each other, Dóra néni explained what I had done and announced to the entire community that I was a confirmed, incorrigible juvenile delinquent. She added that given my pauper background, this did not come as a surprise to her; further, that she knew for a fact that people who were defiant as children often ended up in jail, or even on the gallows. During her little speech I sat erect and motionless as a broomstick. I stared into middle distance and I wished her dead with such intensity that I still don't understand why it didn't work. As it turned out, her disciplinary act of revenge totally backfired. As we filed out of the dining room in silence, kids who had until now ignored me sent me conspiratorial winks and gave me little secret pats on the back. Dóra néni had definitely put me on the map.

I had a treatment that seemed uncanny to me, a sort of exorcism in reverse. Once a week, for the first three months of my stay, at a nonvisiting hour when I was unaware of her presence, my mother came to the Szani and Dr. Révész took blood from her veins. It was stored, and on Tuesdays and Thursdays at four o'clock Dr. Révész administered it into my buttock with a needle that seemed a foot long.

At first I carried on. I vomited, I screamed, I fought, I called for my mother. Then they had me. Like any obedient victim, I entered the infirmary punctually, hiked up my skirt, pulled down my underpants, lay facedown on the examining table, and waited for the pain. I also swore, deeply swore, that once full-grown, I would either kill or be killed in any situation that involved physical suffering under circumstances of coercion.

My mother gave me a bottle of Tokaji Aszu, a thick, sweet wine that I kept on the windowsill above my night table. I was supposed to take a shot-glassful before meals. Then I got some advice from my fifteen-year-old friend Vera, whose father was also a newspaperman who had left for Amerika, along with her mother. Vera had been placed in the Szani by her grandmother because of—and this I had to triple-swear to keep secret—her repeated suicide attempts.

Vera told me that it was by far a better thing to take two shot glasses of elixir, and between meals instead of before. This way, I would see the world, between lunch and dinner, through a glass, less darkly. Occasionally my mother would say, "What? Is the bottle gone already?" I would shrug. "It stands on the windowsill. How should I know what happens to it?"

The only other treatment was lying still on a terrace, watching the sky and the mountains or reading, cocooned in blankets. How to make a cocoon: Take a blanket, put it on a cot, pull it high enough so you can cover a person's head. Lay a second blanket over the first from the midpoint downward. Put a pillow down, and make the person lie on top of the two blankets. Create a hood by bringing the first blanket up to midcrown and tucking the sides under the patient's chin. Pull the right edges of the blankets to the left, and the left edges to the right, fold the bottom up, and so envelop the patient papoose-style. I could stick my hands out of the opening at the top of the cocoon and hold a book. On cold days, we got an extra blanket.

All of us with TB lay on the terrace from morning until lunch. Dóra néni or one of her emissaries fetched us. We disentangled ourselves from the cocoon, went to the dining room, ate, and came back again to lie there until dusk.

Horizontally, the day was divided by activity, meager as it was. Morning: eat breakfast, lie down; afternoon: eat lunch, lie down; evening: eat dinner, retire. It was an orderly, clock-ruled existence.

But the day also had a vertical dimension determined by passing segments of light. As in a silent, grainy movie, the sun and clouds against the mountains made the day die in slow, declining increments of gathering darkness. I hated the process; it frightened me and made me feel very lonely. It was such an inescapable elemental down, down, down, and then again the same thing the next day. Repetition in a nightmare is not reassuring. The fact that each day dies with sleep is not a consoling thought to a sick child.

So I read, and peeked at the disappearing light from behind my book. After about five months, only two of us were still sick enough to remain on the terrace all day. I in my right-hand corner, which Iván finagled for me because I desperately wanted that privacy, and a lady in the far left-hand corner. Once, at twilight, I heard her weep. I pretended not to hear, and silently wept with her. Suddenly she asked, "How old are you?"

What deplorable manners, I thought. We have not even been introduced. At least she should ask my name first, and tell me hers. "Eight," I said.

"I have a little daughter; she is ten. We live in Veszprém. I have not seen her for a year because I am so sick. I miss her. Your mother must miss you and be terribly worried about you."

Lady, you are crazy, a crazy lady. I am not sick. No one misses me, and I miss no one. I am here to familiarize myself with the role of Marguerite in *La Dame aux Camélias*. It will be a very high-paying job when my father comes back and revives it as a Hungarian musical. "I guess," I said, trying to be monosyllabic, so she wouldn't know I was crying. I remembered *my* manners and pulled myself together. "I'm sorry about your little girl," I said.

She started to sob. "Oh my dear little heart," she began, but for once, Dóra néni served a positive purpose. She arrived to announce our release and dinner.

Two days later, I received an anonymous box of chocolates. I waved an indefinite thank you in her direction. The lady never spoke to me again. I understood.

When I got better and no longer had to spend all my time on the terrace, I was made to join Arts and Crafts. There I fashioned the same dreary clay ashtrays week after week. For the drawing assignment, I sketched over and over the same landscape—snow falling on a snow-covered mountain, on top of which stood a single pine tree with white downcast branches.

Because these activities were so unvaried, I was repeatedly sent to the resident psychologist, Dr. Stefi, who informed me in a stern voice that I was:

1. Uncooperative
2. Unreasonable
3. A complete disappointment

She also implied that there was something wrong with me for drawing the same pine tree over and over. I consoled myself by reciting inwardly, to block out her voice, a poem I knew by heart, "The Lonesome Trees" by Heinrich Heine.

> A pine tree stands alone on
> A bare, bleak northern height;
> The ice and snow they swathe it,
> It sleeps there all in white.
> 'Tis dreaming of a palm tree,
> In a far-off Eastern land,
> That mourns alone and silent,
> On a ledge of burning sand.

I knew Heine was a Jew. I guessed he, too, probably missed his brother. Knowing the poem kept me from feeling weird despite whatever Dr. Stefi thought I was. Literature never fails its friends.

Dr. Stefi néni gave up on me long before I was released. At our final meeting, she made a last attempt to set me straight.

"I though you were a bright girl."

I said nothing.

"You seemed very creative when you first arrived. Isn't your father a writer?"

I said nothing.

"I guess I overestimated you."

"Yes, Dr. Stefi néni," I said. I thought of saluting, but I refrained.

I left the Szani within the year, completely recovered. My grandparents' crowded apartment now seemed like paradise regained.

The afternoon I got home from the Szani, Ervin handed me a furtive sheet of folded paper. On it in his elegant script he had written, "I am glad you are home. I missed you. I love you. Eat this note. I cannot face the consequences." He was right. In our crowded quarters, there was no way to keep anything private. Eating it, though, seemed too drastic. Instead, I asked Iván to take me to the bathroom, where I tossed the note, quick as a bug in retreat, into the toilet. "What was that?" Iván asked suspiciously.

"Just some thoughts I wrote down in the Szani. I didn't want them to be read. Worthless stuff."

"Too bad," Iván said. Then, switching languages, "A shame."

"What?"

" 'Too bad' in English."

"How did you say it?"

" 'A shame.' "

"Acham?"

"Not exactly. I so hope we can send you to the English Ladies' Gimnázium when the time comes, as Anyu planned in better days."

"When would that be? When Apuci returns from Amerika with a full complement of hangers-on in tow?"

Iván shrugged. This was not a topic we could discuss. He claimed he loved our father. I did not.

A miracle rabbi from Belz, Poland, came to Budapest, and all the faithful wanted to go ask for his blessing and his intercession with God for their safety. My brother was a total atheist, but he said he, too, would go and ask him to pray for all of us. He wanted to ensure that I remained fully recovered from TB, that we all survived, and that we be reunited with

my father. He waited in line at the synagogue all night. Just
before his turn, they closed the gates. The rabbi, a small, frail,
very tired man, looking out through a doorway, said, "No, I'll
see one more—that blond boy." Later, my brother told us that
he'd asked the rabbi to pray for everything. "Did you ask to
be reunited with your father?" my mother said. Iván went pale.
"No," he said, "I forgot."

MY BROTHER AND I were getting used to our reduced circumstances. Used to being shabbily dressed and painfully poor,
used to always being a little not-full, although not quite hungry. Used to being fatherless.

In fact, the latter had its advantages. I would think back to
a time when I was full, and had a father, and recall that it
hadn't been so satisfying.

My father once took me to Gerbaud's, the most fashionable
place in Budapest to sit outside in the summer and drink iced
chocolate. The staff rushed out to greet us.

"Mr. Publisher, please, which table, which corner, where
will you be happy?" My father tossed an arrogant tip to János,
the maître d', another to Mihály, the waiter. They bowed low.

"Bring a chocolate drink, a chocolate ice cream, and a chocolate cake for the young lady, my daughter, and a triple dark
rum for me."

"Immediately, yes sir, Mr. Publisher."

I was alarmed. "Apuci, I don't want all that. It is too much.
I am forbidden to have so much chocolate."

"You are forbidden nothing when you are with me. You are
Daddy's little bride. We do whatever you want. Taste each
thing, then leave the rest." He winked.

The rum arrived before my order, and he slugged it back.

He ordered another. I wished I were on the moon. I had seen this happen before, but never when there were just the two of us. I put my arms on the table and involuntarily flinched. It was marble, and very cold.

"What is it?" my father asked.

"The marble. It is cold, isn't it?"

My father began snapping his fingers with the staccato noise of castañets.

"A tablecloth for my daughter!" he yelled. "A tablecloth! Her arms are cold."

"Apuci," I whispered, "I am not cold, I want to go home."

"You just said you were cold," he yelled. "What are you, an idiot?"

By now the place was filled with other people, some of them my classmates and their parents or governesses. My overblown, embarrassing order had also arrived. The sight of it made me nauseated. "Apuci, I'm about to throw up," I said, and he knew it was not an idle threat. For some time now, whenever there was a scene in my family, I vomited. They had consulted a number of doctors about me. None had helped. The best of them, the one who was not afraid of my father, had said, as I was told much later, "Tell her to move out. Short of that, feed her bananas."

Finally we left. Gyuri, the chauffeur, pulled up in the car. He helped my father into the backseat, and, tipping his cap, said, "Begging your pardon, Mr. Publisher, but the little miss does not look so well." Everyone in the household knew that I tended to vomit. "With your permission, sir, could she sit up front?"

My father emitted a guttural grunt which both Gyuri and I decided to interpret as a yes.

Once, Gyuri disappeared for two months. In fact, he

absconded with some money. The day he returned, contrite and ready for punishment, my father slapped him hard on both cheeks. Then, without the slightest detectable anger, he asked, "What happened, Gyuri?"

"Well, Mr. Publisher," Gyuri said, the mark of my father's five fingers getting redder and more vivid on his cheeks, "it was not my fault. It was the Mr. Reporter Kelemen's fault. He came here that day in those beautiful yellow leather shoes. I coveted them. When you gave me the money to pay the printers, it was about the same sum as the shoes cost. I have a weak character, Mr. Publisher. I could not resist. I bought them. You can see how it was Mr. Reporter Kelemen's fault, can't you, sir?"

"I certainly can, Gyuri," my father said, laughing, and clipped him again so hard that Gyuri fell. "You are rehired. Get the car keys, wash the car, and be back by five."

"Mr. Publisher, I kiss your generous hands," said Gyuri from the floor.

I felt mostly bad for Gyuri, but I also thought that he deserved what he got. Not for the yellow shoes, but because a few years before, he had betrayed Iván. At that time Iván had entered the first year of *gimnázium* at the Reich Deutsches Schule, the elite German school of the city. Unbeknownst to my poor brother, the custom at that school was for all the boys at each grade level to fist-fight after classes in the schoolyard until only one stood, the grade's champion for the day. The first day, on seeing this, my then bespectacled, literate, bony brother ran into the arms of Gyuri, who was waiting to drive him home. "You must fight," Gyuri said, giving him a little push. "I bet a lot of money on you." All the chauffeurs bet among themselves on their kid.

"I have nothing to fight about," Iván said, getting into the backseat of the car. "Take me home, Gyuri," he added, imitating my father's imperious tone.

Gyuri got mad. He ratted on Iván. "So what we have here is a pacifist, eh?" our father asked, in a threateningly drawn-out, syllabicated manner. "Defend yourself, coward."

He punched Iván on his right eye. "Apuci," Iván began in teary protest. He caught one on the left eye. Before he could recover, he caught one on the chin. He was half the height and less than a third of the weight of our father. He started to cry. He was ten years old.

"I'll stop for now," our father said. "But if I ever hear again that Gyuri lost money on you, I will use the buckle end of my belt."

He did, a year later, when Iván was expelled from the Reich Deutsches Schule for fighting like a savage, in the classroom, in the courtyard, and out on the streets.

AFTER HIS BAR mitzvah, Ervin, like a much-rained-on weed, suddenly shot up toward the sky. In what seemed like a blink, he reached 6 feet, 182 centimeters, my brother's height. Iván was chagrined. Vying, they measured themselves and each other daily, each claiming millimeters of advantage. Slim and loose-jointed, big-handed and bony, one blond, the other dark, they both looked wonderful. To my smug pride, all the girls in the building eyed them all the time and had alternating crushes on them. But they were mine, strictly mine.

Edit Nuszbaum, twenty, formerly a university student, now idle in consequence of recent ordinances forbidding Jews to attend institutions of higher learning, lived with her parents on the second floor. She was a strawberry blonde with green eyes and red, chubby cheeks. She had broad gestures and a husky voice. Among ourselves at home, the boys referred to her as the Rose of Hebron, not quite meaning it as a compliment. On many afternoons, Edit held what she called tea parties—without tea, or crumpets, or a servant, or a program. It was odd. My friends and I guessed that in fact she did have a secret program: the conquest of Iván, with whom she was crazy in love. Mostly he ignored her, in part because he, too, was in love, but with Éva Hirsch from the town of Sárbogárd. She went to school at the English Ladies' Gimnázium, and they had met at a concert. Two years older than he, she was a pianist "of major talent," Iván said. They exchanged letters frequently, and he wrote poetry to her. The one time I met her, I was unimpressed in every way. I thought she was too tall for a girl and her fingers looked to me like weisswurst—stubby, thick, and sickly white. Iván said he hoped I would grow up to be just like her. I decidedly hoped I would not.

My brother also ignored Edit Nuszbaum because she was an expert, clever taunter, and that particular style was not at the moment on our list of most endearing qualities. "Well, Iván," she would say, in front of anyone, "tell us again how brilliant your little sister is. Tell us of her poetic sensibility, her knowledge of literature, her depth. Do tell us. We have not had a lecture on her for at least half an hour. You are overdue. You must feel deprived." Each time Iván blushed and stammered. In repartee he was witty and cutting, but not with her, and not about me. I basked in the exchange. Deep? Sensibility? Knowledge? Is that what he thought? My brother, of me? Impossible! Me. Me?

Memememememememe?

One sultry summer Sunday afternoon, Edit declared, *"Il est nécessaire qu'on s'amuse."* Speaking French was one of her pretensions, like having tea without tea. None of us understood what she said, except for my brother, whose laconic free translation was "All ye who enter here, take cover. She wants to play." Edit proposed a beauty contest between Iván and Ervin. The contestants were to write a brief essay presenting their qualifications. Both boys declined. Never mind, she said; the game would still proceed.

The judges were to be all the girls twenty and under who agreed to serve. That meant Edit and her cousin Rachel, who had been living with the Nuszbaums for the past few months, ever since her father had been arrested by the Nazis and disappeared and her mother had had a nervous breakdown; my brilliant friend Ági; two of the three Kornitzer girls, who lived across the courtyard and one floor below us; and Marika Deutsch from the second floor, a pale, ignored loner my age who was recruited to avoid a tie. And me, of course. Edit said it should be an open vote. I protested feebly. I couldn't do more. A strong protest would have compromised me as much as my vote.

The boys left. We voted. All those for Iván: 3. All those for Ervin: 3. "And you, saintly little sister," Edit asked with malice. "Are you about to spoil the game?"

"No. I vote for Iván."

Edit set about to prepare a list of the results for each of the boys. We all yelled foul. "No," she said, "I am correct. That is what an open vote means. It is open to the candidates."

She called the boys in and handed each of them the specific results. They bowed in turn. We applauded.

Predictably, although I was not smart enough to foresee it, the game had turned into a fiasco. Iván was insulted and sulky that he had won by only one vote; I minded very much having had to declare myself so unequivocally. Ervin was hurt. He said to me in private that evening, "It doesn't upset me that I lost. What upsets me is that I lost your vote."

"I am sorry," I said, feeling terrible. I didn't know how to articulate to him that I thought they were equally beautiful, but my brother was the sadder boy, and therefore he needed my vote more. Also that I could not allow Edit, as she had intended, to drive a wedge between me and Iván.

THE KORNITZERS WERE orthodox Jews and therefore a little strange to me. On the other hand, their father's youngest brother was a journalist of some repute, so my mother approved of the friendship.

There were four children in the family: a boy nearly my brother's age, sixteen, named Ervin like my cousin, and his sisters Ibolya, fourteen, Ellis, thirteen, and Baba, eight, a year younger than I. Ellis had a slight hunchback, not improved by the fact that Mrs. Kornitzer and the other kids in the family punched her in the back whenever they got angry with her, which was often.

Ibolya appeared from time to time with black-and-blue marks on her throat. She was convinced that she could strangle herself to death with her bare hands. None of us girls thought that her technique was particularly efficient or offered much hope of success. We told her so repeatedly, but she kept at it. We suggested lye, but Ibolya said only servant girls drank lye to kill themselves, and besides she did not think lye was kosher.

Baba wore a brace on her right leg as a consequence of a bout with polio. When she was in a good mood she would lie down on her bed, take her brace off, and lend it to each of us in turn. We strapped it on and hobbled around as best we could, but it was hard to do. She shook with laughter at our clumsiness. We laughed, too. After a while she got impatient— we always wanted more—and took back the brace. She strapped herself into it on her bed, got up, and showed us triumphantly how to be properly lame.

Two school friends, Zsuzsi and Évi Éliás, the butcher's daughters, fascinated me. Zsuzsi was my age, Évi a year younger. They were chubby, squat, red-haired little girls, with freckles sprinkled like brown sugar on their faces and on their soft round arms and hands. Skipping toward school in the sunlight, they resembled animated edibles—eclairs, lady fingers. Their pink, starched frilly pinafores reminded me of my former life, and I envied them. No, not them. I knew they were my social inferiors. My mother told me. I knew they were dumb and ignorant. My brother told me, but I knew that anyway. I envied their centrality. The attention lavished on them by their nanny and mama and daddy and all manner of others.

Me, I wasn't a sweet. If anything, I was more like a salami. Long, inelegant, spicy, sharp. Staple, not goodie. Maybe I could have been more properly the daughter of the butcher than of the Mr. Publisher, whose face I was rapidly forgetting anyway.

RUMORS ARE AN inevitable aspect of oppressed societies. The more a government manages formal news, the more "real" news is disseminated by word of mouth—often with results similar to the children's game known as Telephone. At one point rumors were so rampant in Hungary that a law was passed making the spreading of unofficial bad news a punishable offense.

One rumor not punishable, which circulated among us Jews, was that the spirit of the Spanish Inquisition reigned again, and the lives of those who converted would be spared. Our friends and neighbors urged us to convert. My family, defiant by nature and conviction, debated the matter for about a month and finally decided that with the exception of my grandparents, who categorically refused, we would ask for instruction with intent to convert at a nearby church.

This profusion of supplicant Jews who collectively and in the same season saw the light posed a dilemma for our enemies. It was the sacred duty of every Catholic to proselytize and gather converts. At the same time, no one in the slightest doubted our bad faith.

Our particular parish priest solved the problem after a few lessons. He told us, "My children, I can save your immortal souls, but I cannot save your bodies." Rózsi's succinct "To hell with that!" summed up our position and signaled the end of the enterprise. Still, I did get to know and love the beauty of the New Testament, and Jesus too, poor idealistic martyred Jewish boy that he was.

ON WEEKDAYS, I came home from school by noon, two hours earlier than the boys. It therefore became my task to read the newspaper aloud while my grandmother finished cooking lunch and my grandfather continued to work at his sewing machine.

I read in graveyard tones and ghostly voices, dramatizing and relishing every disaster, every death, every new ruling against the Jews.

"Two Joooos walking without staaaars recognized and *apprehended!*" I would render the headline. Or, whispering hoarsely, "Rabid dogs roam the ghetto district!" And so on.

My grandmother got angry. "You are trying to scare us," she said.

I was indignant. "How could I? I am reading the words. I read what is written. Look at it yourself."

"Never mind," she said. "You are trying to scare us. I know it."

I knew it, too.

A glorious week of this, then my Aunt Rózsi, to whom my grandmother had complained, stepped in. She forbade me to read anymore. She said I was upsetting my grandmother too much.

I was thrilled. My voice, my will, my own willful voice, could convey menace she was unable to bear. She shut me up because I had the power to scare her. I have the power. I *have* the power. I have the *power*.

RÓZSI HAD HAIR the color of an Irish Setter's; her friends called her Red. My grandparents and my mother made fun of her. "Red? What are you, a Communist? Ha ha." Rózsi shrugged her amazing shoulders. She walked swinging them as other people swing their hips—left right, left right, two centimeters of advance with every forward thrust. She made her own money and she made her own decisions, without a man. Good, I thought. She can't be abandoned. She would not permit it.

Rózsi was special in another way as well. She was the miraculous owner of a wristwatch, the only one in the family who could tell time exactly without running to the kitchen. Watches are wondrous instruments, I thought. They put you in control of the most precious commodity in the universe:

time. In control of the Now and the Before and What Is Yet to Come. I coveted Rózsi's watch with mean envy and breathless hope. If only . . . if only . . .

One morning, Rózsi, in an amazing gesture of munificence, said to me, "Would you like to wear my watch to school for the day?"

There must be a mean trick here, I thought. I said nothing. I remained motionless. A response would be polite, I thought, but I was too afraid of disappointment.

"Well," said Rózsi néni, "do you want to borrow it or not?"

"Oh yes, yes, please! Thank you!"

My good fortune preceded me by at least two steps on the way to school. My feet lit firecrackers and my heart sparkled with little stars. During the school day I gesticulated as much as I possibly could with my left arm. My watch sent major messages: I am trusted, I am loved, I have a borrowed watch. Thank you, Red. "A watch!" said Szuzsi Éliás, with a question tilting the last two letters.

"Is that your watch?" asked Jutka Schwartz, one among the few of my classmates who actually had a watch of her own.

"I am a partner in it," I replied. "A partner."

IVÁN AND I went to the home of Péter Munk, his classmate and the son of a rich man, perhaps a banker. I was keenly interested in meeting Munk, because he was the boy who, after some silly scuffle on the ice-skating rink, had kicked Iván on the right knee with his skate, causing a cut which needed several stitches. When the cut healed, it left a beautiful scar, jagged and slightly bluish. I badly wanted a similar scar, but by the time it was my turn for skating lessons, there were no skating lessons, and no chance of getting kicked.

The butler let us in. We walked through many rooms, all of

them empty of people, before we reached a study, book-lined and quiet. I had forgotten that this was how we used to live. We sat down.

"Ivan, isn't this like—"

My brother interrupted, "Close. Our view was better."

I had forgotten that, too. We used to look out on the Danube and on the castlelike fortress called the Fisherman's Bastion.

"Could I play that piano?"

"Even if you could you couldn't. It's not done with other people's pianos, remember that. Not unless you are very good." He was very good.

"What will I do while you talk alone with Péter?" That was our arrangement. I could come along if I let him talk with Péter in another room. When I agreed, I had thought another room was an invention.

"You'll read."

"What?"

"My book. I have it here. It's poetry. A French guy wrote it centuries ago. His name is Villon. It's not for little kids, actually. But I will tell you the pages you can read. Don't read anything else. If you do, I will catch you and I will punish you."

"How will you catch me?"

"Easy—you won't understand what you read. You will be curious. Next week, the week after, you will ask me. I will catch you."

"What if I read but don't ever ask?"

"No point in it. You won't know what you have read." As usual, I found his logic unassailable.

Péter entered. His lips were large, his eyes heavy-lidded; he looked hooded, hidden, rich, much more exciting than Villon. "Why do I have to read?" I asked lamely, and trailed off. I knew a deal was a deal.

Villon instantly became my favorite poet. His words intrigued me, his rhythm excited me, his topics felt strange. He was a vast foreign country full of promises, in which I was happy to travel alone.

Annoyingly, the butler interrupted. He asked me if I would like some tea and scones. I said, "No, thank you," my heart breaking. My brother had told me that it is shameful to accept food from strangers when you feel starved.

ONE LATE AFTERNOON I heard Ivàn's whistle from the court-yard. Surprisingly, he motioned for me to come down. I knew instantly that something awful had happened. I took the stairs three at a time. Ivan was waiting for me at the elevator where he supposed I would appear. His cheeks looked sunken, his eyes were circled with blue.

"What happened?"

"You remember this morning Mother gave me the shoe-maker's ticket for her brown suede platform shoes? I picked them up. I paid for them. A lot of money. I lost one shoe on the tramcar coming home."

"What are you saying?"

"I lost one of the shoes. I wasn't paying attention. I was reading. It must have slipped out of the paper bag."

"This is a disaster, Ivàn. Now she has only one pair of shoes left. And the money for the shoemaker is gone, too. They will kill you. This is terrible."

We both lapsed into silence. After a while, I said, "Why don't we say I did it? You gave me the ticket, I lost the shoe."

"Don't be stupid. How could you have traveled that far? Besides which, I would rather die quartered than get you into trouble."

"You are not thinking right. I get away with things that you don't. Leave it to me. I'll fix it."

"Never. They might hit you, and I would commit murder. Think of something else. What should I do?"

"Did you look for it?"

"Yes. I went to the lost and found. I looked on the street. Nothing."

"Be straight. Say, 'I lost it. Kill me.' They can't."

"You're right! It's only our mother's shoe. What can they do? Nothing. Actually, Mother can do something, but it won't be much. Thank you."

"Come on," I said. "Let's go upstairs."

My brother smiled and punched my arm. "Did I teach you about straight?"

"Definitely."

"A good thing, too. It comes in handy in troubled times."

We ascended in the elevator and raced each other in the corridor. Everyone was home and our lateness had been noted with reproof. "What happened?" my mother asked, her right eyebrow hiked to her hairline.

"Well," Iván said, "it's like this: I picked up your suede shoes. I paid for them. I lost the right one on the tramcar. That's it. I am very sorry."

The quiet which followed became dimensional. It acquired the color of storm clouds, the texture of gravel. Suddenly Rózsi said, "I sincerely hope a right-legged amputee found it." The atmosphere ripped. We all exploded with uncontainable laughter. We knew Margit had just been neutralized by competition. Who cared? Iván was off scot-free. The right-legged amputee remained our symbol of unpredictable fortune for some time to come.

OUR FAMILY HAD always celebrated Mikulás Nap—St. Nicholas Day, the traditional children's holiday in Hungary, nonreligious despite the name. In happy preparation, children placed one of their shoes in the window the night before. If they had been good during the year, St. Nick left gifts and sweets in and around their shoe. Judging by Nick's recent performances, our rating had been declining with every passing year.

This night, December 5, 1943, all of us pretended that we had forgotten the date. We children understood that there was nothing left to give us. Still, after everyone was asleep, I got to thinking. What harm could it do to put my shoe in the window where it belonged? Just on the off chance.

Next morning I woke at first bare light and quietly tiptoed to the window. My shoe contained a magnificent rectangular chocolate bar, beautifully wrapped in foil and colored paper.

Iván's shoe was not in the window. I crept to where he slept. His shoes were placed, as usual, on the floor at the foot of his bed, for quick dressing in case of an air raid. On examination, they proved to be empty. In addition to her worry about shortages, my mother must have thought Iván was too old for St. Nicholas. I did not think so.

I returned to my chocolate, broke it, left one half in my shoe, and put the other in my brother's. St. Nick's lapse corrected, I went back to sleep.

I woke as usual to the stirrings of my family. "Mikulás Nap!" I yelled. I ran to my shoe and triumphantly extracted my chocolate square. "Thank you, Édes Anyám. Thank you, my sweet mother." We kissed.

Sitting on the side of his bed, barefoot, my brother grinned. "So Nick thought you were a good little girl. What an ignorant fool he is." I said nothing. He stretched. He yawned. He started to put on his left shoe. His foot encountered an obstacle. Looking puzzled, he brought the shoe up to his eye, peered into it, and retrieved the square of chocolate.

I thought his face looked as if God had come to visit him. "Oh, thank you, Anyu. Thank you very much," he said, and rushed over to her.

Our mother had gone very pale. "I know nothing about this," she said, shaking her head. "It wasn't me."

Iván seemed to contract in all dimensions as he turned to my aunt. "Thank you, Rózsi néni." She, too, looked stricken. "I didn't do it," she said.

Oh, my God! I thought. What have I done? I have highlighted their neglect. I have underscored his second-class status. I pulled the sheet up to my eyes. My brother turned slowly toward me. "It was you," he said. I nodded in full acknowledgement of my guilt and shame.

He walked over to me and fished my hand out from under the covers. Holding it, he drew himself to full height, clicked his shoeless heels, bent from the waist, kissed my hand and said, "Thank you very much. I remain your most obedient and humble servant, forever." He clicked his heels again, turned, and left the room.

THE LAWS AGAINST Jews in Hungary between 1939 and 1944 steadily increased in harshness, bringing more hardships and humiliations. New anti-Jewish ordinances appeared in the newspaper every day and were also posted on the walls of buildings. Jews were required to wear a yellow star four inches in diameter sewn to their clothing above the heart. Rich and poor were forcibly moved into buildings marked with a yellow star. Special food ration cards were issued with reduced buying power. Capricious curfews made walking the streets dangerous. The Allies were preparing to bomb us, and we had air-raid drills in basement shelters. Death threatened everywhere.

Some of the newly created underclass citizens thought killing themselves was the best revenge. They were much criticized as cowards by both groups of survivors, Christians and Jews. After the Germans entered Budapest in March 1944, the number of suicides grew exponentially.

Rumors of deportation and gassing had become facts, reported by eyewitness escapees. The future seemed canceled.

Because Jews could no longer own businesses, the Fischer brothers had transferred the title to the glass and mirror factory to Mr. Poremba, their trusted foreman. As the frequency of air raids increased, working had become altogether impossible, and the factory had closed down. By this time, both my mother and Rózsi were working for Pista Papp, a Christian friend who owned a flower nursery on the outskirts of Budapest.

The flower nursery used a poisonous nicotine concentrate to kill weeds. It was kept under lock and key. The key was in my mother's charge.

Late one Sunday afternoon, Iván called me in from the open-air courtyard corridor in front of our apartment, where I was playing with my paper dolls. A turn on this corridor, forming a corner, had become my new playroom. I was not yet ten years old.

The facts were put to me simply:

Our lives were very bad. Things were going to get much worse. We could get separated. Would it not be better if we all went quietly to sleep together, with no more troubles or fear or hunger?

"Sure," I was about to say, when my brother interrupted. "They do *not* mean sleep. They mean die. They want us all to die together. You have a vote."

"You are the tie-breaker," Ervin said, bursting into hysterical laughter. "Grandfather, Iván, and I voted no. Grandma, my mother, and Margit néni voted yes. Evidently the decision is yours." By now he was laughing so hard that tears were streaming down his face.

I didn't get it. Everyone seemed so very upset, and there hadn't even been the usual fight, as far as I could tell. I looked to my brother. He shook his head almost imperceptibly.

"No," I said. "No. I vote no."

TWO

I WATCHED DEEP CAULDRONS ROILING WITH BROWN MIRE, fervently stirred. A witches' ceremony seemed imminent. Would there be divinations and sacrifices?

In reality, buckets boiled on the kitchen stove. The boys desperately needed shirts. We had no money to buy them, and even if we'd had money there were no longer shirts to buy. The family decided we could do with fewer sheets. Four of the expendable best were selected. The dry goods store had only one color of dye left—brown. Fine. It was a most attractive brown.

The enterprise turned chaotic. Rózsi and my mother nailed strings across the room on which they hung huge brown-tinted sheets that flopped ominously like enormous dead bats for one day and one night. The dye fumes rivaled in stink my mother's defunct perfume venture.

My grandfather cut and sewed the sheets into shirts, two for each boy. I begged for one also, but was told that Grandfather only knew how to make clothes for males. This was not entirely true. Whenever he wanted to console me, Grandfather made some type of clothing for my hard-plastic doll Évike. Évike was everything I was not. She had long lashes and blue eyes that opened and closed when she was rocked. She was not a bigmouth and had no aptitude for argument. The best she could do was say "Maa-maaa" while being tilted back and forth. She sounded like a bleating sheep. She had blond hair braided over her ears, Gretchen-fashion. Except for my grandmother, everyone loved her. I, too, was supposed to—she was mine, after all—but I was not quite sure how I felt. That lucky doll was a lot better off in many ways than I. She was well dressed, and she owned things. She had a backpack sewn by my grandfather in replica of the ones he had sewn for the boys. A backpack was an important accessory. It implied status and privilege; it made the person who wore it look sportive and Aryan. Very unlike the frightened, fugitive Jews with hasty suitcases, among whom I belonged. Évike also had two pantsuits which I coveted. She had a cape, and now, I was sure, she was getting a brown shirt. My family thought that giving things to Évike was like giving them to me. This was a serious error in perception. She and I were separate and not even on good terms lately.

In any case, the brown shirts turned out to be magnificent. They had, however, a significant drawback. They made the boys look like storm troopers. Hilarious, no? Sometimes my family were fools. Each boy at different times had to talk his way out of potentially deadly situations.

THE MISERABLE CONDITIONS of our lives drastically deteriorated. We could no longer possess a telephone, a radio, or a pet. Our movements on the streets became ever more restricted. Jews could go out only between one and three in the afternoon—and all stores were closed during those hours. As a consequence, we could barely acquire enough food to live. My mother would go to the back of the stores she had always frequented, knock, and duck under the half-raised metal gate. The shopkeepers would greet her with I-kiss-your-hands and as a generous favor sell her food at triple the price. This maneuver kept us from starving, but barely.

Some servants helped and even hid their Jewish former employers. Lajos, my parents' butler, visited my mother and offered to go shopping for her. She never took him up on it; she was afraid he might keep the money and disappear. That's when she and Iván began to defy the rules and go out without their stars, trusting luck and their Aryan looks.

There were fuel shortages and water rationing; the pipes were turned on only during certain hours, and we had to store water in buckets to put out fires in case of a direct hit.

One night we were awakened by pounding on the front door. My mother sat up in bed and whispered, "Everybody quiet." She clicked on her flashlight, always near her. "Iván, are you sure the windows are properly blacked out?"

"Of course," he answered, "but I can check." The pounding continued. By this time, of course, we were all awake and terrified. My mother scrambled into her robe and shoes, as we all did. Rózsi and Ervin came out of their room and joined us. The pounding on the door continued, by now accompanied by shouts: "Open up in the name of the law!"

My mother, flashlight in hand, Iván right behind her, opened the door. It was the secret police, which these days meant the Nyilas, or Arrow-Cross—the Hungarian Nazi Party. They were accompanied by the building superintendent, who was our friend. Mr. Lakatos apologized. "Madame Dénes, the gentlemen from the police seem to think there is some trouble." Two rude, burly brutes entered, their trench coats meant to ape the Germans'. They pushed their way into the kitchen and started accusing my mother in loud, threatening voices.

The gist of the accusation was this: We were sending the enemy flashlight signals from our back room in Morse code. "We have no back room," my mother said. This was a fact we could prove, but it offered no consolation. We all knew that once a Jew was accused, even if he was not guilty of that particular crime, another accusation could be immediately invented.

"Gentlemen," my mother said, "please follow me. I will show you all our rooms." Speaking to the secret police, who for these fairly trivial investigations were usually unemployable workers or peasants, recently promoted, was an art in itself, at which my mother excelled. Too much humility in the tone and their sadism would be aroused. Too much hauteur and their abiding sense of inferiority would be aroused. Too much self-confidence and they would definitely want to kill you. The tone had to be modulated to whatever was left after eliminating these options.

My mother took them into Rózsi and Ervin's room, which had windows, but not facing the direction they described. She showed them the bathroom, which had no windows, and then our pantry. It did have a window, and it did face the direction of their concern. However, it was tightly shut and painted black. They opened it, half climbed through it, craned their necks in this direction and that, looked at the motley group of us, three kids, an elderly couple, and two haggard women, and decided that probably none of us was the message-sending enemy of the nation. To save face, they said sternly, "Who lives above you?"

"No one," said my mother. "We are the top floor."

"Ah ha! Then someone must be sending signals from the roof." They withdrew with an unpleasant swagger. We could not even feel the exuberance of having just escaped disaster because we knew that the same thing might happen again in five minutes, or tomorrow, or next week. Who knew who had reported the lights? Who knew if they had even been reported?

On another occasion, a similar pair appeared with corresponding fanfare, again in the middle of the night. This time, they were armed with a warrant for the arrest of one Gyula Dénes, newspaper publisher, Israelite. With a careless little lilt of triumph creeping into her voice, my mother said, "he is not here. He is in New York City, Amerika." At once, Iván and Rózsi looked at her hard. Clearly, she had forgotten that if provoked, they could arrest any or all of us instead. My mother quickly put her hands on her face. With a little sob she added, "He abandoned me and the children. He's getting a divorce."

"We will search anyway," one of the men declared. They had as little luck locating my father in the apartment as I did on the few recent occasions when I would have liked to say something to him. The men left. We returned to bed.

In time, and with recurrence, even danger becomes ordinary.

When Further Restricted Locomotion for Jews was decreed, my family felt stricken—except for my grandmother and me. She was nearly blind, and I looked Jewish; neither of us had been taken anywhere interesting for what seemed like years.

Restricted Locomotion also meant that Iván, Ervin, and I played Kapitoli, the Hungarian version of Monopoly, for hours on end. I also learned how to play chess and three different versions of gin rummy. In time, the boys became bored and irritated; they picked on each other. I ascended to the position of vied-for companion. Could life offer anything more?

All, however, was not flawless. I was often hungry; I was scared and cold. I missed the radio. Not for the music, as my brother did, but as my friend in reassurances. "This is Budapest Radio. It is four p.m. It is raining," a voice would say. I'd look at the clock. It was four p.m. I'd look out the window. It was raining. Ah, I'd think to myself. I am not alone. Others, too, need to be reminded of what's what, even when it is evident.

Sometimes the boys turned on me, together and separately. On one such occasion I learned about Oedipus. My brother said he would teach me how to play the game if I brought him my boy paper doll, Tomi, and one of my mother's knitting needles. I did. Quick as a wink he poked out both of the doll's eyes. "That's the way to play Oedipus," he said.

I was stunned beyond outrage or grief. "Why?" I could barely gasp the question.

"I'm sorry," he said instantly. "It was a joke. A bad joke. A terrible joke. Forgive me. I am so sorry."

"What is an Oedipus? Did you invent the whole thing just to destroy my doll?"

"No. It's a real thing. An actual person in Greek drama. I'll tell you about it. I'll also buy you a new doll. Really, I will."

He told me the story. He also bought me another doll, exactly like the first. But I didn't want another doll exactly like the first. I wanted my old Tomi.

OFTEN THE CITY was saturation-bombed. The Allies would select a sector for total destruction; no building was to be left standing. We were in the city. We were in a building. We could not signal the Allies that we were Jews.

Our bomb shelter was the unreinforced basement, where every apartment had its corresponding storage shed. These were cubicles divided by wooden walls. In peacetime tenants had kept firewood and assorted junk there. The firewood was long gone. The government had ordered everyone to clear out the junk and to furnish the little rooms with chairs, a cot, water, a flashlight, blankets, a shovel—in case of a cave-in— and a bottle of rum. This last item may have been my family's own contribution to the war effort.

Since the battery in the flashlight was precious, we rationed its use and burned candles. We ate whatever little we had, drank rum, and told stories. My mother was a wonderful mimic. On a long night she would do most of the famous Hungarian stage actresses, and all of our neighbors, male and female.

From time to time, against everyone's protest, Rózsi and Grandfather would leave the basement during a raid to smoke in the courtyard. They put themselves in double danger—they might have been hit by strafing planes, or been arrested for sending spark signals to the enemy. Both of them vehemently denied the latter peril, claiming that their dexterously cupped hands made the cigarettes less visible than the little harmless phosphorescent pins we all wore to identify each other in the dark.

Sometimes four nations rose up against us simultaneously, bent on our destruction—the Germans and the Hungarians house-to-house, the British and Americans from the air. How could we not laugh our heads off from time to time—breath-choking, belly-hurting laughter? Even my grandmother would say, alternately clutching her face and her stomach, "Stop! stop! I have to go to the bathroom!" That was a problem.

Usually I fell asleep in total exhaustion before the all-clear sounded. To sit night after night in an underground cubicle and not know whether you will live to see the dawn is no easy matter, to be sure. Still, I did not feel in major danger. I had my family. I could have died, but meanwhile, I had what I needed to live.

Bickering among the adults diminished greatly after we all became equally destitute and imperiled. In some ways the status of the Dèneses had grown, since my mother and Iván were braver than Ervin and Rózsi. Brave meant that despite the fact that had they been caught they could have been arrested and taken to parts unknown, they walked the streets without a yellow star at prohibited times, bought food illegally with ration cards or on the black market, and visited Christian friends and brought back news. Their mobility made them heroes even in the neighbors' eyes. I didn't know that I should have worried.

Since March of 1944, I had regularly received explicit instructions from Iván and my mother about what to do in case I was alone with my grandparents when the building was attacked by the German Nazis or the Hungarian Arrow-Cross. My grandparents were unsophisticated people, and quite helpless. In any emergency, someone had to take care of them.

The drill through which Iván and my mother put me— physically a few times and verbally almost every morning— consisted of the following:

If we were surrounded, I was to sneak out to the street as soon as it was feasible. I was to make a sharp right turn onto Szerdahelyi Utca, where a public telephone was located about fifteen meters down the street. My mother gave me several telephone tokens to keep in a place of my choosing where I could find them quickly.

My orders were to make a call to my great-uncle Dàvid, my

grandfather's youngest brother, whose phone number I had committed to memory and repeated daily. Dávid had been a decorated soldier and prisoner of war in World War I, and so he still had dispensation to live outside of the designated buildings. Also, his wife was not Jewish. After giving a coded sentence, I was to hang up and continue to walk (not run, so as not to call attention to myself) to Dávid's house on Lilliom Utca. As soon as Dávid was notified, he or someone he sent would pick up my grandparents.

Even as I was listening to them, I thought the instructions were absurd. I should leave my helpless grandparents alone?! Uncharacteristically, I did not argue. If the situation arose, I would be on my own and would do as I thought best. Also, I understood perfectly well that the reason for those orders was exactly the same as the reason I would disobey them. In our family we fought, sometimes with an all-out, no-holds-barred, vicious intensity. But we did not abandon each other in the face of outside menace, ever.

Furthermore, I was delighted to have an excuse to visit regularly the hiding place I had chosen for my tokens, the drawer of a white metal night table next to the sewing machine. In it my mother kept her packet of headache powder and an envelope filled with a dozen stiff, sweet wafers called *ostja,* which she would dip in water, spread on the back of her hand, fill with a dose of the headache powder, and fold like a cheese danish, so that the softened wafer formed a sweet casing for the bitter powder. I kept my tokens there to have an excuse to pilfer. I couldn't take many wafers at a time, though, or I'd get caught. The taste, but not the texture, was a little like inferior cotton candy.

In secret, part of me looked forward to the possibility of

being in charge under conditions of immediate danger. Soon enough, it happened. Word came that several of the yellow-starred buildings in the neighborhood had already been surrounded and attacked.

I couldn't understand why everyone didn't run out of the building when the news came. I guess they were afraid of being shot, or captured and punished. My family was different from other people whom I knew. Except for my grandparents, we were completely action- and escape-oriented. I was taught that rebellion was a key to survival. Don't wait until they come and get you. Run. Hide. Disappear. By plan, if possible. If not, improvise. But go, and take your family with you.

As planned, I grabbed my tokens within seconds of hearing the news. "Get ready to go," I said to my grandparents. "I'm coming back for you." They were too stunned to protest.

Downstairs the situation was chaotic. To the left of the building's entrance where other yellow-starred houses stood, people were being herded to the street by the police and by Green Shirts with Arrow-Cross armbands. There were gunshots and screams.

Someone was yelling into a megaphone, "Out! All dirty Jews out! Out!" Some Jews were marching with their hands up, others not. A car horn blared. Don't run, they had said? I did not run. I raced to the telephone.

"Dávid bácsi?"

"Yes?"

"The guests have arrived."

"Fine. Hang up and keep walking toward me."

"No. We will all come together." I hung up.

I walked slowly back. My knees were shaking too hard to do anything else. The raiders had already gotten to the house

next door, and were on their way to us. A new batch of Green
Shirt boys were now beating the Jews with clubs. The screams
had grown louder.

Upstairs, I found my grandmother wringing her hands, wai-
ling and walking aimlessly back and forth in her unsteady, blin-
dish way. My grandfather, who had put on his jacket, had
grown into a very fat man in the few minutes I had been away.
I had the overwhelming urge to laugh.

"Why do you look that way?"

"I am saving things. Under my coat."

"What things?"

"Things." I unbuttoned his jacket. A dozen or so kitchen
towels fell to the floor.

"Leave the towels. Let's go." I got my jacket and my grandmother's. I had to yell at her to pull herself together. Then I
checked to make sure that none of our garments had a star
sewn on it. We headed downstairs. An old couple and a kid.
Obviously homeward bound, scrambling away from the
neighborhood of the dirty Jews. Three good souls, God bless
them.

Soon we saw David coming toward us. By rehearsed routine, none of us gave any sign of recognition. David passed us,
then crossed the street, and turned to walk parallel with us
toward his home. We arrived without incident.

Later that day, my mother came to fetch us. She'd learned
that the Green Shirts had left, and on this occasion it was safe
to return to our apartment.

THE MORNING OF October 16, 1944, was oxen-gray and
unseasonably cold, with gusty winds and a sparse, steady rain.
I had tonsilitis, and had spent the previous week in bed, except

for running twice each day to the air-raid shelter. In the morning the British bombed us, at night the Americans. Like clockwork.

Still, the day was promising. The specter of tubercular relapse made everyone pamper me whenever I came down with a fever. My grandmother fixed my favorite food—egg *nokedli* with cucumber salad. My brother read me *The Last of the Mohicans* in the style of a radio serial. Ervin and I played cards. Not a bad life at all.

As we sat down to breakfast, the news came, brought by Pista Szabó, a neighbor's son. Like a whirling dervish he ran round and round the courtyard corridor of our floor, knocking on every door without waiting for anyone to appear, yelling breathlessly, "They have surrounded the yellow-starred house next door. They are coming toward us. They mean business. I saw them shoot a man. Hurry!"

My family panicked. Each of them jumped up, rushed randomly to some other part of the room, gesticulated, and barked contradictory orders that made no sense. I sat. My mother caught sight of me.

"You un-for-tu-nate im-be-cile, don't just sit there!" she screamed. "Get dressed. Immediately!"

For some reason, in Hungarian, the adjective "unfortunate," when pronounced slowly, in carefully articulated syllables, is a major insult. Coupled with "imbecile," it had a devastating impact. I scrambled into my clothes.

Meanwhile, lines of division became clarified. My brother said, "We'll go hide in the attic." My cousin said, "We'll march out with our hands held high."

"You are insane," my brother said. "They'll separate us and take us away to God knows where. Then maybe they will shoot us."

"I am insane? No. You have gone mad," Ervin said. "They will definitely kill us in the attic. Escapees are always shot."

During this argument the Green Shirts had entered the building and were now standing in the courtyard yelling instructions through megaphones. "All filthy sons of Abraham, all you Israelites, all you dirty Jewish pigs—females and children included—march downstairs. Hands high. Yellow star displayed. Stragglers will be shot. Resisters will be shot. Every ugly, big-nosed, racketeering, cross-eyed shit Jew who is not down here in three minutes will be shot. Long live Szálasi."

"Do they have to be so insulting?" my grandmother asked.

"We've got to hide," Iván said.

By now, a small group of our neighbors had reached the courtyard and were being shoved into formation with the occasional encouragement of a rifle butt, producing sporadic screams of pain. A few families, in their panicked rush to obey, temporarily lost track of some of their members. The sound of running feet became intermingled with strangled cries of "Where is Zsuzsi?" and "Find the baby!" The Green Shirts continued to yell orders and curse us through their megaphones, shooting quick rounds at the sky and hooting. From breakfast peace to catastrophic chaos took less than fifteen minutes.

"We are trapped," said Rózsi. "We will die today."

"Not me," said my brother. "Not any of us, if you follow me." He took my mother's arm and my hand. "Come on, we're going to the attic."

"No," Ervin said. "We're going to surrender and survive." He seized Rózsi's hand. My grandparents stood immobilized between the opposing sides. Which way?

"You come with us," my brother said, pointing a stern finger at them. "Now." The authority in his voice made them start toward us. Ervin shrugged. "Have it your way," he muttered in disgust. "Idiot." He prodded his mother out the door and toward the stairs.

"Good," my brother said. "Now this is what we'll do. I'll lead, then Magda, Grandma, and Grandpa follow. Mother will be last." I could see the logic in this arrangement, although I didn't like it. He was flanking the feeble. Dammit, I thought, I am not the weakest link in this chain. Grandma is. Right. That put me exactly one up from the bottom. God, if only I were four years older! Adult—fourteen, like Ervin.

"Walk sideways with your backs completely flattened against the wall of the corridor. That way we'll remain invisible from the courtyard. Don't rush. Don't step forward from the wall. When I get to the back stairwell, I will duck in. You continue to walk until you reach me. I'll pull in each of you in turn, as conditions allow. Let's go."

Once inside the stairwell, we could see that others had had the same idea as Iván. Pista Szabó was there with his mother, and other neighbors from our floor and the floor below. At a later count, the total came to fourteen, five of whom were our family. The most important people there, however, were Mr. Pike and his beautiful blond wife, Christians who lived catty-corner to us. Mrs. Pike and I were old friends. We became acquainted when I first moved in with my grandparents. I had curtsied to her in the elevator. She invited me for jam and bread. She let me help her pour the tea and dry the dishes, and helped me practice pronouncing the letter *l,* with which I had a little trouble.

Her husband was a a slight man in his thirties, employed as a waiter. I am certain that Mr. Pike didn't think of himself as a hero. But on this day, his deep character surfaced. He could not passively watch his neighbors being slaughtered. He stepped in, risking his life and the life of his wife. Jews were hated, but those who helped them were hated even more. If he had been caught, they both would have been tortured before being killed.

Now he stood in front of the door where the staircase led to the attic. "All of you," he said, "climb up fast. Hide under the boards. Don't let me down. I'll guard the door and swear that you are not up there. Be silent. Don't let me down."

"We won't," said Iván. "And thank you. Thank you eternally." They shook hands. People started to climb up quietly. To us, my brother said, "Hide under the first boards. Nearest the door." My mother stopped short. "That means we'll be shot first, if we are discovered."

"That's right," my brother said. "Would you prefer to see everyone else shot before us? They will certainly shoot everyone if they catch us. You know that."

"You are right," my mother said. "We'd best be first. It will be easier, particularly on the child." We climbed on.

"Mother, does being shot hurt?" I asked.

Before she could answer, Ivan said in a stage whisper, "Like the dentist. About the same as the dentist." That was fine. I had several times survived death at the dentist.

"Are you sure?"

"Of course I'm sure, ignoramus. Keep climbing."

Back then in Hungary, attics were the equivalent of today's basement laundry rooms. To ensure the proper evacuation of water, the attic floor was made of wooden boards built about sixteen inches over a concrete base, on either side of a concrete passageway. On top of the boards washtubs were placed at intervals. Between them stood ironing boards. Above both, clotheslines hung from wall to wall, stretched under the eaves. Two rows of windows with wooden shutters faced each other, one set of windows opening to the courtyard, the other to the street.

On an ordinary day, several washerwomen would have been laboring there, scrubbing laundry on corrugated washboards. Thick, hot steam would have been rising from the overflowing tubs; stark white sheets suspended from the lines would have billowed in the breeze. Rivulets of water spilled below the floorboards would have collected into puddles, emitting the sweet, slightly sickening odor of soap, sweat, lye, and bluing. One of the women might have been singing, probably a mournful gypsy tune. The others would have hummed in harmony.

The attic, on the rare occasions I was allowed to visit it with our washerwoman, Piroska néni, invariably seemed a place of exotic mystery. On this day it was different. The window shutters had been tightly closed by a provident Mr. Pike. Twilight and silence prevailed, mixed with our dirty smell of fear.

Fortunately for us, the boards were set high enough for a normal body to squeeze itself underneath, flat on its back or belly.

We scrambled under the boards. My mother and I were together. Iván was somewhere in back of us with Pista Szabó, and even farther back, to the right, were my grandparents. We waited. In the courtyard, the orders shouted through megaphones continued, but now they were muted and incomprehensible. From time to time an uninterpretable scream reached us. Each noise made my mother shudder violently. We heard a round of bullets.

Suddenly, Iván appeared next to us, having slid on his belly without making a sound. "Pista thinks we ought to escape through the street windows," he whispered. "We could run from roof to roof and come down in another neighborhood, then go free. What do you think?" My mother was silent. "Well, what do you think?"

"Who? Who could do that? The child? Your grandparents?"

"Right," said Iván. "I'll go back and tell him no."

Discouraged, Pista also changed his mind. We waited. Suddenly, we heard Mr. Pike's voice. "*Nem vannak fent. Senki nincs fent.* They are not upstairs. No one is upstairs. I came here to guard the door. No dirty Jew got past me. What do you think? I cannot smell a Jew pig? Believe me, I can. I worked for some of them. Filth, I tell you. No tips. No consideration. Pushy, rude. Kill them all first chance you get, I say. I spit on them. Killers of Jesus. I hate them. I hope you shoot them all. I wish they had come this way. They would have learned what's what at the end of my knuckles. Eh, brother? Long live Szálasi!"

He certainly was convincing. Silence followed. We waited. Time passed. Then we heard Mr. Pike's voice again. "Oh, the pigs? The brothers took them long ago, thank God. They shot some. The rest they took. We will breathe easier without their stink. I'm guarding the door so they can't escape upward. Eh? Long live Szálasi!"

Time passed. Silence. We waited. Mr. Pike's voice surfaced again, several octaves higher than before. "Of course you can search, brother. Go ahead. A fine thing. A charming thank you. I stood here all day to protect the door from Jewish pigs and now you doubt my word. Search, then, and apologize later. Ha!"

"Well, brother, I didn't mean to offend you. I am sure if

you took care of it, they are not up there. Long live Szálasi! Heil Hitler!"

"Heil Hitler."

Silence. Time passed. No, that is wrong. Time did not pass. It hovered in the air. It became a palpable aspect of danger, a hungry vicious bird with an ugly beak, set to devour us.

Pista Szabó's alarm had come at about nine in the morning. It was now late afternoon. Since we climbed to the attic we hadn't moved, eaten, drunk, or gone to the bathroom. I didn't mind any of that. I just wanted us to survive. I thought if perhaps I could make myself into a small, barely visible ball of pure energy, I could explode at will and send a lightning bolt through the sky into God's garden, to fall at His resting feet and alert Him that He was needed immediately.

Mr. Pike's urgent whisper came through the half-opened door. "They are gone for the moment. Come out fast. You must disperse. Be quick!"

Be quick. Throats had gone dry, limbs had turned numb, spirits sagged in despair. Quick? A demoralized bunch of disoriented citizens in various degrees of terror filed slowly down into the stairwell.

"Go," said Mr. Pike, pointing at two people. "Now. Before the guards come back. Go." They left. "Next, you," he said to Iván. Hesitant, Iván turned toward my mother. "Go," she said. "To the flower shop." Iván nodded and left for the shop owned by his godmother, my mother's best friend, Ilonka. The process continued. When Mr. Pike got to my grandparents he said, "Indig bácsi, do you have someplace to go?"

My grandmother started to cry. "No," she said. "We have nowhere to go anymore. Dávid may be in trouble, too."

"Of course you do," my mother said. "Go to Piroska néni,

our washerwoman. She will put you up until I can get to you. Now go." They left.

A shrill whistle shattered the air. "Oh, my God. My sweet Christ," Mr. Pike said. "That's the warning of a friend of mine. They are back. I can no longer help you. Go downstairs into the men's toilet that opens from this building into the bar on the next street. It is so filthy that no one but a drunk would use it. It's your best chance. Hide there. Good luck!"

I looked around. Four of us were left, abandoned. Pista Szabó, his mother, my mother, and me. "Well," Pista said, "let's hurry." Nobody moved. He got angry. "Dear ladies," he hissed, "if it's not too much of an imposition, could you rush a little? Our lives happen to be in the balance." As one, we started running down the stairs.

From my current perspective, the one-person toilet into which we all crowded does not exist. It never did. How could it? The size of it was about four by four. The actual urinal was a hole in the ground. The peeling walls and the broken floor were covered with urine, fecal matter, snot, phlegm, blood and other unidentifiable excretions which, combined, appeared to be sufficiently noxious that even breathing them would cause a plague.

"Don't lean against anything," my mother whispered.

Right.

We heard voices. One of them said, "That's where they are probably hiding. The filth. Those goddamned Jews. They have so much. They are all bankers, you know. And black marketeers. We have so little. Let's go in there and catch a few."

My breath started up in loud gasps. Loud enough to be heard on the other side of the door. "Shhh!" said Pista.

"Quiet!" my mother said. I could not help it.

"She'll get us caught," Pista whispered, once more in a rage. "Stop her."

My mother studied the map of the damp ceiling, barely visible in the semidarkness. I clamped both my hands on my mouth.

"You want to go in there? Go ahead," said the other voice. "I'd like to see you step into what's in there. Shit. A few mice. A rat. Go ahead. Let us catch some Jews."

"You think I am afraid?"

"I don't think anything. I just want to see you go ahead."

To my immense relief, Mr. Pike's voice came through. My breathing quieted almost at once. "Good evening, brothers," Mr. Pike said. "What's going on?" He sounded entirely conversational.

"He thinks Jews are hiding in there. He wants to catch them," said the first voice.

"In there? That's a very good joke!" Mr. Pike burst into laughter. "Why don't we go for a beer around the corner, brothers? You will be my guests." He laughed again.

"Yeah," said the first voice. "Let's go for a beer. The brother invited us." We could hear them shuffle away.

"Now! Fast!" Pista said. We dashed across the courtyard toward the Teleki Tér exit. Pista ran through the wrought-iron gates. Before we could reach the gates, Mr. Lakatos, the building super, stepped in front of us. "Go back," he said. "Pista was lucky. The new guards are just crossing the street. They mustn't see you leave."

"We are stuck," Mrs. Szabó said. "We'd better go to our apartments." My mother panicked. "I cannot do that," she said with barely contained hysteria. "I will not go. Rózsi is lying in there shot to death. I know. I cannot enter that place. I will not. She is in there dead. I know it."

Mrs. Szabó looked at me. I shrugged. "Fine," Mrs. Szabó said. "Stay with me in my apartment. It is too late to go anywhere, and we need some rest if we are to escape tomorrow."

Nobody said it, but I sensed that we had become considerably imperiled by this delay. We ended up lucky. No one came to search for us in the night. The two air raids helped. It kept the Green Shirts in the shelters. To us it was welcome cover fire.

Mrs. Szabó's apartment, that morning a neat, comfortable home, had been looted and vandalized. The floors were littered with broken glass, torn papers, and general debris. Someone had peed on the couch. Most everything movable had been taken. Whatever was left was damaged. Mrs. Szabó burst into tears. My mother wept with her. I needed to go to sleep.

Mrs. Szabó had hidden some jars of jam. She brought them out and we each ate a few spoonfuls. "This will be your bed," she said. "It's Pista's. Undress to your underwear and lie down. I will cover you with this comforter. I hid it for Pista. I hope he is all right."

"Thank you, Mrs. Szabó. I, too, hope Pista is all right. Good night."

"Good night, dear."

My mother seemed to have disappeared. Before I could worry about her, I fell asleep. I dreamt that I heard a dog bark. I could hear him wail and gnaw as if eating off his extremities in a desperate attempt to escape from a trap. I woke after a few hours of sleep to the sound of a bereft dog barking in an empty apartment—probably the wolfhound Attila on the third floor. Dawn came soon. We were all up before it could turn from mist to light.

"So," my mother said, "we have to leave today."

"Yes," said Mrs. Szabó. "You will have to get the child's coat from your apartment. It is cold outside. She will be conspicuous without a coat."

My mother's obsession that Rózsi had been shot in our apartment and was now lying there dead had not abated during the night. She based her belief on a single particularly piercing scream, followed by rifle shots, which we had heard while hiding under the attic boards.

"No," my mother said, clenching her teeth.

"All right," Mrs. Szabó said, "I will get it."

"No!" my mother said. "I don't want to find out that my sister is dead while I am alive."

"I won't say anything," said Mrs. Szabó, the soul of practicality. I laughed. Enraged, my mother turned on me.

"You find death funny? You find your aunt's murder funny? Very funny. Right? Your father, too, would have found the situation funny. Only he is not here. He is in Amerika. That is funny. Right?"

"I didn't mean anything, Anyu. I will need my coat. You know that. And what Mrs. Szabó said was funny."

My mother remained enraged. "You have a mouth the size of a large city gate. Keep it shut."

"Everybody calm down," Mrs. Szabó said. "I will lend her one of my suit jackets. It should fit her almost like a coat."

The suit jacket did not fit me like a coat. It didn't fit me at all. I looked like a clown, dangerously different. I said so. Mrs. Szabó concurred. My mother was adamant. "I know Rózsi is lying dead in the apartment. I do not want it confirmed."

An hour passed. It was time to contact the super again about the changing of the guards. We had to find a small free window of time through which to slip out between their exits and entrances.

My mother went to see the super with a few hundred pengös scraped up between her and Mrs. Szabó. She returned with the news. "They are not budging. When they do, the super will let us know. It will be difficult." We sat. Two hours passed. Four hours passed. We ate jam. More hours passed. The super knocked. "Time for you to go." It was midafternoon, close to early-winter dark. We raced down the stairway to the exit. "Good luck and thank you," my mother said to Mrs. Szabó.

"Good luck," Mrs. Szabó answered. We went our separate ways.

"We'll take the tramcar," my mother said. "It will be safer than walking. We will go to Ilonka's. Iván is waiting for us there."

"Are you sure?"

"Of course. That is where I told him to go."

Seated on the tramcar, I felt that overnight the city had changed. As in a fairy tale turned wicked, the world had revealed its layers of menace. The well-known streets through which we traveled had turned alien. There was no more Budapest. We were in a bewitched city of evil populated by hidden monsters. One accusing word, one pointing finger, could get us instantly killed.

"Don't pull your neck in," my mother whispered. "You are not a turtle."

"What?" I whispered.

"Don't whisper," my mother whispered. "Look confident, dammit."

I nodded. Confident. Sure. In Mrs. Szabó's suit jacket.

In a while the ticket taker shouted, "Ferencz Körút!" Our stop. We got off and walked the half block to Ilonka's flower shop was.

As we approached, we could see that the corrugated iron gate had been pulled down halfway. It was near closing time. We entered to the tinkle of a little bell above the door. There was Ilonka, her mother, Miszlai néni, and, our bad luck, a customer. A man buying roses.

"Good evening," my mother said.

Ilonka turned to her. "Good evening, madam. Unfortunately we are closed. This gentleman is our last customer for the day. We cannot help you."

My mother turned a shade paler. "Yes," she said, "I thought you might be closed. I saw the gate drawn. But it is the child's name day and I promised her a corsage."

"Name day" was good. My mother was quick. Only Christians had name days. And if the fellow asked me what my name was, I would have to pretend to be mute. He looked at me. I could see him thinking, The poor have funny notions. The kid doesn't even have a coat, but she'll get a corsage. I turned toward my mother and hid my face in her clothing before conversation could develop. Shy as a violet.

"Sorry, madam, we cannot help you," Ilonka said again very firmly.

The man came to our rescue. "But you must. Really. Just wrap my roses. I am ready to pay. You heard, it's the child's name day. You must help them."

"All right," Ilonka said.

"Thank you," my mother said to the man. I remained in hiding.

Finally he left. Ilonka pretended to look for corsages as we all listened in silence to the sound of the man's receding footsteps on the pavement.

"Where is Iván?" my mother asked. "Is he upstairs?"

"No," Ilonka said. "Miklós is upstairs. Olga's husband. I couldn't hide two."

"But he was here, wasn't he?" I asked, unable to contain myself.

"Yes," said Ilonka. "He was here last night. I cannot hide two. Miklós gave him the address of a factory on the outskirts of town. The owner is friendly to Jews. Iván went there last night."

"You let Iván go?" my mother asked in total astonishment. "You let him go at night? Without papers? Ilonka, what have you done?"

Up to this moment, I had liked Ilonka very much. Before opening the flower shop, before having gotten terribly fat, she had been a talented and famous character actress. She also performed in musicals. Once she had a part in one of my father's shows. I had seen her on the stage, although I barely remembered that. She was not my godmother; I didn't have one. Still, every Christmas she sent me my own little tree, two feet high, decorated with pink ribbons and candles on every branch, and draped with white angel hair. Those were beautiful little trees. Where was my life now? What had happened to Before?

"I could not help it," Ilonka said. "I had to send him on. You must also go. Right away. You were seen coming in. You must be seen going out. It is past closing time. You are endangering all of us. Let me jot down the address of the factory."

"You cannot do this, Ilonka," my mother said. "It is almost dark. Let me leave Magda at least."

"No!" Ilonka and I protested in unison.

"I am going with you," I said. "I am not staying here. I want to see Iván." I started to cry.

My mother took the slip of paper from Ilonka. We left without saying goodbye. The iron gate slammed down hard behind us.

"Do you think Iván is at the factory?" I asked, as we were walking toward the tram stop.

"I don't know," my mother said. "Once Ilonka didn't take him in, I don't know where he went. I just don't know."

"And everybody else? Where do you think everybody else is?"

"Stop nagging. Enough questions already. Walk faster."

"There is nowhere to walk, fast or slow. We are at the station."

"Stop it! Stop nagging. Insolent bigmouth. Fresh child. You know as much as I do."

If that was true, it was not much. Night had come. Yesterday's rain had been chased away by a chill fall wind, which was now blowing through Mrs. Szabó's suit jacket. We had not eaten anything since the spoonfuls of jam earlier in the day. I decided it was pointless to mention it. She would just get angry again. Anyway, I was not hungry. In fact, all day my stomach had felt as if I had eaten lead dumplings for breakfast. Where was my brother? What was to become of us? Worry about the unthinkable is the most harrowing worry of all. It is like walking blindfolded in unfamiliar, possibly mined terrain; it is like being struck mute when to save your life heroic oration is called for.

The tramcar stopped in front of us. A little on the late side, my mother urgently whispered, "The address where we are going is the home of your grandparents. Grandma is a little sick. Their name is Viradó. Ours is Dénes. You know nothing about a factory. Nothing."

I nodded. We got on. Lurch. Screech. Clatter. The tram proceeded. We traveled through neighborhoods I had never seen. The home of gnomes. The kingdom of warlocks. No benevolent majesty ruled. We arrived and again we walked in the wind.

At the factory, my mother knocked on some large, beautifully carved wooden gates.

"We are closed. Come back tomorrow," said a stern voice.

"Please," my mother said. "Ilonka sent us."

"I don't know any Ilonka."

"No, Miklós sent us. Olga did. Please."

The gate opened, barely wide enough for my mother to push me in and slip through after me. The man inside was a curly-haired laughing giant. "Whoever sent you, you are obviously Jews. Come in. Come in."

"Is my son here?" my mother asked. "He is a very tall blond boy, with blue eyes. He looks like a Nazi. His name is Iván. Is he here?"

"Oh, is that your boy?" said the man, his grin widening. "A very nice boy. A really wonderful boy. He slept here last night. He left early this morning. He was going to some flower nursery. He was worried about you."

"He left?"

"Yeah. Come on in," said the man.

"He left?"

"This morning," the man said. He turned to me. "What is your name, little girl?"

"Magda. Was my brother all right when he left?"

"Of course he was all right. He was just fine. Come on in."

I was beginning to hate this man. "My brother, did he leave us a message?"

"No, he thought you were going directly to the nursery."

We went in. "In" was hell. My brother had read to me sections of Dante's *Inferno*. I thought maybe Dante had been here just before us, perhaps that morning.

Distorted shadows were moving around in candlelight, over piles of sheet metal. Murmurs could be heard, but no speech. "Quiet," said the man, putting a finger in front of his lips. "In here, the sound carries. You must sleep on the metal sheets. Do the best you can. I am sorry I have no blankets to give you, or food."

"Oh, that's fine," my mother said. "We ate earlier at my friend's house. And we don't mind where we sleep. Thank you. Thank you very much. Curtsy to the gentleman," she said to me. Weary of everything and of all of them, I waved to the man and allowed myself to sink down on the sheet metal with my full weight. A small ripple through the metal made faint eerie music.

"Come, my little mother," my mother said. "Come cuddle close and let's go to sleep."

Next morning, the man woke us very early. "You have to leave," he said. "The workmen are due to arrive at six, and they must not find you here."

My mother had brought with her, in her pocket, a small comb and a lipstick from Mrs. Szabo's apartment. She put on lipstick and combed both of us. We thanked the man again and left.

"Where to now?" I asked.

"We'd better go to the nursery and find Iván." We set out on foot.

For fugitives, safety lies in the absolute absence of others, or in crowds. Everything in between is laden with risk. To be ordinary, inconspicuous, to blend, to melt—to be melody, never counterpoint—is the trick of the successful fugitive. On this day, we stuck out like black donkeys on a snow-covered field.

"Forget yesterday," my mother said. "Today this is the story. We live in Ó Buda. Our house got struck by a bomb two days ago. Your aunt, who was staying with us, died. We escaped. Now we are trying to find your paternal grandparents. Their name is Csaba. Attila and Márja. Our name is Csaba, too. We lost our papers in the fire that ensued in the wake of the bomb. Your father is on the Russian front. You have no brothers or sisters. No other relatives at all. Can you remember all this?"

"Of course I can. I can also remember my grandparents' name from yesterday. They were called Viradó. Why can't you keep it the same from day to day? No one has even asked us yet. I mean, we haven't used up the names, have we?"

"Be quiet," my mother said. "Be quiet. Don't make me nervous. I have enough to think about without being nervous. Are you hungry?"

"After two days without food? Definitely not."

"Why do you have to be so insolent?"

I relented. "Anyu," I said, "it doesn't matter what I say or do. We're in terrible trouble. We don't even know where Iván is, or the others."

We kept walking. As the streets became more populated we hopped a tramcar. Eventually we made it to the nursery.

The first person we saw there was my mother's friend, the owner, Pista Papp. A former member of Parliament, Pista had bought the flower nursery when his politics became dangerously unacceptable and he had to resign his post. Also, some disease had damaged his eyes so badly that he could no longer pursue any occupation that required reading and writing.

"A bad mistake, Margit," he said as he caught sight of us. "A very bad mistake to come. You are well known around here. They know you are Jewish. What the devil were you thinking of?"

"Is Iván here?" my mother asked.

"No," Pista said.

No. Things became soft and undulating all around me. I felt nauseated and suddenly tired enough to lie down right where I stood. Also, something had gone wrong with my ability to breathe.

"I mean, he is not here right now," Pista continued. "He arrived yesterday. I thought the safest thing would be to treat him like the other workers. We had to make a delivery. I sent him out on the truck, with three men. It is safest, believe me."

My mother said nothing. Still, the world reacquired some of its solidity.

"You have to leave, Margit," Pista said. "You are endangering Iván, me, everyone. I will not have it."

My mother nodded. "We will leave. But we have not eaten in two days. You have to feed the child."

"All right. Just come along. Come, little bug. You must be pretty hungry."

A bathroom at last! Soap and towels. Hot food. Normalcy. The talk during the meal was not heartening, however. "You cannot stay," Pista said. "Neither can Iván for more than three or four days. The story we sold to the other workers is that he is back on leave from the army. His home was bombed out, and he couldn't find his family. He worked here before, so now he came back. That story is good for a week at most."

My mother was close to weeping. "I don't know what we should do."

"I don't know, Margit. You may not be in as much danger as you think."

That was a line we were to hear over and over again from people who were turning us away.

I spoke for the first time. "Pista bácsi, can we see Iván?"

"I don't know. If he gets back in time, sure. But you cannot wait for him." He turned back to my mother. "You have been here too long already. Long enough for the authorities to be notified."

That was another lesson we learned: Quick in, quick out. Before the enemy's mind has had time to turn to murder.

"What plans should I make?" my mother asked feebly.

"I don't know, Margit." He turned to his wife. "Sárika, pack them some sandwiches."

Suddenly my mother was in a total rage.

"Na! Just wait a second. Just wait a little second here. We have known each other since our youth. You owe me a little more than sandwiches. I am hunted. My children are in danger of being murdered. You sit in your safe kitchen offering me sandwiches? You ought to be ashamed of yourself. You owe me more than that. In the name of humanity you owe me more."

We all turned to Pista. He stood up. To his eternal credit he said, "You are right. You are absolutely right. I am sorry. I was frightened. You cannot stay here; it really is not safe. Go back to Ilonka's. I will phone her right now." Ilonka was his cousin. "You will wait there. Together we will plan something for you."

As if on cue, my brother appeared in the doorway.

THREE

"WELL, A REUNION. WHAT A PLEASANT SURPRISE," MY brother said with a crooked little grin. "Fancy, all of us still alive. Did I not tell you civility continues to reign abroad in this land?" He aimed a tiny wink at me. We both expected our mother to become enraged at his levity. Instead she staggered up from her chair toward him.

"Oh, Iván," she said, then burst into tears. My brother embraced her, patted her, murmured words of consolation.

At that moment, the light of him was eclipsed. For all his bravado, his eyes looked scared. He was covered with mud and dirt and dust. Some of it he had acquired in the attic; some of it, as it turned out, had been applied by Pista.

"Any trouble on the truck?" Pista asked.

"No," said Iván. "We were stopped twice, but I guess your mud trick worked. We were waved on."

"Good. Sit down and eat. We have to make plans. Margit and Magda should leave. We will all get into trouble."

"You *should* leave," Iván said, turning to my mother. "But

first I have to tell you something. Don't get angry. It is a good thing, particularly now. Magda knows. For the past six months I have been a member of the Zionist underground. The Boy Scout meetings I told you I went to on Wednesday nights were actually Hashomer meetings. They will help us now, tell us where to hide, give us false identity papers that look totally real. Stop worrying. We will be fine. It will only take a few days."

I chimed in. "Iván has been saving Polish and Romanian Jews for months. Taking them from place to place. He is a runner for the Shomers."

My brother looked at me with dark reproach. Oh God, I had done what I'd sworn I wouldn't do. I'd told Anyu I knew. "I thought by now it was all right—"

My mother interrupted. "I see," she said at her iciest. "You trusted a ten-year-old child more than your mother who gave you life. Beautiful."

"No time for this now," said Pista. "You must leave. Go to Ilonka's. We'll meet there and make plans. People come and go in the shop during business hours. You won't be as conspicuous there as you are here."

"Is Iván coming?" I asked.

"No," the three of them answered me in chorus.

"It is safer to split up," Pista bácsi said. "You leave with your mother."

He was obviously as eager to get rid of us as my mother was anxious to stay. As for me, I did not care what we did. I wanted to be where my brother was. If that was impossible, the rest was a matter of total indifference.

Iván leaned down to hug me goodbye.

"I'm sorry," I whispered into his ear.

"Never mind," he whispered back. "I will see you at Ilonka's."

"Yes."

After all-around handshakes and hugs and emphatic assurances of fealty and forgiveness, we left.

Outside, to my surprise, the street looked ordinary. The sun shone. There were passersby, some with packages. There were cars, a bicyclist. Three girls about my age were playing hopscotch.

Still, I felt encased in some invisible substance that stood between me and the world. It was as if my eyes were not quite seeing what they saw. As if my feet touching the pavement stayed up in the air with every step. I did not believe my hands could actually grasp an object and feel its substance. To others I probably looked normal, but I knew the world and I had ceased to be contiguous.

My mother's urgent whisper roused me from my thoughts. "Hurry!" Suddenly she pulled me by the hand with a force that practically severed my arm. "Two Arrow-Cross men who know me from the nursery went by. They might have recognized me. Hurry up!"

"I am hurrying."

From behind us we heard a man scream, "I recognize you, dirty Jewish whore! I'll kill you!"

A shot followed. My mother shoved me forward with all her might so that I stumbled and nearly fell.

"Run!" she yelled. "Run! Jump on the tramcar."

The tramcar was about a third of a block away; it had just started moving. The man fired another shot. It left a little trail of disturbed air above our heads. I heard my mother running directly behind me. I knew she was shielding me but I could not reverse the situation. I kept running.

"The tramcar is moving," I gasped, totally out of breath.

"Jump on the steps. Jump on the steps," my mother yelled. A third shot flew our way.

We reached the tramcar, which had gained momentum. I knew exactly how to hop on a moving tram; Ervin had taught me. But my mother didn't know that and would have vehemently disapproved. I decided this was no time for pretense. I grabbed the metal handle on the side of the tram, slightly above the steps, ran a few beats to get into the rhythm, then jumped forward and up. My mother did the same. We made it.

From inside the tram, a gravelly male voice cried out the Arrow-Cross salutation, "Courage, sister." A uniformed arm, arrow-straight, shot out in our direction, fingers extended. We did not make it after all, I thought. But I was wrong. The man, a little drunk, executed a small balletic twist, grabbed my mother's arm, and helped her into the car, then me. "You should not hop a moving tram. Ever," he said, wagging a flirtatious forefinger in my mother's face. "No sense risking those beautiful legs. They are beautiful, madam."

My mother answered, with a throaty laugh, "You know how it is, brother. Women chat too much. My husband will kill me if we don't pick him up on time at the factory where he works. So bad-tempered." She gave her shoulders a little undulating shrug.

"Married, eh?" the man said. "Too bad. Me, I am single. The old lady died few years ago. She turned yellow first. Liver trouble."

They continued to chat. I knew perfectly well what Mother was doing. His uniformed presence protected us. To the world we looked like a nice little Arrow-Cross family. I did not like it at all, but I kept quiet, as I knew I should.

When we got off to go to Ilonka's, I asked my mother, "Do you think those bullets were real?"

She rolled her eyes and said nothing. I guessed they were real.

We reached the shop, then hung around outside looking at the window display until the one customer finally left. Ilonka greeted us much more warmly than she had the day before.

"Pista telephoned," she said. "You are to go to the upstairs room and wait for him and Iván. They will be here about an hour before closing time. Also I have some very good news. Dávid stopped by. Your parents are at his place, safe. It seems the washerwoman put them up for a night and a day, but then her son, who is a party member, was expected home, so she had to ask them to leave. They walked to Dávid's without any trouble. Naturally, they cannot stay there for long, so plans must be made for them."

Plans, plans, I thought, what are these plans? First we had a good home, then we had a bad home, now we have no home, and plans to make. The lead-hopeless, fatal fatigue of fugitives descended on me.

"You should go upstairs now, before some customer wanders in," Ilonka said. "Sit on the bed. Don't move about and don't talk. We must not arouse any suspicions."

My mother nodded. "Did Dávid say anything about Rózsi or Ervin?"

"Unfortunately, no."

We climbed the steps to the upstairs room. It was small, with a low ceiling and a heavily draped window. Most of the space was taken up by the bed, next to which stood a night table with a lamp. My mother motioned me not to light it. We sat on the bed, side by side in the near darkness. I opened my mouth to say something, but my mother motioned again to be quiet. We heard the tinkle of the shop doorbell. A customer. In seconds, another one. The conversations drifted up to us, but only a word here and there was clear. We sat. One left, then the other. The bell sounded again. A new customer. We sat. Time seemed to fly with badly broken wings around here. At last we heard Pista bácsi's voice. Ilonka and he seemed to be talking of roses. I did not hear Iván. No one approached us. Finally we heard the bang of the corrugated metal gate being lowered.

Pista appeared in our doorway. "Quietly now," he said. "Come down. I will tell you what the plans are."

"Where is Iván?" I asked.

"We thought it better that he not come," Pista bácsi said. "It is safer for all of us." He hesitated. "Well, actually, he went to see his Zionist friends about hiding places and the false papers that you will all need. For now, this is what we will do. Margit, you will stay with Ilonka overnight. Tomorrow, Iván or I will telephone and give you further instructions."

Ilonka cut in, "I cannot stay in the shop. My mother is expecting me at home. Besides, the neighbors know that tonight is not my night to stay."

"That's all right," Pista said. "You can lock Margit in. Then tomorrow she can sit upstairs. Or appear as your first customer. Iván said he will have made arrangements by noon. Have you given them anything to eat, Ilonka?"

Ilonka looked embarrassed. "No, of course not. How could I? There was no time. I didn't eat either. I am going home for supper."

"Fine, fine," Pista said. "I just meant that we don't know when Margit will be able to eat next, so you'd better give her whatever you have now."

"Some wine, two tins of sardines, a piece of bread, a jar of sour pickles." Ilonka recited the contents of her larder like a chastened schoolgirl.

"Margit, you eat as soon as we leave," Pista said. He turned to me. "Little bug, can you wait two hours for a fabulous feast?"

I nodded. "I am not hungry, thank you. Not at all."

I really was not. I knew that I would hate what came out of his mouth next. It would stamp my fate for the worse, if such were possible.

"I came with the truck," he said. "I will drive the child to my sister-in-law's. My brother-in-law is about three steps to the right, but he is a decent fellow. Besides"—Pista burst into a deep, full-hearted laugh—"he owed me quite a bit of money until late this afternoon."

No one laughed with him. "Will she be safe?" my mother asked.

"Of course she will be safe. She'll be fine. You know them. They have no children of their own, although they want some. They will adore her."

"Pista, would you entrust your child to them?"

Pista looked at my mother with a hard, steady gaze. "Given no choice whatsoever? Definitely. Come, little bug," he said to me. "It is getting far too late. We must go."

"Mother," I cried. "Anyu! Where am I going? What is to become of me? I don't want to go."

My mother stepped forward to embrace me. Half bent, she kissed my face. "*Menned kell kisanyám. Menned kell kis csilla-gom.* You must go, my little mother. You must go, my little star. I will come and get you as soon as I can."

I burst into tears. I sank to the floor. "I do not want to go," I began to wail.

Pista clamped a hand over my mouth as he lifted me into his arms. "Shut up," he said with fury. "Shut up. You will get us all arrested."

"Iván said you should go," my mother said.

"No, he did not. I didn't hear him. Édes Anyám, dear Mother, don't let him take me. Please don't let him take me." I was yelling again. Pista's hand was on my mouth again. Ilonka had raised the iron gate halfway. Pista ducked under it and ran toward the truck with me struggling in his arms.

I had never ridden in the cab of a truck. It didn't have the same odor, at all, as cars and taxis. This one smelled faintly of manure, which I did not find unpleasant. I loved, however, the smell of cars, especially of a particular car my father bought when I was little. It was huge and had the combined smell of new leather, car polish, aftershave, and petrol. It smelled of speed, of distance, of excitement, and of Major Grown-up Romance. I figured then that when I grew up I would be driven by a chauffeur in just such a car, with my long blond hair blowing in the wind; many young, handsome, uniformed officers with medals and monocles would pay me court as they praised my profile.

I was not blond, I had no profile, no father, no home. I was not even grown up. I was a short junior editor stuck in this shit-fouled truck cab with an abductor who was driving me away from my brother, on back roads, in the darkness, to God knows where, in order to save my life.

"Na, my little bug," Pista bácsi said. "You have to memorize a few things before we get to where we are going. This is very important. You could get yourself and all the rest of us killed, even Iván, if you forget."

"I know."

"You are going to the home of my wife Sárika's brother and sister-in-law. You are to call them uncle and auntie. When the three of you are alone, you can do or say whatever you want to. If anybody comes in whom you don't know, a neighbor, or friends, the milkman, anyone who is a stranger to you, act shy and say as little as possible. If questioned, your name is . . ."

Here it comes. I bet it isn't Viradó or Csaba, I thought. They all seem to be enamored of inventing false names. "Yes?" I prompted. He looked at me, surprised and a little irritated.

". . . exactly what it is. You are Magda Dénes. No? Now here is the important part. You come from Szeged. You were bombed out twice. Once in your home, once in the church to which you fled after your home was destroyed. Your father is on the Russian front. You and your mother got separated in the second bombing. There was a big fire. You ran. You remember almost nothing else. Someone brought you to this house. These are your uncle and auntie. Stick to the story. Leave all other answers to the grown-ups. If pressed, act stupid. Distracted. Shy. Not frightened, shy. Do you understand? Can you do it?"

"Act stupid? Naturally."

"This is not a joking matter. Anyway, it will not come to any of that."

We rode on in silence. The night was very dark. After a while, I asked, "What is their name?"

"Uncle and Auntie. You are a little shell-shocked. You forgot the rest. It is better that way." I knew he was thinking that if we were stopped, I might give them away before we even got there.

"Of course. Especially since it won't come to any of that."

Pista bácsi glanced at me sharply, but said nothing. He
didn't have to. I knew I was impossibly sarcastic, bigmouthed,
insolent, and far too smart for my own good. I had been told
that. Often. Be it resolved then, I thought, henceforth, for all
time, I will be nothing but shell-shocked, imbecilic, ignorant,
and stupid, stupid.

A while later, Pista turned off the ignition and the head-
lights of the truck. In the dark, we coasted quietly next to a
small house. It, too, was in total darkness, in conformance
with blackout regulations. As we walked toward it, Pista
bumped into a flower pot and nearly started to curse, but
caught himself at the first hiss. We reached the front door and
he knocked almost inaudibly. The door was opened at once by
someone who whispered, "Come in, come in." We entered,
the door was shut, and the light switch clicked on.

The person who had opened the door was a blond, freckled
young woman, a little plump, with a pretty smile.

"*Szervusz*, Pista," she said. "So this is the child."

"This is Magda. Greet Auntie," he said to me.

"*Küss die Hand,*" I said. She did not offer her hand to kiss
or to shake. I was not sure whether a curtsy was called for
under the circumstances, so I refrained.

"Come inside," Auntie said. "Come to the kitchen. Have
something to eat."

"Not me," Pista said, looking at his watch. "I have to get
back to the nursery. But please feed the child. Where is your
husband?"

"Asleep. He couldn't wait up. He starts work at five."

"Oh well. I'd better be going. I'll be in touch tomorrow or
the next day, latest. You have the story of her arrival straight?"

"Yes. Of course."

"Be very careful. We are like a castle of cards. We cannot afford any mistakes."

"Of course. I know."

Pista shook hands with her, then hugged me. "Be a good little girl," he said. "I will be in touch soon."

Auntie switched the light off. Pista slipped out. She turned the light on again. I wished she hadn't; it illuminated my circumstances with the vengeful glint of a deadly blade, aimed straight at the heart. I was a stranger in a strange house. My family was dispersed. My name was variable. I had no address. Everything I had ever known had lost its fixity. What force could shape this chaos into a life again?

"Magduska," Auntie said. "Do they call you Magduska?"

I considered the question. I could nod and let it go. Magduska Csaba Viradó. Why not? I felt too lonely to do it.

"My mother mostly calls me that when she is angry with me," I said in full honesty.

Auntie laughed. "Pista bácsi said you were smart. Come and eat something, Magda."

"Please forgive me," I said, "but I am not hungry. I am very tired. Could I possibly go to sleep?"

She showed me to a bathroom, then to a bed, full of soft pillows and covers. I had not brushed my teeth in four days. Would I ever again? I was too weary to pray. I waved good night to God and went to sleep.

Peculiar days followed. I met Uncle. He was big, cold, and surly. I didn't care. Auntie laughed a lot and tried to draw me out, without success. There was no news of Pista or my family. "No news is good news," Auntie asserted. Mostly I sat. The torpor in my soul had turned my body into wood.

Unexpectedly, neighbors dropped by. Auntie told my story. I kept my eyes to the ground.

"Oh, my poor lamb! Oh, this accursed war!" They addressed questions to me. Before I could answer, Auntie told them that I was shy. Out of the corner of my eye I saw her making the traditional finger-twirling gesture indicating there was trouble inside my head. To me, she said, "Go play in the backyard, little mother." I sat in the yard for a few hours, in the pale autumn sun, and watched things die. Leaves, summer flies, flowers. I was venomously tempted to help a few busy ants meet their Maker, but the idea that someone might be waiting for them somewhere stopped me. At last, the neighbors left.

I never learned which, but either the neighbors' visit or my airing triggered near disaster.

The next afternoon, while we sat in the kitchen, the front door was almost broken down by violent kicks and bangs. There were also shouts of "Open, open! Now! Instantly! This is the law!" and curses.

Uncle jumped to the side window and peeked through the curtain. "Fuck it," he said. "Two gendarmes. Now we are in for it." The uproar intensified. "I knew this was a mistake."

Auntie picked "this" up in her arms and urgently whispered: "I'll hide you in the bread oven. It's big enough. It hasn't been used for months. You'll be fine. For the love of God, stay quiet. Don't move, and whatever happens, don't come out until I take you out. It will be ten minutes at the most."

She shoved me into the oven. While still in forward motion, I heard its broad metal door slam shut, then the clang of the safety catch as it fell into place. In a loud whisper Auntie said, "Move all the way into the back."

The oven was large enough for me to sit with knees drawn to the chest and head bent. I was in total darkness, but to my surprise, the interspatial acoustics were excellent. I heard every damned terrifying word spoken.

"Courage, brothers. Long live Szálasi!" Uncle said. I heard his heels click. "What an enthusiastic entrance."

I could imagine his right eye forming a misguided wink. "To what do we owe this pleasure? Come in, come in." This was the jackass whom my mother had put in charge of my life. Indirectly, to be fair. I heard the heavy clatter of spurred boots.

"Please sit down, brothers. Sit."

"We have come to see the child," said a pleasant baritone.

"Oh, you have found her mother! What a relief," said Uncle without missing a beat.

"No," said an older, uglier voice. "We heard you were harboring a Jewish fugitive of approximately eight years of age, right here in your gracious home."

Eight! What was I, a runt?

"A Jewish fugitive? You hear that, Macza? That's some joke." Uncle slapped his thigh and laughed quite believably. I might have underestimated him. "Oh, brother! You must have an enemy, or a very funny friend. They set you up for a little joke and wasted your time. We do have a child here. She's my godson's sister-in-law's little girl."

Relational distance in these lies seemed very important, I learned in time.

"They were bombed out. Twice. At home and in the church to which they fled. The mother seems to have disappeared. The father is on the Russian front. The child is a little weak in the brain. But a Jew? Don't insult me. I would not let a stinking Jew sit at my table. Please!"

"Perhaps we could speak to the child herself," said the baritone.

"Yes," said the older voice. "We should interview the witness—I mean, the accused." Embarrassed by his error, he became belligerent. "And right now!"

"Of course," Uncle said. "She should be back anytime now. We sent her out to play."

"We will wait," said the baritone.

I knew that I was in more danger with every passing minute, but I was less and less afraid. What worried me most was that the grotesque humor of this overheard exchange might make me burst into a belly laugh.

"You should wait," Auntie said. "She is a very sweet child. Worth meeting. A little shy. Meanwhile, why don't we all sit down and have a little rum?"

"Kissing your hand, madame, I would be glad of some," said the older voice.

I heard the noises of people arranging themselves for a party. As the gendarmes took off their helmets, they jangled against the table. I did not hear the whoosh of the rooster feathers with which they were decorated, although in my mind's eye I saw them bobbing.

"To your health," Uncle said.

"And to yours," Oldie said.

"To Szálasi and to the party," added the baritone.

"To all of us," Auntie replied. Glasses clinked.

What seemed like two hours passed. Then three. My legs began to cramp. My neck hurt. I started to wonder where my air supply came from and how long it would last.

"We must make a search," said the drunk baritone.

"Right. Guns at the ready," said the old voice, equally drunk. "No child stays out this late."

I heard guns being cocked.

"You are right," Uncle said. "Where is my head? I must go

out and search for her." He bolted before anyone could stop him.

"And don't come back until you find her! No matter what!" Auntie shouted after him.

This was standard procedure, as I learned later. Men, who were usually in greater danger, fled; the women stayed to flirt, and if necessary to put out, trading dignity for survival. When it worked it was thought to be a good bargain.

"How about another round?" Auntie offered.

"First we search," the baritone said.

"Go ahead." Auntie seemed to be leaving the room.

I froze as I broke into a sweat. I didn't think I could hold my head bent anymore. I didn't think I had enough air left. I thought I would scream. "You are a bread, you are a bread," I said to myself. The wrong palliative: Over-yeasted, I will rise and burst through the door. Or else I will be baked. All right. Not a bread. Whatever I am, I am alone, in dreadful danger.

"Hey," called the baritone, "don't you go following her. We both have to search."

"Sherch, sherch. You are, you are . . ." He trailed off.

A derelict to duty, I wanted to say out loud. Iván would have laughed.

They opened and banged shut a few cabinet doors and some drawers. They were nowhere near the oven.

"Satisfied?" asked Auntie, who had returned to the room. "How about another round?"

"Hey, where is your husband all this time?" asked the baritone.

"Gone to look for the child."

"We better search some more. I bet that child is a Jew and

is hidden right here." Suddenly he sounded angry and more sober.

Auntie began to cry. "Brother, I'm ashamed to admit it, but he has another woman. He runs to her all the time. I swear to God I don't know where the child is. She is not normal." By now Auntie was racked with sobs.

The baritone relented. "Well, it's late. We probably did get the wrong report. You do look like a full Aryan, patriotic, beautiful woman. Perhaps it was your husband's mistress who telephoned us. Who knows? Do you want me to investigate her?"

"No, brother, thank you. You know how it is. These things have to be solved at home." She giggled.

"In bed, eh? He is a fortunate man. Well, good luck with finding the dimwit." He clicked his heels. "Courage, sister," he said, and clicked again.

"Hey," he shouted at the other stalwart protector of the soon-to-become-fully-Aryan-Hungarian nation. "Wake up, Jóska. It's time to go. I will explain everything."

I heard the fellow jump; his heels clicked. "Long live Szálasi! Courage!" he yelled.

Almost immediately, the oven door opened. Six hours had passed.

"Oh my baby," Auntie said, now truly weeping. "Are you still alive? Did you have enough air? Can you move?"

I was shaking so hard that I was unable to respond. She pried me out of the oven, put me to bed, and made me drink several glasses of water.

The next thing I knew I was at Ilonka's in my mother's lap. Saved. Reunited. Never to be parted again.

"Where is everyone else?" I asked my mother anxiously.

"It is all good news," my mother said. "Rózsi and Ervin have returned unharmed from the Tattersal. What happened to them is a long story, but now they are fine."

She told me that with hands held high the entire route, Rózsi and Ervin had been marched to the racetrack of Budapest with hundreds of others. Rózsi was worried because they both stuck out—Ervin was too tall; she was too redheaded and wore a very good pantsuit. She took the jacket off to blend in better, but then she was too cold.

At the racetrack, men and women were separated. Rózsi became hysterical. She drifted near one of the Arrow-Cross guards and started chatting him up. "You see that tall boy in the green knitted bomber jacket? That's my son. He's very tall, but he's only fourteen. Even if we're not together, please let us stand near each other." Rózsi had a great deal of charm. The Nyilas brought Ervin around and allowed both of them to lower their arms. They were kept overnight and then everyone was let go. One more exercise in extreme harassment. No one got killed and only one young girl was raped, over and over, by many, all through the night. She screamed and prayed for death, but she did not die.

"Now, as for us," my mother continued, "Iván has arranged everything."

"What do you mean?"

"Well, he got in touch with the Hashomer. They have access to various houses under the protection of the Swiss government. The Swiss are not part of this war. Rózsi and I are staying in a house on Vadász Utca. Until yesterday, Iván and Ervin were in another house on Vekerle Sándor Utca, but they have moved over with us to Vadász Utca. That building has been officially designated an annex of the Swiss consulate. The

Zionists are using it as headquarters. We are forging Christian birth certificates and letters of protection by the dozen." My mother laughed. "I am in charge of filling them out, because my handwriting looks so official."

"And the old ones, where are they?"

"Rescued also. Iván took them to another building. A safe house on St. Istvàn Park."

"Why are they not with you?"

"Well, there are many reasons. The building on Vadász Utca is small. Already almost four hundred people have crowded into it. There isn't enough room. Also, all those who are there work for the Zionists. Iván and Erwin are runners. Rózsi and I are in the office, forging documents, routing people to various safe houses, keeping records, and so on. It is a very busy place. No old people have been allowed to move in." She paused. I waited. She looked away, then resumed in her I-want-no-arguments voice, "Sanitary conditions are extremely poor. Everyone sleeps on the floor. Food is very scarce. So there is really no place for children either."

I could not believe what I had just understood, although it had not yet been fully said. All I could think of was that I was six inches too short to remain with my family. My creeping conviction, acquired in the TB sanatorium, that children are disposable rubbish was true. My childness was like a plague that endangered everyone who came in contact with it. I was an embarrassment, a burden, a reluctant obligation to be fulfilled under the hard, chafing yoke of duty.

"I want to speak to Iván," I said, and began to cry.

"You can't. It is too dangerous for him to come here. I will give him the message. Anyway, we have to leave in the morning."

I had two mothers: the one I pursued and the one who was present. The iron mother.

"Where are we going?"

"Well, dear, as I told you, Vadász Utca is a very dirty place. Extremely unhealthy. Not fit for a former TB patient. Not fit for children. I want to keep you safe and well. It is important for you to have fresh air."

"Where is St. Istvàn Park?"

"What do you mean? That's not where you are going."

I started to sob. Why did I have to be all alone again?

"I want to speak to Ivàn. He will take me to Vadász Utca."

My mother raised her right hand in the impending gesture of a slap. "If you don't stop the hysterics, I will hit you. Stop it!"

Instinctively, I crossed my arms in front of my face. She became even more enraged. "Don't you dare defend yourself from me! Down with the arms! If you deserve to be slapped, I will slap you. Down with the arms!"

I considered letting fly the strychnine-tipped darts stored in my heart. But what would become of me without her? In any case, the fight had gone out of me.

"Where am I going?"

"Oh, to a wonderful place, under the protection of the Spanish Red Cross. On Rózsadomb. It is totally safe, organized by the Zionists especially for children. Clean. It will be practically like a vacation for you."

"Of course. And on the way there why don't I whistle a funeral march?"

I did not see it coming. What I saw were the myriad little lights the slap exploded in my head.

At dawn we set out, hand in hand. Evidently there would

be no sunrise. The cold morning air smelled of yesterday's rain and of imagined snow. The sky was the color of gravestones. Nothing shined. Nothing reflected. My mother looked tired.

"You know the routine," she said. "Except we're using our own names. I have our forged papers with me, so we're relatively safe. Anyway, I will do the talking."

"Of course. How much farther?"

"A kilometer, maybe two. Listen, I have nowhere else to put you. This is the safest place. Really. I am trying to do what is best. I love you."

"I know, Anyu. I love you, too."

"Tomorrow I'll bring you some clothes and food. The call from Pista was so abrupt, and Ilonka wouldn't let us stay another day. I am doing the best I can."

"I know." We walked on, uphill, slightly out of breath. A blond boy in a Nazi uniform stepped out of the mists. "Halt," he said. *"Wo gehen Sie?"*

He looked very much like my brother. A desperate yearning overcame me. I beamed up at him. I waved. *"Szervusz,"* I said. "Hello." He burst out laughing. "Servus," he replied as he patted my head. He waved us on.

"Don't ever do that again," my mother said with suppressed anger. "It is much too dangerous."

I shrugged. "It worked, didn't it?" I said, as if I had planned the action. We trudged on.

"Mother, please don't leave me. I will be good. I don't care about the dirt. I don't care about beds. I don't care about anything. I just want to be where you are. Where Iván is. Please."

"Don't start in again," my mother said curtly. "There *is* no other place."

"Yes there is. We could turn back right now and you could take me with you to Vadász Utca. Please. I will be very good. I will be no trouble at all."

"Stop it. The decision has been made."

The iron mother had decided.

"Does Iván know where you are taking me?"

"Of course. He arranged it. It was not easy, believe me."

I abandoned all hope. It also began to dawn on me, as yet in the form of a mere glimmer, that perhaps influence and distance stand in inverse relation to each other. Living with Iván, Mother had clearly gained the upper hand.

A pockmarked, angry-faced Arrow-Cross guard halted us. "Your identification papers." His foot tapped a menacing beat.

My mother's handiwork was about to be put to the test, probably for the first time. She rummaged in her handbag at great length, as any unfrightened woman would do.

Survival in the midst of the enemy is a circus art. It requires the balance of the aerialist. The skill of the magician. The speed of the juggler. The resilience of the clown. The cunning of the midget. The courage of the lion tamer.

"Oh, these big stupid bags," my mother said. "Na! At last. Here you are, brother."

"Just like my wife," he muttered. "It takes her half an hour to find a box of matches when I need a light. What is it with women and pocketbooks?" He barely glanced at the papers. "Go on, go on," he said. "Make the next checkpoint guy happy."

My mother's arm shot out. "Long live Szálasi."

The Spanish Red Cross was housed in a beautiful villa on top of a hill, with stunning views of large oaks, chestnut trees, and acres of lawn. It was, however, not all my mother cracked it up to be. It didn't have enough beds for everyone. No blankets. No towels. No real food. Only one bathroom worked. I hated the woman who gave us all this information, indirectly indicting my mother. She did, however, promise to take good care of me. My mother kissed me and was off. Desertion must be swift, like a knifing. The perpetrator gone before the unbelieving, rounded eyes can accuse or plead.

The woman, whose name I had forgotten, but whose presence was too repulsive for me to want to ask again, ushered me into a large communal room. The floor was carpeted; the windows were enormous and probably flooded the room with sunlight on a clear day. That day, their hugeness merely admitted more of the gray-metal outside, making me feel that I was about to drown in the murky waters of a pool in an underground cave.

"This is Magda," the woman said brightly. "She is the newest member of our little family. Let us all welcome her."

Where the hell does this idiot think we are? In kindergarten at ice-cream time? I did not want a new little family. I just seemed to have been irretrievably dumped by my old one.

A few children gathered around us. Many more sat in the back of the room, but they appeared to be about as interested in the proceeding as I was. Thank God.

"This is Julika."

"*Szervusz.*"

"*Szervusz.*"

"This is Péterke." "*Szervusz.*" "*Szervusz.*" "And Tamás, and Erika, and this is Mimi. She is our youngest, three years old."

Mimi stuck out a mean tongue at me. I made a gesture as if to catch her tongue, but instead of being amused, she burst into tears.

"Now look what you have done," said the woman.

Mimi had more sense. When I opened my arms to her, she ran into them at once. I lifted her. "Now, Mimi," I said, "this is the plan: You and I are going to go to a quiet corner in this room. We are going to sit on the floor and we are going to think. All right?"

Mimi nodded yes into my neck.

I speedily excused myself from the woman, whose mouth had not yet closed.

Mimi and I did exactly as I told her. She nestled into me and I closed my eyes to think. On sober consideration, my situation seemed dire and quite hopeless. My mother was obviously dead set on leaving me here. I had no way to get in touch with my brother. These two exhausted the list of my available resources. The only other option I had was to run away. But to where? I had not been taught to commute, so I didn't know how to get anywhere from anywhere—a fatal omission I had permitted in my upbringing, I now realized.

I was roused from my thoughts by The Woman, as I had decided to call her.

"I have to feed Mimi and put her to bed. Do you have any luggage at all? A blanket? Anything to eat?"

Naturally. I have this invisible portmanteau chock full of *gulyás*, goose liver, homemade bread, feather comforters, a brother, a cousin, several mothers, and all the United States of Amerika where my father lives, racked with constant concern about me.

"No. We had to leave in a hurry. My mother said she will bring me some things tomorrow if she can."

"Well, all right. I'll lend you a blanket and some food. You will have to pay me back tomorrow."

"Thank you. Pardon me, but I did not catch your name."

"I am Mrs. Ungár. Mimi's mother."

To my astonishment, I burst into sobs. I tried to cover them, pressing my hands to my face as I pretended to have a coughing fit.

"You must be catching a cold," Mrs. Ungár said. "I'll be back in a few minutes."

On returning, she handed me a blanket, a glass of water, and some bread and jam. "I am sorry," she said, "but food is very scarce."

I nodded. "Thank you very much. Actually, this is quite extraordinarily decent of you."

She laughed. "What grade are you in?"

"I started the fourth grade, then the saturation bombings and everything else happened. I had to stop."

Mrs. Ungar sighed. "You seem to like this corner. Stay here. Wrap yourself tightly in the blanket. It gets cold at night up here on the hill. Good night."

I dreamt of an earthquake and of bridges crumbling. No, I did not. I simply thought that if I dreamt of such things it might make me a poet and therefore entitle me to something. Perhaps to be rescued.

In the first hours of the next day, I thought again, This is not a good place. In the early afternoon, my mother arrived with blankets, a pillow, a toothbrush, clean underwear, a bottle of milk, fresh bread, and an obscene quantity of food of a quality none of us had seen for years. I am done for, I thought. I have just been supplied with my last supper.

"I had to get through several checkpoints. I barely got here," she said breathlessly.

"Why do I have to stay here alone?" I asked her point-blank, fixing her eyes with mine. "Why?"

Her eyes wandered, returned, darted away, closed.

"Because. Because it is better for you. Because it has been decided."

"Why? I am not safer here than at Vadász Utca."

"Of course you are. Safer than anywhere else."

It is finished, I thought. She means to lose me. So be it.

"Well, so long, Anyuci," I said. "I am missing Ping-Pong in the recreation room." She didn't get it.

"Oh, fine," she said. "Fine. Goodbye." We kissed.

This was our parting for life, as far as I knew. Or for death, to be more accurate. What have I done? I thought. What have I done so grievously wrong, so despicably bad, as to deserve this? Surely, I must deserve this, or else I would be reprieved.

Days passed. A week. More time. I steadily declined musical chairs, sing-alongs, and twenty questions.

We each ate alone, at odd times, in secret, in corners. I was ashamed of all the food I had, but afraid to offer it around. In a minute, it would be all gone and I would have none left. Still, chocolate began to choke me; sardines stuck in my gullet. I wished to die.

Rumors began to circulate that the Nazis would attack the building and remove the children to parts unknown. I did not care. Mrs. Ungár said rumors were the same as lies. She was a little simple-minded. Still, when a number of children were taken away by parents or relatives, and one escaped on his own, her countenance darkened. I did not care very much.

One afternoon an older boy, almost my brother's age, announced a poetry reading. The performers were all *gimnáz-ium* kids who lived together in one room upstairs. I could not resist. They read Ady, Babits, Kosztolányi. I was transported to better times.

Incautious in pleasure, forgetting the world, I cried out at applause time after an Ady poem, "My favorite, my favorite, my very most favorite!"

The organizer boy gave me the fisheye. "Well, dear," he said, his voice winking at his friends, "name us another favorite. We are like gypsy musicians, ready to oblige requests."

My mind went blank: my brain turned to soapsuds. I could not remember a single line of poetry. Nothing. Amid resounding laughter, I retreated in haste to my corner and wept with my face turned to the wall. Where was my brother?

Next morning, surprisingly, a few new children arrived. One of them was a boy about thirteen. He was not brought but came alone, and was much admired for this feat. The resident children and Mrs. Ungár surrounded him. From the center of his circle, he nodded at me in the corner. I smiled back.

Soon he walked over and lowered himself next to me on the floor. "I am Ervin," he said. "What is your name?"

"Magda."

"How come you are so corner-trapped? Why are you so sad? Are you hungry? I am. Is there anything to do around here? Why do you look like a sailboat without sails? Are you alone?"

I started to laugh. So did he.

"You see," he said, "I have my uses. I wanted to demonstrate them to you. Now your eyes no longer look mouse-shit scared. They are bright-green beautiful."

I laughed again. He'd said the word "shit." It was very daring, I thought. "Are you really hungry?"

"Starved. Ravenous. Famished. Skeletons rattle in my stomach but do not dare to bite me because I would bite back. I have not eaten since yesterday morning. Don't worry, though, I will promote some food for us soon enough. Who could resist giving a little handout to a boy like me? Many little handouts add up to a lot of edibles."

I was laughing again. "You don't have to do that," I said. "I have plenty of food. You can eat as much as you like." My relief at his presence was overwhelming. I laughed again for no reason.

"Wait," he said, suddenly serious. "You don't have to give me your food. I really do know how to live by my wits. You obviously don't."

"Please. I would like to."

"Well, then, that is an entirely different story. We will have a picnic. Spread the blanket. Make sure no ants get on it. I'll scrounge around to see how we can make this table a little more festive."

He returned without a smile. "I found an old dirty bar of soap. I didn't think there was enough time to fashion it into candles. That's all I found. It's amazing how stripped this whole place is."

"Don't worry. The food I have is exceptional. Get some glasses of water."

We sat on the blanket and chomped away. He ate systematically, as if he were filling an empty barrel. I had not had such a good time since the Green Shirts rousted us on the 16th of October, or perhaps even for a while before that.

"So tell me all about yourself," he said. I giggled. It was a phrase that Iván and my cousin Ervin made fun of.

"I guess you have brothers," he said. We both laughed.

Other than living in almost constant danger of being murdered, this was the most astonishing thing that had ever happened to me. Here was a boy I didn't know, but looking at him made me happy. What a puzzle. How could I have guessed that by age ten, the war would have initiated me into the two major existential mysteries of life? Death and Love. Love and Death.

"It is good food, isn't it?"

"You know it is." He took another length of *kolbász*. "It is excellent. How come?"

"My mother brought it. She means to leave me here for the duration. You know, 'Till death do us part.' "

"Fuck it. Do you want to be my *bachurah*?"

"What does that mean?"

" 'Fuck it'?"

"No, I've heard that before. What does *bachurah* mean?"

"You are amazing," he said, truly exasperated. "You are in mortal danger. You are hiding for your life. You may have to run any minute and you don't know the simplest things. How do you expect to live? *Bachurah* means girlfriend in Hebrew."

"What does it involve?"

"Well, we share our food."

We both laughed so hard that Mrs. Ungar came over to ask us if we were all right. When she left, Ervin said, "You know perfectly well what I meant. I told you you didn't have to give me your food. I would have gotten some for both of us."

"I know. What else does it involve?"

"At night I'll lie down next to you in this corner, although I hate corners. I'll put my arm around you and you won't have nightmares."

"What else?"

"You are too young for the other stuff."

"What do you mean?"

"Forget it."

"What else?"

"Forget it, I said!" He was yelling.

"All right."

I thought perhaps he really liked me. An idea formed. "Listen," I said. "Do you know where Vadász Utca is? Would you know how to get there?"

"I just came from there," he said.

"From Vadász Utca? Now? Why? How? Tell me!"

"What's the big deal? It's a day's trip, with luck. If the gendarmes don't stop you. Why are you so excited? What is at Vadász Utca?"

"My brother. My cousin. Everybody. How can it be so easy? You must be crazy."

"I will take you there today, if you like. We can run away from here easily. I don't care where I go. But why Vadász Utca? It's not a terrific place."

All of this was beyond comprehension.

"I have to think," I said. "Please just let me sit here a little while, alone."

"Of course." He started walking away.

"Ervin," I called after him, "are there kids there our age?"

"Some. What is this thing with you and Vadász Utca?"

"Never mind. Just let me think."

About an hour later he returned, laughing. "I think I know who you are," he said. "You have a brother named Iván and a cousin who is my namesake, or used to be. True?"

"What do you mean, used to be?"

"His name is Simcha now. He adopted a Hebrew name. He has a *bachurah*. Her new name is Shoshana. She's eighteen. Very pretty."

"Just a second. My cousin's last name is Guttman. He is very tall, but he is fourteen."

"Yeah, the same fella. Your brother has a *bachurah* also. Only she is a *shiksa*. A judge's daughter. She lives in Buda, across the river. Your brother keeps running over there, to everybody's amusement, since he is so committed to saving all the Jews of Budapest."

"You are insane. You must be insane. I have to think."

This news was incredible, astonishing. Intuitively I was aware that it had major implications for my life, but I was unable to particularize its significance. Or unwilling. I sat, turning the words over in my mind. *Bachurah*, Shoshana, judge's daughter. Some conclusion had to emerge.

The boy is lying.

Wrong.

This has nothing to do with me.

Wrong.

Well, what then?

It is hard to say.

Judge's daughter, *bachurah*, Shoshana.

Come on, conclude! Conclude!

In the past I had been the sole, the exclusive, the only important girl in the boys' lives. Evidently, through absence, my status had collapsed. I had to rush to Vadász Utca most urgently to see what I could salvage from this rubble.

Now you have it!

Fine, I thought. But what do I do? I could escape with this Ervin and he might take me there. Or not. We could get caught. Separated. I knew I did not know how to survive alone in the city. Also, I was scared to go. Terrified. Better try a letter first. I found Ervin.

"Listen," I said. "I will write a letter to my mother to get her to rescue me from here. If it doesn't work, I'll become your *bachurah* and we'll do whatever you say. Is that all right?"

"Of course. There are two imperatives you should observe in writing that letter, if I may say so. I don't know why I am advising you, since I hope you fail."

"Yes?"

"Principle number one: Grovel. Adults like that. Principle number two: Grovel."

We laughed.

I asked Mrs. Ungar for a pencil and a piece of paper. She provided them and assured me that a courier would pick up the letter the following day. Every two or three days there were runners between the safe houses of Budapest carrying news and mail. How strange that in all this time my brother had not been assigned to come here.

The letter I sent, translated verbatim into English, is as follows:

My Sweet Dear Little Mother!

Please send someone for me urgently. Do not come yourself because for you it is dangerous. About fifty children were taken from here and three escaped. If possible send the car for me.

I am very anxious here regarding all of you. It is better to be together. My little mummy, take me to you without fail. My sweet only little mother, I cannot bear it without you. My dear little mummy, come today or send someone for me. My little mother, if we cannot be together I don't know what I will do.

How are you all? Sweet little mother of mine, have you heard of the ground raid? If the radio announces a ground raid, then with five days' worth of food one has to go to the basement. I am so nervous if you are not with me. Dearest little mother, it does not matter if there is no food, if there is no decent blanket,

I just want to be with you. My little one, how are Rózsi néni,
Ervin, Iván, and the old ones? My little mother, I beg you to
come for me.

I kiss you a thousand times and hug each of you separately.

MAGDA

As I wrote, every phrase, like fulminating acid, burned into
my flesh and rotted it with shame. To this day the question
remains: Was I ashamed for groveling in order to manipulate,
or was that the pretense? Were these sad, naked sentences an
unguarded revelation of what I truly felt—a beggar, forsaken?

More rumors drifted our way. The days of this shelter
appeared to be numbered. It was said that someone from the
German High Command had warned the Zionist leaders that
the children would be arrested and shipped to Poland anytime
now. Still, the Zionists mounted no organized rescue opera-
tion. That could mean one of several things. 1. The rumors
were untrue. 2. They could not find a suitable place for us so
quickly. 3. We had been written off. 4. There was no one left
to help us.

The atmosphere palpably deteriorated. As before a thunderstorm, the air was heavy with electric energy, ready to ignite.
The younger children shivered and tried to hide, like small
animals who sense some nameless impending doom. Everybody wept more. Fights broke out. At night, many more
dreamers groaned or screamed in terror.

Ervin said we should escape. I said I wanted to give my
letter a longer chance.

My mother did arrive. She came in the "company" car, one
of several vehicles with diplomatic immunity which the Swiss
consul occasionally lent the Zionists for rescue missions. I was
awed and overjoyed.

My mother had also heard the deportation rumors, which had augmented the impact of my letter. I didn't care how it happened. She had come, and I was going with her.

We both thanked Mrs. Ungar. I hugged Mimi and went to say goodbye to Ervin. My mother had given me permission to offer him a ride. "Naw," he said. "Vadász Utca isn't a good place. It's overcrowded and boring. I may go to a safe house in Buda; I've heard better things about that one. Or I may not go. Who knows?"

"Your parents—where are they?" It was the first time that I had dared to intrude. Or perhaps because my mother was with me, I had the courage to ask.

"Shot. Both of them. Trying to escape a roundup."

I had in my hand a bag with my remaining food. I lifted it toward him.

"Take it. Please."

"Thank you," he said. "Just look how profligate you are, in every way. You could have been my *bachurah*."

In the car, I was struck again by the disparity between the communal world and individual destinies. I rode, for the moment in safety, with my mother. Ervin was alone. All alone.

Several weeks later the news came: A day or two after I was taken by my mother, everyone at the Spanish Red Cross was arrested. They were herded to the ramparts of the Danube— Mimi and Ervin and Mrs. Ungar and all the rest of them— and shot into a turbulent, watery grave. This may have been, of course, only a rumor.

Some gentiles stood in a cheerful, chatty circle around a newspaper kiosk. The sun shone. God was not in his heaven. I was in the safe car racing toward Vadász Utca.

"What is it like there?" I asked.

"Where?"

"At Vadász Utca."

"We are not going there."

I was stunned. She couldn't know what she was saying. This was not like when I was bad and we skipped the circus. This was not like when I refused my vitamins and she canceled the zoo outing. This was not no dessert because I hadn't finished my main dish. This was my life. I *needed* to get to Vadász Utca.

"How can you do this to me?"

"For heaven's sake! You have been told before. It is not a fit place for you. I am tired of this constant nagging."

"I thought you were taking me to be with you."

"I am taking you with me to Ilonka's."

"You will stay there too?"

"No, of course not. There is no room and I have to get back to Vadász Utca."

I guess begging does not beget love, I thought. I felt at the edges of myself. Raw as burnt flesh, jagged as a saw, full of sorrow. It is finished, finished.

At Ilonka's, my mother told me that I would have to be a very good little girl. During the day, while there were customers in the shop, I was to lie on the bed in the small attic room. I was not to move, not to pee, not to read. The rustle of the pages might be overheard, and anyway, there was not enough light in the room for reading. When the shop closed at midday I could come down, stretch my legs, go to the bathroom, wash, have lunch, converse, and behave normally. Then go back up again until closing time and supper. At night, sometimes Ilonka would stay with me in the same bed; at other times I would be locked in on my own. On those nights immobility and silence must be observed, because the neighbors would expect the place to be empty. I was to ignore air-raid sirens at all times.

"Is all this understood? Is it clear?"

"Yeah. Clearer than you can imagine."

My mother left, surprised and offended that I didn't want to kiss her.

We started our new routine with supper. Ilonka's mother, Miszlai néni had brought it over from their home nearby. Evidently this was not an unusual practice, so it wouldn't arouse suspicion. Ilonka often stayed late to work on the books or to organize the shop and have dinner here with her mother.

To me, the meal was a miraculous resurrection of happy memories. My grandmother kept a kosher home; my mother had not. Our old cook, Irma, had made bean soup exactly like this, full of pieces of pork and bacon and ham, which we then ate, my brother and I, on a separate plate with black bread and mustard. Just like now.

I had not eaten mustard since my father left. My grandmother considered mustard an immoral food that ruined your kidneys. Come to think of it, she had many odd indicators of moral turpitude deserving the deepest contempt: eating anchovies, biting your nails, wearing sunglasses (obviously to cover the oozings of trachoma), stuttering, sucking on an aching tooth, or trying out ballerina steps seen at the sideshows of a local flea market.

I was shown to bed and told that tonight I would be locked in. Air-raid sirens woke me. Through the double-shuttered windows, they sounded faint, ghosts whistling an eerie dirge in the dark. A message from the netherworld: Hell was poised in the sky, ready to fall to earth in fire.

The explosions started before the third round of warning

was over. Antiaircraft guns responded in furious staccato. I wasn't very frightened until later, when I heard the detonations come nearer and nearer. The building seemed to stand under the path of aerial retreat. An astonishing realization struck. I knew only the first two words of the Jewish prayer for a time of danger and dying: *Shema Yisrael.* I could not die all alone, without even God for company. I would have to do what I had learned not long ago: kneel and say their prayer. "Our Father who art in heaven." It didn't seem right. It seemed humiliating to address God in Christian in the hour of my Jewish death. I thought I should learn *Shema Yisrael* in its entirety. Fast.

The glass in the window began to rattle in a most alarming manner. That tended to be the sign of an imminent bulls-eye. Even if the bomb strayed a block or two, the glass would shatter, there would be fires, the injured, the dead, rescue squads. Death squads to me.

My assessment of the raid was wrong, I learned the next day from Ilonka. What I had heard was something brand-new: planes in such concentrated numbers, in such mind-boggling quantity, that their vibrations created shock waves of sufficient strength to affect the stability of what was below them.

My insides could attest to this.

Breakfast was a brief but rather pleasant affair. I seemed to have earned some stripes through my silent endurance of the previous night's raid. Ilonka gave me two sticky buns. God knows where she got them; I hadn't seen any in years. And hot, sweet coffee with milk. Another rare luxury. Then, up to bed with me for the day.

In the forced twilight of the room, as in a bewitched kingdom, everything stood still. I turned inward. I took my pulse.

I counted my teeth with my tongue. I measured my heartbeat while holding my breath. I tried out old shadow games which did not work. I dozed. I dreamt. I woke. I dozed. I remembered.

When you come down to it, fear is an entertaining emotion. It keeps everything inside you buzzing. It keeps you taut, tingling, alert, prepared to jump, ready to invent lies, set to overcome odds. Fear contains in itself possibilities of the spectacular.

But the most pervasive emotion in me was not terror. It was disbelief. How could all this have happened? How? Could it have been foretold? Prevented? Had my father known? Was that why he had left? Why had he then not taken us? But even aside from him, how could this have happened?

I was no longer afraid, and even that didn't frighten me, although I knew it to be the nadir of defeat. Let what comes, come. Let what is, be. My previous life receded. I was only this: a body on a bed. Why should anyone want to harm me? I was disappearing anyway.

These were my thoughts on bad days. On good days I fretted. I couldn't recall when I'd last had a bath. I washed myself every night in the sink downstairs, piece by piece, hopping on one foot to stick the other under the running water and scrub it with the foul-smelling soap Ilonka provided. Still, I felt dirty all the time. I also felt exiled. I thought I might have appendicitis. I suspected the constant artificial twilight would make me go blind. I worried that I had forgotten how to read. I knew for a fact that I could no longer remember how to analyze the grammatical structure of a sentence. I also knew that if I were to complain of this to Ilonka she would think I had gone insane. I forgave her, though, because we kept eating mustard.

Sometime during this period my head began to itch, at first just a little, then with growing intensity. Scratching it turned into a major imperative pleasure.

When Ilonka noticed, she became alarmed and suspicious.

"What's wrong with your head?"

"It itches."

"Why?"

I shrugged. Who could fathom the dark mysteries of an itch? Itching usually comes as a surprise, suddenly, like an accident. It can be set in motion by some internal disruption that in time blossoms forth in the form of a boil, a pimple, a sore, a rash. It can be caused by contamination like a mosquito bite or touching poison ivy; also by contagion, as when you see someone else scratch. It can even come by suggestion, just from thinking about itchy things.

I remembered the summer I turned four. We were in a rented country house. It must have been late in the season, because the house was surrounded by piles of freshly cut hay.

"Doesn't it look inviting?" Iván had asked.

"What?"

"The haystack, dummy. We could climb the ladder to the roof of the porch. It juts out a bit. If we aimed ourselves properly we could jump right into the middle of the stack."

We were both barefoot and in bathing suits. The roof seemed far away. The ladder looked rickety.

"I don't think we are permitted."

"Of course not, dummy. Nothing fantastic is permitted, but who would know? Up, down, out. It would be a less-than-four-minute adventure."

"We might get hurt."

"We will not get hurt. The hay is soft. Come on."

"No."

He got angry. "You are scared. Admit it. You are a coward. Cow-ard, cow-ard! Spoilsport! I knew it." He was yelling *sotto voce;* our parents were in the house.

"Yes." I hung my head. Guilty as charged.

"Fine. Just fine. You wait here, coward. I will go by myself." He started toward the ladder.

"No!" I said quickly. "I'll come." I didn't want him to get hurt alone. Or to be punished alone, if that was to be the case.

He stopped and smiled. "We will jump together hand in hand. Is that better?"

Infinitely. Anywhere. Always.

Our descent is still a tinkling thrill in my heart. The whoosh of air, the upward-flying sliver of sun, the drumroll of blood in my ears. My brother's hand in mine.

We landed smack on target. Then we sank, way down into the pile. I feared we would drown. We did not, but we did have to shout for help. The hay was piled too tightly for us to fight our way out sideways. Tarzan was eleven years old.

Rescued, we had to be rushed to the doctor. We had welts all over our bodies, and ticks in some of the welts. We itched painfully for more than a week, which our parents considered enough of a lesson.

Over the years, whenever the incident came fully to mind, I itched all over and grinned.

Later in my life, remembering, I itched and wept.

"Well?" Ilonka asked, exasperated. "What do you have to say?"

I shrugged again.

"Stop shrugging. It is very rude. I'll call your mother to come wash your hair. Perhaps that's all you need. In the meantime, don't ever scratch while there are customers. They might hear you."

"Thank you. Please forgive me." Mentally I shrugged twice. Ten times. I didn't give a damn about anything anymore. Not even about a visit from my mother. She was coming to wash my hair. So what? I liked scratching.

Two or three days later, my mother arrived, triumphantly holding up a bottle of shampoo. "Look at this!" she said.

"You are incredible!" said Ilonka. "Shampoo! Sweet Jesus. You are a magician."

Closeted in the small toilet, my mother said, "Ilonka is worried that you have head lice. If you do, she won't keep you here any longer. She is afraid of catching them. You'd better not have lice, because I have nowhere else to take you."

"Is it an optional matter, Anyuci? Can I decide not to have them? If I am good, will they abscond? How does it work?"

She lost her temper, as I meant her to do. "The whole world is on fire, but you alone don't change. Fresh, insolent, big-mouthed, sarcastic. Just like your father. What is wrong with you?!"

"Lice, I guess, Anyu. What do you think? Lice I acquired at the wonderful Spanish Red Cross place. You remember. 'Practically a vacation,' you said."

"Good Apuci's darling little daughter, I will wash your hair now. Lean over the sink."

She grabbed my head and pushed it forward and down. I was too short. My head did not reach the sink no matter how forcibly she stretched my neck. Disgusted, she unlocked us and went in search of a footstool. There were many scattered around the store; Ilonka kept the expensive crystal and less expensive glass vases on the highest shelves. With the stools, she could reach them quickly, before a romantic costumer changed his extravagant mind.

A cat's cradle was no puzzle compared to my life. Why was everyone always angry with me? If I had lice, had I, unbeknownst to myself, invited them? Had I written: "Dear Madame and / or Monsieur Lice. Would you do me the great honor of attending the invasion of my head, Tuesday next, October 30, at four o'clock in the afternoon? R.S.V.P. All gifts to be donated to charity."

My mother returned with the stool. "Step on it," she commanded, "and let's get this over with. I have a pass only until six p.m. After that I am endangering my life for you."

Nice. I nodded. I stuck my head into the sink and I left. Where to go? Where to go? Not to Gerbaud's for chocolate with Daddy, I thought, and laughed out loud.

"Something is funny again?" my mother hissed angrily.

"No, nothing is funny."

"Stick your head further into the bowl and stop being so difficult." She scrubbed my head hard, twice. Then a third time. "It's no use," she said while rinsing.

"What is it?" By now I had gotten off the stool, and I stood facing her with an old, frayed towel hanging over my wet hair.

"You are full of head lice—larvae and live bugs. They cannot be washed out. We would need some medicated liquid or some gasoline to get rid of them. Neither is possible to obtain."

It was cold in the toilet, and I began to shiver and to shake.

"Stop the hysterics," my mother said in a stern voice. Her face, in contrast, looked stricken, as if she were about to burst into tears.

"What now? What does this mean?" I asked.

"You will have to stop scratching. Not just upstairs while

there are customers, but at all times. You may not scratch at lunchtime or in the evening or ever when the Miszlais can hear you."

"How will I do that, Anyu? I itch. I itch a lot."

"I don't know how, but you'll do it. Ilonka suspects that you have lice. I'll lie to her. I'll say your hair was simply dirty. If she catches on, she will throw you out. I have no other place to take you. None. You must stop scratching, no matter what."

At first, not to scratch seemed impossible. Back on my bed, the itch kept growing, like the monster shadows that small objects cast when illuminated by a haunting light.

I am vermin-infested, I thought, and immediately fell asleep. Soon, I woke. I am vermin-infested, I thought, and could not fall asleep.

I knew similiar disasters had befallen others before me, but I could not remember who. Was it Job? Was it Gulliver? Who?

Eventually, I realized something else. A mobile dimension had been added to my static existence. My head now was host to a world of live creatures. They fed, met, multiplied, traveled, parted, and died. My hair was the jungle of their struggles. My ears and neck appeared to be worlds beyond their world. Barren and exposed, they were probably considered dangerous territory, forbidden by the elders who had been scratched in the past.

From time to time I removed a louse from my hair and held it up between my thumb and forefinger. This exercise did not occasion noise. Fat, bloated, and drunk on my blood, the louse wriggled its legs in what I imagined to be terror. Ah, your turn now, my friend! I thought. Are you Jew or Nazi? Whichever you are, you smell bad and you disgust me.

I ached to kill the louse, but that presented a dilemma.

Wherever I crushed it, it would explode with my blood and leave a stain, the origins of which I could not explain to Ilonka. I put the louse back in my hair. Did it then go among its tribe and preach that it had been spared through unfathomable, or perhaps earned, mercy? If yes, I ultimately must have harbored a worshipful sect, because I did this a dozen times at least, with self-torturing fascination.

Meanwhile life at the shop proceeded in the usual routine. I came down for lunch and dinner. I put food on my plate. I smiled. I said thank you. My hands were quiet and clean.

One noon, Miszlai néni said, "The child does not look well. She eats half of what she used to. Her face is drained and much too pale. Look at her."

Ilonka looked at me. How strange! How rare! No one looked at me these days. Looking at another's face must be motivated by some passion—by love, hate, fear, rage, curiosity, or at least by the implicit expectation that looking will soon arouse one of these emotions. I was an abandoned child in hiding. Why would anyone look at me?

"What do you expect?" Ilonka said, irritated. "She has been indoors for weeks. Do you expect rosy cheeks? A tan, perhaps? What is the matter with you, Mother?"

Miszlai néni was a stubborn old lady, not easily intimidated. Pulling her thickly knitted, heavy cardigan tighter around herself, she said, "This is different, I tell you. The child has no appetite. She looks drained of blood. She barely speaks. She reminds me of the gypsy children of my village when I was a young girl. They were eaten away by head lice. Margit must have made a mistake. You'd better call her to check again, before we all end up with bugs crawling in our hair."

My heart missed a beat, but Ilonka was also stubborn.

"Mother," she said, "we are not in your village anymore. I have not seen or heard this child scratch since the day Margit washed her hair."

"I don't itch," I said quickly, and to my astonishment I realized that I was only half lying. Itching had ceased to be the issue. I lived under water, under deep water, without being fish or algae. What surrounded me was totally unfit for my inherent nature, yet I survived. I survived through some mysterious, encoded talent in my being, through some unshakable ancestral commitment to hang on and keep going.

As is often the case, someone else's random disaster touched off the disaster we were expecting. Thus do contingency, chance, and the accidental circumstance determine fate.

A bullet strayed off its intended trajectory, and a man died, leaving a wife and three children under the age of fifteen. The wife worked in a factory. She couldn't afford to miss work and lose money, even though they were both good Arrow-Cross party members and were widely known to supplement their income by informing on the Israelites and on their errant Christian neighbors.

The day of the funeral arrived sooner than Mrs. Veres—that was her name—had calculated. She decided to get up extremely early and stand in front of the neighborhood flower shop until it opened. She intended to buy a ready-made wreath and carry it herself to the funeral parlor. Every penny counted.

It was seven in the morning. Ilonka had stayed the night and we were having breakfast. The iron gate rattled faintly. Ilonka must have thought—I don't know what she thought. I do know that I watched in horror as she hurried to the door, opened it, and flipped up the gate.

There we were. Mrs. Veres—bird-faced, bony—and I, staring at each other. She was all eyes. Ilonka's mouth hung open.

"I came for a wreath," Mrs. Veres said, after what seemed a long while. "My husband is to be buried today. I will take whatever you have ready. Who is the little girl?"

"Oh. Mrs. Veres. Yes. The girl? A wreath? Aren't you early, I mean late, for your husband? I mean, I will see what I have ready. My condolences."

Ilonka was terrible at this game, I realized. She should have seen my mother in action. She could have learned a thing or two!

Mrs. Veres hooked me with her gaze. I shifted my eyes away and down to my bread, which I started to chew with great concentration.

"You are a pretty girl," Mrs. Veres said. I continued to chew. "And you like your bread, don't you?" I chewed on. I hoped to God Ilonka remembered that I was supposed to be shell-shocked.

"Can't you speak, little heart?" Mrs. Veres asked, honey dripping over irritation. "Or are you a spy in hiding? Ha, ha."

I looked her fully in the eyes. "My father is dead," I said, and looked back down at my bread.

Perfect shot. She began to weep. "So is my husband. We are burying him today. Oh, these are terrible times. I don't know what is wrong with me. I keep seeing what's not there."

I knew with absolute certainty that I should go through the routine again, only this time say, "My mother is dead." It would scare and disarm her. We would be safe. I knew it. I could not do it. I was too superstitious to utter such a sentence. Instead, I kept chewing on my bread with downcast eyes. Not a good move.

Ilonka returned with a large wreath, which she offered to Mrs. Veres at a 50 percent discount. Another suspicion-arousing mistake. Wreaths on sale? Was there a shortage these days of dead bodies? Or was resurrection imminent?

"Who is the little girl?" Mrs. Veres asked sweetly. "She is so good, eating away at her bread."

"Oh, she is my brother-in-law's sister's godchild." Ilonka launched into my story and, thank God, remembered to end it by letting the woman know, behind my back so to speak, that I had a few screws missing.

"Ah, the poor thing," the woman said, not at all behind my back. "The poor thing. These terrible times."

"Yes," Ilonka said sadly. Then she said, "I am only keeping her for today. They arrived about an hour ago and they will be gone by tonight. The countryside is safer, as you know. Actually I opened the gate so early because I thought you were them."

They talked further, but I didn't listen. "Gone by tonight," Ilonka had said. If my mother indeed had nowhere else to take me, I would be at Vadász Utca tonight. Vadász Utca! Dream of my heart. Hope of my soul.

Half an hour later, Ilonka telephoned my mother.

Later in the day, two strangers entered the shop together, a man and a woman. There were no other customers. By now the die had been cast, so I had been allowed downstairs. The strangers identified themselves to Ilonka at once, using the signal agreed upon with my mother on the telephone: They asked for a ready-made wreath. It had seemed funny to me when I suggested it. The couple looked Christian and of the right age. They carried false papers for the three of us, probably filled out in my mother's hand. The arrangements were an attempt to protect Ilonka and Miszlai néni, in case Mrs. Veres had already notified the authorities and the store was being watched. We got into a car and drove away. We were not stopped or followed. The baroque maneuver of my rescue had been executed without a hitch.

The night was very cold and very dark by the time I passed through the hallowed portals of Vadász Utca 16.

My mother and brother were waiting for me beyond the doors, behind the Zionist young men standing guard. We rushed toward each other. My mother hugged and kissed me. My brother was about to rumple my hair, as was his custom, when he checked the gesture in midair and pulled his hand back.

"Stop it!" my mother hissed at him. "Stop it. Your hand will not catch head lice."

Iván blushed. "It's not that," he muttered, obviously feeling bad. He leaned over to hug me at arm's length and to give me one quick gingerly kiss. "I am glad you are here," he said.

I nodded. Not exactly the reunion I'd expected. Where were the trumpets? The rose petals? Where was the celebratory fifteen-cannon salute for the prodigal?

"I am very tired," I said. "Could we go to where we sleep? Or do I sleep somewhere alone?"

"No, no," Iván said. "You sleep where we sleep, of course." He bent down to whisper, from some distance, into my ear. "Pay attention to me," he said. "I am very sorry to be afraid of lice. But you're still my best buddy." He grinned the old grin of our long-ago conspiracies.

I nodded again. Right. Your leper buddy. I tried very hard to control myself. Weeping was no way to start a new, long-coveted phase of your life.

"Come on, Anyu," Ivån said. "Let us put the child to bed, metaphorically speaking." He winked at me and laughed. I looked away.

We ascended a flight of stairs and reached what in dim candlelight appeared to be a very large office floor. There were desks, chairs, and filing cabinets scattered all about. Every available horizontal surface was occupied by a person wrapped up for the night. The coverings varied from expensive fur throws to raincoats to, in one case, a single torn, yellowing sheet. Led by Ivån, we picked our way carefully among the bodies. We reached a cozy space between a wall and a desk, set up with pillows and blankets.

"This is our spot," my mother said. "This is where we sleep." The area did not look large enough for three.

"You will sleep crosswise at our feet," my mother said.

Naturally.

She started at once to make my "bed."

"Mark her pillow," Ivån whispered. My mother shot him one of her "Now you are dead" looks. "I mean, we all have our own pillows, right? Now she has a pillow of her own, right? That's all I meant." My brother was flustered again.

"Good night, Ivån," my mother said. "Enough. Go to bed."

Evidently some normal rituals still remained. We picked our way back to a large communal washroom with four sinks and four toilet stalls. We washed, brushed our teeth, and got into our modified nightclothes. Nightclothes here, I learned, were street clothes which you did not wear by day. The idea was to be able to run instantly in case of a ground raid by the Nazis or an air raid by the Allies.

Back at "our" nook—their nook really, because, situated at

their feet, I was exposed to the rest of the room and became for them an unintended bulwark—I climbed, exhausted, into my bedding. My mother sat down next to me. "Do you want me to say your prayers with you?" she asked.

The question surprised me. It knocked me off balance. What prayer? A child's prayer? "Now I lay me down to sleep"? I still prayed, but not that way anymore. Not in other people's words. I spoke to God directly, and I berated Him as often as I begged. These days I did not praise Him. It didn't matter. He didn't care.

"No, thank you," I said.

"You look very pale," my mother said. "It's the lice. They are bleeding you. I could not get anything with which to kill them. But I did trade some food with a Romanian man for a lice comb. It has very thick, close teeth. I will pass it through your hair every day. It will get rid of the live lice. They will no longer feed on you. You won't itch anymore. The larvae will remain, but each day as I comb out the live ones, there will be fewer and fewer of them left. You can stop worrying. I will take care of everything."

My brother, unnoticed until now, was looking down at us from his six-foot highness.

"Mother, if you keep whispering to her and if she keeps weeping at the same rate as she has done for the past half hour, I calculate that by four a.m. she will drown on her pillow. Elementary, my dear Watson."

I giggled. My mother smiled. "You are right," she said. "We should all go to bed. It has been a very long day." She hugged me hard and gave me many kisses.

My brother lifted my arm, bowed, and ceremoniously kissed my hand. This ruse for staying away from my head did not fool me, but I forgave him.

"La Dame aux Camélias, I bid you adieu. I truly regret that I am totally unwilling to marry you. *C'est la vie.*" We both laughed. "Well, now," he said. "Quickly: What is the slightly distorted reference?"

I melted, but I waved a dismissive hand.

"Lastly, an opera. A novel before that. Perhaps vice versa. I am too tired to remember. Go to bed, you fool."

I was alive again.

Settled in, humanity breathed all around me. The night was full of lovely noises. Full of groans, snorts, coughs, snoring, the rustle of bedding, the crunch of turns. I felt blessed, even by the occasional stifled cry of another's nightmare.

FOUR

I WAS BARELY ASLEEP WHEN AN OBJECT CRASHED DOWN on my head. Then another. I was startled but not hurt. Still, I heard myself scream hysterically. "Oh, God! My head! Oh, my head!" I woke up everyone in my vicinity. Some lit precious hoarded candles here and there in the room in an attempt to locate the source of the screams. Caught in the spotlight, as it were, I thought I should improve my performance. I thrashed about. I pummeled my bedding. I kicked, I wailed, I held my head. Curiously, the more I fussed, the more fitting it felt. Yes, I *had* been hurt. Hurt? Mortally wounded! So what if not by these fallen objects?

Meanwhile, my brother jumped up and stood over the desk that defined one side of his and my mother's nook. Illuminated by flickering candles, he looked gaunt and threatening. A man, I realized, not a boy. This, too, happened while I was elsewhere, I thought bitterly.

The desktop over which he hovered served as a bed for a woman of about my mother's age, Lily Bauer, a friend. The fallen objects were her shoes, which she had placed side by side next to her feet on top of the desk. This was a logical precautionary measure against possibly urgent escapes in the night occasioned by pressing internal needs, or by the Nazis coming on land, or the Allies by air. As Mrs. Bauer turned over in her "bed," she accidentally knocked over the shoes.

My brother yelled at her with astonishing rudeness. "What's the matter with you? Are you stupid? Don't you care about anybody? How can you drop shoes on my little sister's head? You . . . you . . ."

My mother also stood up, lit candle in hand, and yelled at Iván. "Stop it! That's enough! Apologize to Mrs. Bauer." My brother turned his back on both of them.

I felt like laughing. Clearly this was a new, enchanted, topsy-turvy world, laden with possibilities. I began to climb back into my bedding when both Iván and my mother leaned over me. "Is your head all right?" Iván asked.

"Yes, thanks. Fine." Experimentally I added, "Except for the lice." My brother's face turned dark red.

"Well, good night," he said, and waved. I waved back, smiling. I had gotten it right, after all. He was yelling at the lice, not at Mrs. Bauer.

By now all the candles had been snuffed except my mother's. In its eerie light she kissed me gently good night. As I drifted off to sleep, I felt, for the first time in a long while, safe.

Next morning, Iván explained the lay of the land. In addition to the office space where we were housed, the building had a courtyard, two basements, and one long, convoluted attic. "The basement to the left is the Hashomer hideout," he said. "The basement on the right is occupied by the religious

Jews, only some of whom are Zionists. The attic is for bohemians, students, and other free spirits—in a manner of speaking."

The owner was Arthur Weisz, whose glass-brick factory had been located here until the Germans entered Budapest in March and closed down the business. Through his connections with Swiss colleagues and friends, and through complicated bribing ceremonies of certain German and Hungarian Nazi officials, he had managed to have the building declared an annex of the Swiss consulate. Consequently the grounds were now considered foreign territory protected by the neutral status of the Swiss government. Guards stood at the gates—Jewish boys inside, the bribed Nyilas outside—and no one could enter the premises without their joint consent.

The Weisz family kept their baronial apartment at the level of the offices on the opposite side of the courtyard. Even now, they sometimes gave parties for a select few, among whom, Iván said, he was always counted. I was very impressed.

"Iván, how did you get to be so important?" I was looking up at him as at a tower. Even hunched, as he sometimes carried himself, he seemed two feet taller than I.

"I don't know. To tell you the truth, I've been thinking about that myself. Perhaps it's because I'm not afraid to go out into the city. Actually, I am afraid, but I can't stand being cooped up. So I meet Christian friends, eat at restaurants, do the habitual things. Perhaps it is because I speak German and look like a Nazi. This is awful, but I'll tell you anyway. I love looking like a Nazi. It makes me feel free." He shrugged. "I shouldn't talk like this to a child."

"You always talked to me. Always."

"It is different now. I am a man. I do things and think things children shouldn't know."

"Oh, yeah? Like what?"

"Like I'll administer the seven deadly knee holds if you don't stop asking questions."

"When?"

My brother laughed. But I knew, and he did, too, that something (what was it? What *was* it?), something atmospheric, porous, painful, and totally irreparable, had crept between us. His attention flickered around me. It was no longer as it used to be—dead-center, charged.

"Well, what else?" I asked. "Are you in command?" I was careful not to alter my tone with the last question. My brother gave me a hurt, oblique look from under his acres of lashes. Hoppa! I too could wound. "No, of course not. The titular head is Mr. Weisz. Well, not exactly titular, because he does own the building, and he has many connections, and he contributes a great deal of money. Still, the real bosses are a committee. They are all Zionists, mostly Hashomer, although some other factions are also represented. They decide everything and take care of everything."

"Like what?"

"The distribution of protection money, the food, the safe passes—who receives them, who delivers them. Who is allowed to come in here, where they are to sleep—everything. I'm not a member, so I don't know all the details, but many of the members are my friends. So is Mrs. Weisz."

"Is her father a judge?" I asked, looking at the ceiling. After my stay at Ilonka's, I was a master of ceilings. From the corner of my eye I saw my brother blush and get mad.

"What's wrong with you?" he yelled at me in a whisper. "Are you practicing to become a junior Old Hen? Stop it! It was not my fault that you weren't here with us until now.

Anyu decided. She was worried about your lungs. It's crowded in here, and dirty. She tried to protect you. She was right."

"Yeah. I've been told that already."

I would have liked to say so much more, and I could have, I could have to my brother, if only we were back in our battered bathroom at old Teleki Tér. Sitting on the closed toilet, puffing on my pretend cigarette, I could have said, "You should not have been part of the treachery. You should have seen more clearly and rescued me. It was her plot to be just with you. Now there is an unbridgeable chasm between us. It hurts. I hurt. Help me."

I was surprised to find that the contents of my despairing soul amounted to so few sentences. But for all its brevity, what I had to say seemed at the moment unspeakable. We were in a crowded room, seated on office chairs, on opposite sides of a worn-out wooden desk, or Mrs. Bauer's bed, depending on the time of day. So I shrugged and said instead, "What else?"

"Well, come along and see," Iván said. "I will give you the grand tour." We walked downstairs and exited to the courtyard. Looking up, I could see a slate-gray, snow-menaced sky and blind windows secured with black paper according to air raid regulations. The building walls were striated gray, the flaking paint exposing darker gray beneath. The cobblestones underfoot were gray on gray, caked with mud. Only one thing stood out. In the center of the courtyard stood a structure like a long, narrow prayer house made of textured glass bricks that absorbed and reflected the accumulated grays in a magical silver shimmer. I caught my breath and nudged my brother with my elbow. "What is that?"

"Stop elbowing. It's the latrine," he said.

"The what?"

He rolled his eyes. "Dear God, how ignorant can a person get? The latrine. To make doo-doo and pee-pee in."

I laughed, a little embarrassed at this off-color joke. I was also a little relieved that we were getting back to normal. "Tell me the truth. Don't joke. It's beautiful, like a temple."

He shook his head. "I just told you. The latrine. Really."

We both fell silent. After a while I asked, "Who uses it? How is it used?"

"The people who live in the basements. There are no toilets down there. Certain times are reserved for women, other times for men. They all come up at the appropriate hour and use it."

"All the women together at the same time?"

"Yes. It is necessary. There are many people. Don't worry about it. Upstairs, where we live, there are regular bathrooms. You used one last night."

"Are you sure?"

"Absolutely. Come on."

By now my mother was waiting for us at the left corner of the courtyard. "Hurry up!" she shouted. "What has kept you? Hurry up."

"We're coming," my brother answered, scanning the sky.

My mother was standing in front of some high wooden shelves on which buckets of paint, brushes, hammers, saws, nails, rags, pliers, and other assorted building tools and materials rested. "I thought we were going to the basement," I said.

"Just wait," my mother said, undulating her shoulders with glee. "Just wait and see."

A couple of brawny young men leaned against the shelves.

On seeing us they both straightened up. *"Shalom,"* said one. *"Szervusz,"* Iván said. They shook hands. *"Szervusz,"* said the other. *"Szervusz,"* Iván said. They too shook hands. "This is my little sister, Magda."

"Szervusz."

"Szervusz."

"Szervusz." We all shook hands.

The fellows slid the case of shelves to the side. It glided effortlessly, revealing a heavy, locked wooden door. One of the young men knocked on it. Some mysterious words were exchanged. The door was opened from the inside. Beyond the door, steps led down into darkness.

Amazing. Amazing. What an amazing, wonderful world! After weeks of watching only a ceiling. Holmes! Poe! *The Princess Magda and the Hidden Cave of . . . ?* The end of the title would have to await the facts.

"Go ahead." my brother said, motioning me forward.

"No," said my mother. "I will lead." She offered her hand. I grabbed it and we walked down, lockstep. My brother followed.

The bottom of the stairs was lit by a dim single bare bulb, hanging on a wire. The shadows it cast made it difficult to discern what lay beyond. As my eyes became accustomed to the darkness, I saw a long, very narrow basement with a row of wooden bunk beds built against each wall, leaving only a tight walkway between them. The bunks, upper and lower, were occupied by an astonishing number of persons in a variety of positions. Some were in repose; others seemed to sit in rigid vigilance. It was very cold. Many were dressed in overcoats or parkas, in hats of all types, gloves, mufflers. Some were bundled in blankets, including their heads so that only their thin transparent faces showed. From the murmur of many low-voiced simultaneous conversations, an occasional word or phrase escaped and hung in the air out of context:

". . . I assure you . . ."

". . . *gulyás* . . .

". . . in the third movement . . ."

The smell, corporeal in its rankness, hinted vaguely at a variety of sources that added up to an assault: dried urine, unwashed bodies, putrid food, cheap tobacco, hunger-induced halitosis, damp walls, damp pillows, damp blankets, farts, not enough oxygen. Fear.

I noticed my grandparents seated to the right, quite near the entrance, on a lower bunk. The upper tier had been dismantled and the supporting beams left intact, giving the impression of a four-poster without the canopy. They looked more frail than I remembered them. But perhaps that happens. Perhaps the first glance after a long separation often reveals terminal vulnerabilities which we choose to overlook in day-to-day contact. My grandmother had a silk kerchief on her head, as if she were about to light Sabbath candles. She wore a dress, a sweater, an open coat, and, incongruously, bedroom slippers over heavy socks. My grandfather was also hatted, and the never-absent home-rolled cigarette dangled from his lips, unlit.

Glad as I was to see them, I recoiled and stopped short. "How come they are here?" I asked, letting go of my mother's hand. "You told me they were safe, but you never said that they were here. How long have they been here? How did they get here? Who brought them?" All my nasty quivering jelly suspicions were at once transformed into a prickly ball of hard certainty in the pit of my stomach. Yes, I had been excluded. Excluded, personally. Me. Only me. By this woman next to me who claimed to love me.

"That's a very long story," my mother said, sounding a little nervous. My brother let out a low, appreciative whistle at the length of the breath I exhaled as I clamped my lips shut.

I didn't know whether he misunderstood or deliberately misinterpreted me, but he said, "It's not all that long a story. It was an emergency. The committee got word that the Nyilas were rounding up all the people living at the safe houses on St. István Park. You probably remember that that's where I took the old ones in October when they had to leave Dávid bácsi's. The Nyilas were about to march them all to the ghetto, from which they were to be deported. When I heard the news, I told the committee I had to go get my grandparents. They authorized it. They gave me false arrest papers, made out for the immediate detention of Mr. and Mrs. Indig. So I went.

"When I got there, it was total chaos. Six, seven blocks of Jews, five to a row, mostly old and some kids, all clutching their nothing belongings. Many of the Jews were crying. The Nyilas were screaming and shooting rounds into the air. I walked up to the head guy, saluted, showed him the arrest papers, and told him I had to get two particular bastard Jews, and on an afternoon, yet, when I could have had a date. He laughed. Four of his front teeth looked newly capped in shiny gold. He told me there were no names here. They were herding everyone to the ghetto. Those who couldn't keep the pace, protested, or fell out would be shot. It was the simplest way to get a shit job done. 'Just a minute, now,' I said, in my best imitation of the currently fashionable fourth-grade-educated intellectual. 'I have this here arrest paper in my hand. The lieutenant at headquarters will not appreciate it, thank you very much, if I bring him the two wrong shit-Jew prisoners. You'd better help me locate them, brother. Long live Szálasi.'

"His right hand shot out like a puppet's. I nearly laughed. That damn sentence never fails. It's like pulling strings. Whenever I say it, I feel like the Magician to their Marios, except they are evil, not I."

"Wait, wait," I said to Iván. "Don't go into literature. Weren't you afraid?" By now I had ceased to exist as offended, betrayed, or anything else Magda. I had become a concentrate of attention. My brother was magical, indeed. His words conjured up a world of sound, colors, action, danger. My heart barely beat as he talked, and then it raced, and stopped and started again.

"I don't know," he said. "I never think of it. I get a creepy-crawly feeling all over my skin, and I'm very excited, but I guess I'm not scared. If they caught me, I would be scared. I would collapse and die. Meanwhile, it's a game of who is smarter." He trailed off.

"Then what happened?"

"When?"

"Ivááááán!"

"Oh, not much. The guy said, 'Take them. Take as many as you want. Shoot them. Drown them in the Danube. I don't care. I wish they would all drop dead and I could go home.' He offered me an armed guard to look for my prisoners. I told him I could take care of this trash without a guard. What were they, after all? Garbage Jews. I made him salute again.

"I strolled down the street looking at every row. I was lucky.

I spotted them in half a block. Then it occurred to me that the Old Hen—" He stopped and cast a scared sideways glance at our mother, who appeared oblivious. "—that Grandma might give us away by throwing her arms around me. So I circled the row and approached on Grandfather's side. I said, 'Indig, you and your wife are under official arrest. You are to fall out of formation and follow me.'

"You won't believe this, but Zsigmond actually gave me a wink. Then he gave Emma's arm a sqeeeze so hard I thought he would break it. 'Yes sir,' he said loudly. 'Let's go, Emma.' They followed me. Later I told them to march ahead of me. Eventually we got here. That is the whole story. No sinister plot, no premeditation."

I guess my brother did understand me.

By now my grandfather had noticed us, and he waved with a big smile. "Come on, come on. I have been waiting for you, Magduska," he said with the outgoingness he was known for everywhere except at home. "How are you?"

"I am fine, Grandfather." He leaned over to kiss me, but I warded him off. "I have head lice."

He laughed. "It is fashionable these days," he said, and kissed me anyway.

My grandmother and I shook hands. Dutifully I said, "I kiss your hand, Grandmother." Rózsi and a man stood up from the adjacent bunk to greet us. Rózsi and I kissed. The man patted my right shoulder.

Who the devil was he? He looked old and gaunt, but vaguely familiar. It came to me with a shock. Guba! Ervin's father, Rózsi's ex-husband. He was here too? Everybody but me? Who else? Mrs. Szabó? The school band? "Guba bácsi," I said, "I am glad to see you."

I really was. I had always liked Guba bácsi. Except once—the unforgettable time when they were visiting, before Ervin moved to Budapest, and Guba beat Ervin's bare backside eleven times with the hard buckle end of his belt. For breaking the violin, he kept saying. For breaking the violin. Ervin did not break the violin. I did. Actually, neither of us did. The violin broke itself. Ervin forgot to hook the lock on the case, and when I pulled it to put it elsewhere, the violin fell and broke itself.

Seeing what had happened, Ervin said, "Oh, my God, we will get killed." I burst into tears. He was nine; I was five. "Let's think this through," Ervin said. "For me, it will be a beating. For you, it will be Margit néni owing more money. A beating is fast, and it's over. Let me confess."

"No," I said. "I have to do it." We both knew that in our family there were no accidents when it came to breakage and children. Blame had to be assigned, punishment had to be meted out. Ervin got angry. "Absolutely. Do it. Confess. By all means cleanse your soul at the cost of your family's comfort. Let them eat air. Why not?"

"Ervin, I love you."

"Then trust me," he said.

He confessed. Guba bácsi belted him. I crouched in the farthest corner of the room, whimpering, while Ervin remained stone silent.

"Where is Ervin?" I asked. Guba's face darkened.

"He is in the back."

"Can I see him?"

"Not now," said Guba. "He is in the back."

I looked toward the back, but I could see nothing beyond dark, endlessly stretching bunks. "So if he's in the back, why don't we go get him?" I asked. Iván surreptitiously motioned me to stop. I did not want to stop. I repeated the question. No one answered.

The air suddenly filled with sticky-sweet romantic accordion music. To me it sounded very sad and heartbreakingly beautiful. There was a general hush as everyone listened for a moment.

"What is that? Who is that?" I asked.

"That is Ervin, playing an accordion," Iván answered.

"What do you mean? Ervin plays the violin, not the accordion."

"In love he plays the accordion," my brother said.

"In love!" my grandmother cackled with her usual scorn. "A child. A fourteen-year-old boy and an eighteen-year-old whore. In love. So is my left slipper with my right one. She is twisting him around her little finger and using him."

I was always fascinated by the sayings my grandmother made up and passed off as folk wisdom. I knew that in general she thought of love as a boomerang which, if let loose, returns to kill the one who launches it. But right then I was much more curious about the facts. I tried to back into the main topic by asking the smallest question that picked up where she left off.

"For what is she using him, Grandmother?"

"Don't stick your nose into everybody's business," my grandmother said. "Look at this girl! The insolence! She has barely set foot in the place and she has to know everything already."

"But Grandmother, I just—"

"Never mind what 'you just.' You are too smart for your own good. Always have been, since the day you were born."

"At it again," my grandfather muttered.

"Don't be fresh to your grandmother," my mother said.

"Don't be fresh," Rózsi echoed my mother.

Nothing had changed. My grandmother was still a Soul Skinner. She was a Despair Alchemist. No matter what the substance, she could transform it into misery in an instant. She was also highly contagious to her daughters.

Iván picked me up and put me on his shoulders. "I have to go now," he said. "I am taking Magda upstairs with me. *Au revoir.*" Under his breath, he added, "*Mon* definitely *not* plaisir."

I was in an excellent position on his shoulders. As he walked, I got hold of each of his ears. I threatened to pull hard if he didn't tell me about "the Ervin Situation."

"Don't be an insolent market fly," Iván said, using one of our grandmother's favorite expressions. We both laughed so hard that I let go of his ears and he nearly dropped me. Upstairs, I begged. He claimed I was too young to know. I countered with the weight of my recent independent fugitive status and my literary knowledge of Romance. He gave in.

"It's a complicated story," he said. "It hinges on political conviction, on status identification, on philosophic commitment, and on hormones. Mostly hormones."

"Are you saying Ervin has gone mad?"

"No. Not mad at all. He has gone 'native,' as it were. He met this girl Zsuzsa, now called Shosha. She's an old-time Zionist through her parents. A Hashomer, meaning a Communist. I always suspected Ervin of having a bit of the prole in him. Anyway, now he wants to emigrate to Palestine with her, and he wants to fight for a Jewish state. I don't even know what that means. Jews are intellectuals, not farmers or soldiers.

It's all rather sophomorically naive. His *nom de guerre*, only he claims it's his 'true' name, is Simcha. He drives the family crazy by not answering if they address him as Ervin."

I was stunned. This was much more elaborate than anything I had imagined. I had so many questions. Most of all I wanted to know about my Ervin and this Shosha. And Iván?

"Wait. Aren't you a Hashomer?"

"In name only. I am a firm believer in capitalism. Better yet, in a meritocracy based on intelligence. I don't want to build a state. I want to be a professor of literature at the university. I like my name. They tried to sell me, too, on my Jewish name in Hebrew, Moshe. Look at me. Do I look like a Moshe to you? I refused."

"But you work for them. You are a runner."

"I do it for people, not for politics. I'm just a guy who wants to survive and who wants to help other people not to die. I am interested in the Homeric wars, not in future warring. Ervin and I have lost all points of contact."

"But why is everybody so mad at them?"

"Aha! The heart of the matter. They incurred the wrath of the Adult Gods—and we are approaching the hormone issue—by living together as a married couple, without being married."

"Ervin can't be married. He is too young."

"You know what I mean."

I nodded. The truth was, I did and I didn't. I had heard rumors, far too outrageous to be believed. No one had ever explained any facts to me. It was a secret not to be questioned by children. The technicalities escaped me. The word "womanizer" was related to it.

Womanizer. Whatever it meant, the word had figured in my

nightly prayers for years. My father was a womanizer. While
we lived with them, Grandmother had informed us of this fact
with great frequency. She made it sound like our fault, so I
took care of it: After I said my usual prayers aloud with my
mother, I always added in silence, "And give us some more
money. And make my father not a womanizer. Amen."

In a few days, Iván did take me to see Ervin and to meet
Shosha. They lived way back in the cellar in a lower bunk made
private by blankets hanging down on the sides and in the
front, a very cozy arrangement. I wondered why everyone
didn't do this, but I guessed there weren't enough blankets.

A man standing nearby greeted Iván. "Come to see the
honeymooners, eh?" He winked. "Well, just knock. They will
climb out eventually. They do, from time to time."

I was very excited at the prospect of seeing Ervin again at
last. After all, how much could this Shosha person interfere
with us? How much brighter and prettier could she be than
all the other girls at Teleki Tér in whom Ervin was never, ever
interested? Did she know as much about poetry as I did?
Could she even rhyme? I doubted it. The more I thought of
it, the more I realized that the family had completely misread
this "situation." Ervin would come out, he would pick me up,
we would hug and kiss. Then we'd go upstairs and talk fever-
ishly in whispers, interrupting each other in our eagerness to
tell what had happened since we last spoke. Ervin would move
upstairs with us. We would play chess. Or if there was no chess
set, we would play *Malom*. Everything would be fine. I got
impatient at the momentary delay of this magnificent, inevitable future. "Knock louder," I said to Iván, a little irritably.
"Tell him I am here."

Just then, Ervin climbed out from behind the front blanket.

He was even handsomer than I remembered him. He looked more grown, and he glowed. He smiled broadly as he said, "*Szervusztok*. How are you, Magda?" He seemed very happy, but not particularly at seeing me.

"Thank you, I am very well," I said formally, as if I were talking to an adult stranger. I was tempted to curtsy and to ask, as I had been taught, "And you, sir? How are you?" Instead, with great care, I examined the ugly cracks in my ugly black shoes. My disbelief was oceanic. So was the instantaneous correction of my convictions. Of course. I was a short, ugly, Jewish-looking, head-lice-ridden nothing with barely healed holes in my lungs. Whatever could I have been thinking of? Stupid, stupid.

"Na, here is Shosha," Ervin said with an expansive gesture of his arm that embraced her without touching. I remembered that gesture well. Shosha and I said *szervusz* and shook hands, but I couldn't see her. I was stuck with the sight of tall structures crumbling in slow motion, the bricks of which until recently had had the word "hope" etched into them.

Back upstairs, I more or less settled down. I was introduced to the only child my age, a boy named Imre, or Imi for short. My mother gave us paper and pencils and told us to play. He was a nice boy who said that the dots I drew on faces for eyes were very expressive. Dope. I couldn't help thinking of him as my consolation prize. What an absurd notion that is—to regard as a prize getting what one doesn't want. To think that getting anything less than what one wants can be consoling. As if with loss one's wants would turn retrograde and rogue.

When I wasn't playing with Imi, I watched my elegant mother. She sat at a desk, a knitted cardigan thrown carelessly around her shoulders, and typed counterfeit papers all day.

Occasionally she exclaimed, "Another good Christian has just been born." After a while I got tired of the joke.

Other women, including Rózsi, stamped the documents with fake official seals and signed them with variously colored inks. The runners picked up the papers and delivered them to all parts of the city. We believed that this sometimes saved people's lives, although no one ever knew for certain.

Lately, after each run, the messengers complained that things were getting too tight. The roundups were more frequent. The checkpoints had multiplied. Many resigned, as did Ervin. Only my brother laughed. "A bunch of scared old hens," he said, making a clown face. "I have no problems."

I did. I worried about him all the time. About two weeks earlier, Iván had committed a foolish error, of which he was very proud. He exchanged winter coats with an older friend who left the building for another hiding place. Iván gave away his old tattered cloth coat for a fabulous green leather German officer's greatcoat. "What generosity! What a coup!" my brother gloated, showing off the coat.

"You un-for-tun-ate im-be-cile," my mother said, close to tears. "Why do you think the bastard did this?! He duped you! This coat is dangerous. It is lethal. You have nothing else to wear now. You must not go out again."

"Oh, Anyu," Iván said, waving away her objections. "Look at how I look in it. Look at me."

"I can't bear to," my mother said, turning her back. This exchange took place while we were standing up in our nook. The people near us kept their eyes and ears steadfastly elsewhere, as dictated by the conventions of courtesy in these crowded quarters.

I became, as of old, his audience of one. "You look magnificent," I said, in total sincerity. Iván the Conqueror, the Luminous, the Grand. He smiled, then smiled again behind his smile. "A great coup," he said. I considered saying nothing, because I wanted to stretch this moment into forever. But I had to. It was my duty. I took a deep breath. "I think Anyu is right," I said. "The coat is a mistake. It is dangerous. You look too good in it. Too beautiful. Too provocative. You must get rid of it."

The smile disappeared. "Oh well, yeah," my brother said, jerking his head up and down in quick little nods of bitterness. "Yeah. Well. Actually, it's none of your business." He walked away, flinging the coat around his shoulders.

In a day or two, God answered my prayers to protect Iván. He came down with typhus, like many other people in our section of the building. He couldn't go anywhere.

He was put in the VIP sickroom on our floor. Since there were no mattresses, he lay down on straw covered with blankets. He tossed with fever, he was delirious, he lost weight. He was thirsty all the time. Because of the many recent breaks in the city's pipes, the water was filthy. He drank it anyway, as we all did. The line his female visitors formed around the corner became a standing joke. Each brought her treasure: Half a salted black radish. A quarter of a cup of soup. A postcard of Venice to tack on the wall. A bit of jam. The partitura to some obscure music. As if commanded by communal will, he recovered in a week.

Next our mother became ill. As a favor to Iván, the committee allowed her, too, to stay in the VIP room. Despite a newly decreed quarantine, Ivan and I took turns sitting with her during the day. No one else came. Typhus had turned into a rampant epidemic and everyone was afraid.

My mother looked moribund. She had diarrhea, she vomited. She fainted in the bathroom.

"And if she dies?" I asked, barely able to utter the words.

"She won't," Iván said. "She's tough, like you." It was a joke, but I couldn't laugh and I wasn't reassured.

At night, he sat with her and gave her dirty water to drink. He patted her face and held her hand. He told me to go to sleep in our nook. What else was I to do?

In a few days, my mother stood up. "Well, let's get on with it," she said. We both applauded. She was as yet unaware that we could not quite get on with it.

While we were focused on typhus—and, incidentally, only the lung-rotter escaped it—we had missed the many discrete downward steps in our deteriorating conditions.

The Nazis, in fiendish cleverness, had billeted soldiers in the building next to ours and built a latrine in the courtyard. They installed antiaircraft weaponry. From the air, the two sites were indistinguishable. In consequence, the Allies' strafing became more frequent and savage. Their bombings also became more concentrated. They did a lot of peripheral damage, but, amazingly, neither the Germans nor we sustained a major direct hit.

After our mother recovered, one of the last boys still running brought us very bad news. Two days after I came to Vadász Utca, Ilonka's shop had been demolished by a bomb. It happened around noon. A customer was instantly killed. Ilonka's left leg was badly injured; she might not walk again. Miszlai néni lost an arm. The bed on which I would have been contemplating the ceiling in silence was blown to bits. My mother started to cry. "Oh my God! Poor Ilonka! Poor Miszlai néni!" she kept repeating as she sobbed. My brother went

very pale, but he said nothing. Ilonka was his godmother, and
I knew he loved her.

Me, I was mostly ashamed. I felt terrible for Ilonka and her
mother. But I also wanted to dance like a ballerina, twirl like
a top, and shout to the world, "See!? God loves me! He saved
me! He saved me again in the nick of time!"

Why had he? How did he decide? Kati, Ervin, the other children, and Mrs. Ungar, shot and fallen to the bottom of the
river, had probably by now turned into fish. The Miszlais were
in hospital with parts of their bodies mangled and missing.
And I, I stood here composing celebrant prayers of gratitude.
"Anyu," I said, "could I sit on your lap?"

"Now? Have you no sensitivity at all?" my mother said.
"None? Can't you see that I am upset and crying? Don't you
know that Ilonka is my best friend and she may be dying?
What's wrong with you?"

"Everything. Everything," I said under my breath.

"*Ne motyogj!* Don't mutter! Haven't I told you not to mutter? It is rude. Servant girls mutter and they get fired for it.
What was it you said?"

"Nothing," I said inaudibly.

"What?"

"Nothing!" I yelled. "Nothing!"

"Incredible," my mother said. "Insolent as a market fly, and
at such a time."

I walked away. As far as I was concerned, God could go to
hell.

Other calamities had befallen us as well. The office area
where we had been living was hit and had become uninhabi-
table. All the windows shattered, and some of the furniture
splintered to bits. The pipes and the toilets in the bathroom

burst. Miraculously, no one was severely injured. Mrs. Bauer and some others caught flying shrapnel that made them bleed but left no permanent damage. The committee ordered everyone to relocate to one of the basements. Ours, naturally, was the basement of the Hashomer.

At the outset, the committee had estimated that the building would be able to house about four hundred people. By the time we moved, there were 3,600 of us in hiding. Those who lived in the attic had to remain there despite the danger from more frequent bombings, because there was no room for them anywhere else.

The Hashomer basement, like every other place, was filled far beyond capacity. Iván moved to the back with the other young Zionists, near Ervin. My mother and I were crowded into a bunk with my grandfather and another man where until now only one had slept. Rózsi and Guba moved over to grandmother's "four-poster" across from us.

Then more people came. We tripled and quadrupled until we reached a degree of crowding that permitted each of us to sleep only on his or her side. When I needed to turn, I alerted my mother. She yelled out, "The child needs to turn." Then she on my right, my grandfather on my left, and two more people on either side of them had to push themselves up on one arm to create enough room for me to turn. Shortly, my need to turn became worse than any itch, an urgent, sweaty, panicky imperative. I had to turn over and over, or I would die. But I couldn't turn, because I couldn't whimsically disturb so many people. No one in history, I thought, had ever died from not turning. I evolved a solution. Snakelike, I slithered downward until my knees cleared the bunk. Then by vigorously kicking my legs back and forth, I eventually touched

ground and stood up. It was not a good solution, because
both my mother and grandfather woke. They sat upright (with
my absence they could do this) and asked in unison, "Where
are you going?"

To the Philharmonic, because I hate the opera. "I am just
standing here."

"Well, don't," my mother whispered angrily in the near
darkness. "Get right back here." I sliddled back. Bodies had
expanded during my maneuver, and now I had even less room
than before. No matter. By morning I would be gone, to a
fabled country of magical castles that twirled perpetually.

Our days were no improvement over our nights. We sat, we
hungered, we despaired. The worst thought was, what if there
is nothing at the other end that makes all this suffering worthwhile? Is it assured that we will all end up in a heaven on earth?
And what would that be? I thought it was a deep, clean tub
full of sudsy hot water, and as many hot boiled potatoes to eat
as would satisfy the soul.

Commerce with the city had become virtually impossible,
so we had very little food left. Twice a day the men in charge
of food distribution gave each of us very thin pea soup, more
like thick water, and a very small piece of moldy bread. The
taste was so foul that I ate it as if I were taking medicine, like
cod-liver oil. I held my nose, swallowed, opened my mouth to
air it out, held my nose, and started again.

One afternoon, I overheard my mother whisper to Rózsi,
"Last night some idiot urinated into one of the soup buckets.
I will never have soup again. Not here, anyway."

"Don't be stupid," Rózsi whispered back. "It's a crazy,
malicious rumor. Probably a scare tactic to make the soup last
longer. Guba would know. He's one of the men in charge of
the soup distribution. He has said nothing."

My mother remained silent, but she was as good as her word. Henceforth, she traded with the man who slept next to my grandfather—a recent escapee from we didn't know where—her piss-laced soup for moldy chocolate wafers, which she fed to me against my will. Their stale, sweet, suffering taste stuck in my guilty gullet for years to come.

Body lice infested the cellar. They were many, and savage as tartars. Everyone scratched all the time. It was awful. On the other hand, I was no longer an outsider. My club had been joined. Although it is a blood sport, hunting lice can be done without a license. You catch a louse in your clothing, you put it on your thumbnail, and with your other thumbnail placed opposite, you crush it. It crunches and spurts its blood. Simple. Nevertheless, whenever I did this—often, because it was the only game in town—I thought, What if, in another part of my clothing, a family of lice is anxiously awaiting the return of this one? The intrepid I just crushed? What then? I didn't ask my mother, because I knew she would say I was melodramatic. I couldn't ask Iván, because he was too far back in the dark.

Bombings and strafings increased exponentially. The basement was no longer a hiding place from just the Nazis. Now we were hiding in earnest from the Allies. This made any number of simple things extremely difficult to do. Relieving oneself became a race against danger. Divisions among sexes and age groups had ceased. We huddled at the cellar exit, humiliated, jumping from foot to foot, and often many of us shamelessly grabbed or covered our genitals, desperately trying to stem a long-held-back tide. Finally, the Hashomer in charge yelled, "Go!" Men, women, and children galloped to the latrine. Speed was the issue, not privacy. The only direction toward which our eyes wandered was up. Frequently, before anyone was finished, the magical striated glass bricks started to splinter, grazed by bullets.

Once at latrine-sprinting time my mother stayed behind in the courtyard corner with a bucket of black water. She tried to wash my underwear, because I had nothing clean left. The water froze. My underwear froze. Her hands froze. I was angry, not grateful. Look at what that stupid woman has done, I thought. Her beautiful, delicate hands looked like raw meat.

The weather worsened and the basement turned even colder. Each exhaled breath was clearly visible. Now would be the time, I thought, to pretend to be smoking, but I had no toilet paper.

We took to wearing all our clothing at all times, layer upon layer. I dressed in two skirts, a shirt, two sweaters, and Mrs. Szabó's suit jacket. Still, I was cold most of the time. I rubbed my hands together and stamped my feet often. So did the others. At night I welcomed our inability to turn, because the tightly squeezing bodies of my mother and grandfather warmed me.

A man, a lawyer, who slept in an upper bunk, decided to entertain us in the afternoons, a gray blanket draped around his shoulders, a striped woolen muffler draped over his head and tied under his chin. He sat on his bunk cross-legged and described slowly, in a honeyed tenor, the detailed preparation and serving of elaborate, sumptuous dinners. He chopped chives and parsed parsely. He ground, grated, mashed, simmered, and reduced until, finally, the meal was ready. He might start with freshly roasted goose liver sprinkled with almond slivers, and end with a chestnut mousse cake topped with sweetened whipped cream. We, his audience, sat mesmerized in total silence. Our heads were tilted up toward him in reverence. As he spoke, the air filled with the smell of half-forgotten feasts, and we salivated in communal bliss.

Occasionally, like any good popular performer, he asked for requests. People were shy. No one could think of anything nearly as good as what he had already described. On one such occasion, I put my hand up. At his nod to me, I said, "Bean soup."

"Bean soup? What kind of bean soup?"

"My grandmother's."

Everyone burst out laughing. When the merriment died down, the man said, not unkindly, "Then let your grandmother tell it." Another burst of laughter.

I looked at my grandmother. She, too, was laughing hard, with her right hand held in front of her mouth. At the same time, she shook an adamant no with her head.

Otherwise, the cellar settled into an ominous hush. The Hashomer in the back stopped singing their songs, even "Hatikvah." We heard no accordion music. People barely spoke to each other. Everyone was conserving energy. Deprived of adequate air, of light, food, and warmth, we needed to concentrate on survival.

Then the most feared happened. Despite bribes, promises, favors, agreements, and oaths of honor, the building was attacked by a joint detachment of Nyilas and Nazis. They beat up the Jewish guards at the gates and forced their way into the courtyard. The news was brought by a young runner in charge of the twenty yards between our gates and the basement. One of our own door guards, Samuel, explained the situation to us in a fast near whisper. Another one ran to the back to do the same. "Be very quiet," Samuel said. "Don't even breathe.

Blow out all the candles. Just sit. I'll put the false wall in place from the outside. Then I'll leave for the street. It is a great sacrifice. You must survive. You owe it to me. *Shalom.*"

In seconds, we heard the false wall snap into place. We obeyed Samuel. No one moved. No one whispered, no one breathed.

An hour passed, two, many hours. Survival is a tedious activity, I thought. Death might be more exciting. What is death anyway? Riding into the fog on the tail of Beelzebub, as I once read somewhere? Throwing a coin into the River Styx? Ascending to heaven? What is it? It must be like sex—off-limits to children, with no adult ever wanting to answer any questions about it. I am safe then, I thought. Children may not know of death; therefore they may not die. I knew I was lying to myself, but I liked it. There were certain lies I very much favored. My brother said that lying bespoke moral turpitude. I disagreed. Some lies were like toffee and rainbows and circus clowns. Some lies filled your empty belly, as those of the man in the upper bunk had done for us. Then he got tired and stopped. That's the real problem with lying. At some point, you always feel you must stop. That's when you get into trouble.

"Stop muttering to yourself." My mother elbowed me. I stopped. A short while later, we heard the false doors being moved. For several terrifying, breath-held seconds, we didn't know who would enter. Friend or foe? Had we survived, or were we to be murdered? The man who appeared was Samuel. "It is over," he announced loudly, but with no particular joy in his tone. "For now it's over. The Nyilas are gone."

Details emerged the following morning. The Nazis had crossed the front gates and penetrated the courtyard by only a few yards. They never reached anywhere near our entrance. Mr. Weisz and some other members of the committee rushed down to negotiate with them. A runner was speedily sent to fetch the Swiss consul.

Mr. Weisz still had quite a bit of cash. He offered the Nazis a lot of it in exchange for their retreat. He and everybody else hoped that the consul would arrive and cut a different deal, since the cash had been allocated for badly needed food, and for smaller emergency bribes. In a massive attack, offering this much was dangerous. The Nazis might get even greedier and return in ten minutes.

The negotiations were prolonged, but not long enough. The runner was stopped at several checkpoints and at one roundup. He was a brave young man, talented at deceit. He got through, but with hours of delay.

Mr. Weisz had to surrender the money. The Nyilas agreed to retreat. Throughout the talks, their guns were at the ready. On their way out, one man turned around, aimed randomly at the committee but away from Mr. Weisz, and pulled the trigger. The woman was buried later in the courtyard.

Shortly after her murder, the consul did arrive. Regrettably, all he could do was pay his respects to the bereaved. "Would anyone care to join the *minyan?*" someone asked. I saw my mother's restraining hand creep onto my grandfather's elbow. No one volunteered. This was a Hashomer hideout. Fierce and godless and scared.

Two days after the foiled coup, Ervin announced to his parents that he was leaving with Shosha for a safe house in Buda. The Swiss annex had proved itself to be vulnerable, he said. He and his Hashomer friends calculated that the building would be attacked again soon, and there was no cash left. He thought it was his duty to save Shosha, and for her sake to save himself.

Both Guba and Rózsi argued, admonished, cajoled, and begged in whispers, without success. "My mind is made up," Ervin whispered back, again and again. I was not part of the fight, but even I felt like slapping him. Finally I heard him say, in normal tones, "I will think it over."

The next morning, he sneaked out unobserved. He took Shosha with him.

Although I periodically overheard murmured sorrows and rages regarding the following letter, I did not actually read it until after Rózsi's death, when I found it hidden among her effects. It is written on lined white paper in neat, surprisingly elegant script.

Dear Parents:

I am sorry that it is only in this manner that I am able to inform you of my departure. Unfortunately, you alone are to blame for this. I am leaving for my personal safety. I know you do not believe this, but I know that I am right.

I would not have believed that I would ever, for any reason, have to act this way, but you must see that it has become necessary.

I am going with Zsuzsa. It is to this fact that you are hostile. In this matter, also, I am convinced that I am right, inasmuch as my friendship with Zsuszsa can only be beneficial to me.

We are going to an entirely safe place. Do not worry. Almost certainly it will be within my means to be in contact with you, even if not in person. If this should not take place, it will mean nothing.

Do not pester my friends about anything. None among them knows either where we are going.

I hope you can agree that this step was necessary, not only for practical reasons, and that it will not lead to a complete break between us. I trust your objectivity. All the best, and I kiss you and my grandparents too, countless times.

Take care of yourselves,
ERVIN
Budapest, 1944, Dec. 18.

ON DECEMBER 31, 1944, a date I was unaware of at the time, I sat way back in our bunk fretting about the state of my intellect. I had noticed that I could no longer recite to myself flawlessly any poem that I used to know. I was worried. Was I going crazy, or just becoming stupid? What exactly was wrong with me? My mother's approach interrupted my musings. I smiled, glad of the distraction.

"Iván has gone out," she said breathlessly, looking ashen.

"What do you mean? What do you mean, 'out'?" I yelled. I get very irritable when I am frightened.

"Out, out, out. To deliver a *Schutz*-pass, a *laissez-passer*, a what-do-you-call-it."

"But why? You forbade him. He promised."

"I know. I know. He told me earlier today that he wanted to go. I said no. He said yes. He had to. The fellow who needed the thing was a very fine man. Besides, Iván wanted to go to Ildikó's, the judge's daughter, to wish her a happy New Year. I got mad at him. We quarreled. He walked away. I ran down to the guards with his coat. I showed it to them and said, 'Don't let a boy who wears this coat go out.' They said fine, we won't. I trusted them. There was a change of guards. He slipped out after that. He is gone. I don't know what to do." She looked so drained of blood I worried that it had all collected in her ankles and she would spring a leak. I imagined her ankles turning into a five-pronged sprinkler, the kind Pista bácsi used to have at the nursery. But instead of water, she would spray blood.

"It will be all right," I said, not convincingly and unconvinced. In a flash of certainty, I knew this was a disaster, a catastrophe. My blood felt not drained but frozen. In the ice of it, piercing the skin, a blade was carving the words "dead," "murdered," "dead."

"How long has he been gone?" I asked.

"He should have been back by now."

"How long?"

"Six, seven hours."

"Don't you know?"

"Seven. They change the guards at three in the afternoon. It is ten in the evening now."

"He can't come back in the dark. You know that. We shouldn't even count the past four hours. If he didn't finish delivering the safe pass and visiting Ildikó by six, he couldn't come home. There is a curfew. He probably got delayed and stayed at Ildikó's house, or at one of the safe houses. He'll be back in the morning. Don't worry, Anyu. He will be back."

All night, my grandparents, Rózsi, Guba, Mother, and I huddled together on the four-poster, wide awake and wordless. At ten in the morning, my mother decided to go look for Iván. All the adults vehemently objected. "It is an insane, suicidal plan," Guba said. "You can't rescue him. You can only get yourself arrested. You have an obligation to your other child. You must not go." What other child? I wondered.

"But I must," my mother said. I returned to our bunk and climbed into the back. For no reason at all, I started remembering our neighbors at Teleki Tér, particularly Ibolya, the oldest of the Kornitzer girls.

My mother got back at curfew. She walked toward us very slowly and sat down hard on the four-poster. She looked as if she had lost ten pounds since yesterday. Her lips were chapped, her eyes looked sick, and she trembled with cold or fever. It was hard to tell. "Nothing," she said, her voice cracking.

In a rare gesture, my grandfather patted her shoulder. "Tell me," he said. I feared that he would burst into tears. Instead, he became vague, and said, in irrelevant sadness, "Such times! And I have nothing to give you to eat."

"Go on, Margit," Rózsi said gruffly, trying to normalize the situation.

"Nothing," my mother repeated. "He never reached Ildikó."

Mother told us that she had spoken to Ildikó's father, the judge, a very elegant man, nice. He told her how fond he was of Iván, how much he respected him. Anyu asked him to help her look for Iván, to please use his connections. He declined—kindly. "Madame," he said, "I, too, have children. I must protect them. You understand." A fireplace blazed. The room smelled of fresh pine. Champagne goblets had been set out for lunch.

"It's New Year's Day, you know," Anyu said. "It occurred to me that I could cut his throat if I broke one of the glasses, but I just thanked him and left." She lapsed into silence.

Rózsi pressed again. "Is that where you were for all these hours?"

"No," my mother said. She paused for fifteen heartbeats by my count. "Arthur Weisz gave me the name and address of a police captain in our pay. Villi Klein on the committee gave me the name of a detective. 'He's an old school chum,' he said. The man is a Nyilas, but loyal to Villi and to Villi's friends. I went to see both of them. They each made phone calls to the detention centers where they had connections. Iván was nowhere. The captain clicked his heels and said to me, 'Go back to the annex, dear lady. You are endangering yourself. I remember the name and the description. I will continue to look for your son. Go home.' Then he turned beet-red."

She fell silent. I no longer had a heartbeat to count. She started again, with the sudden, surprising spurt of a run-down wind-up toy. "Buildings are on fire all around. The castle in Buda is burning. Other buildings are spilled on the ground in broken bricks. There are barbed-wire checkpoints everywhere. And no street signs. I got lost several times. Here in my own Budapest." She trailed off again.

"You must have some hot soup," Rózsi said. "Guba, go get it." We all knew my mother could not possibly have eaten in twenty-four hours.

"No soup," my mother said, tightening her lips. I felt a little hopeful for the first time in two days.

"I'll see what I can rustle up," Guba said. "Schluff," my grandfather said tenderly, breaking a long-standing rule imposed on him by the family never, ever, to speak Yiddish, the despised language of the Jewish lower classes. *"Schluff, my tochterle."* He kissed her on the forehead.

"Come on, Anyu," I said. "Let's go to sleep." We climbed into the bunk and positioned ourselves on our sides. I threw my left arm over her.

Two seconds later, Guba shook our legs. "Get up, Margit.

I brought you something." We both sat up. Guba handed her a bowl full of what he called tea.

For a wild moment, I thought it was heated urine, but in fact it did smell like tea. Then he handed her a rather large piece of stale bread smeared with bacon fat, on which lay three pieces of bacon, each a quarter of an inch square, hot off an open fire. How wondrous.

"Eat it, Margit," Guba said. "You need it."

My mother smiled. She wasn't quite herself yet, but to my immense relief, she was getting there. "You are a magician, Guba," she said. As she bit into the bacon, her teeth splattered a little fat. "Have some," she said to me. "Have a piece." She broke off a generous third of her bread, with bacon on it.

"No, Anyu, thank you. I am full. Guba has been feeding me this bacon all afternoon. He must have traded something for a cache of it. He is so extravagant." I counted on Guba not to give me away.

"Oh, well, I'm glad you ate," my mother said. "I was worried about you."

We sardined ourselves back into our bunk. Before I could ask her anything, she was snoring.

What did all this mean? She went here and there; Iván was not anywhere. Had he been murdered? Was he alive? What had she actually found out? She never quite said.

Next day, collected again, my mother said, "I found out nothing. I wasted yesterday. He must be at one of the roundup centers. There are so many. I will speak with the committee later today and try to locate him."

"What will that do?" I asked. "What if you locate him? He will still be arrested. He will still be condemned."

"No," she said. "The trick is to ransom."

"What?"

"To ransom, to buy him back for money. The committee owes him that. If I could locate him, I would persuade the committee to buy him back. Do you see why I had to go yesterday to try to find him?"

"Yes, I see. I do see."

The shift in perspective didn't shift my extreme despair. Where was my brother? I tried to imagine it, but I was bitterly limited by my lack of experience. What did I know? I knew a basement, an attic, the Red Cross shelter, a flower shop. He was at none of these places, I was sure. I knew being shot at, but not being hit. Was he hit? Was he dead? If dead, would I really never see him again? I began to weep. To hide it from my mother, I told her that I was tired and needed to lie down. She nodded.

I climbed into the back of the bunk and silently sobbed for a long time. Just as I thought that I would never be able to stop, I heard my brother's voice in my head. "Don't be so melodramatic," he said. "You are not the heroine of this drama."

"Oh, yeah? Then who is?" I replied in the tone we always used to counter a challenge-gambit. He did not answer. Still, I thought, if I could hear him so clearly a moment ago, then perhaps he wasn't dead. I asked him, "Are you dead, Iván?" He did not answer.

DAYS PASSED. THE basement was colder than before. The food supply dwindled. Candles were rationed, so we sat in darkness a great deal of the time. No one spoke very much, but my family had gone nearly mute. What was there to say? All topics were meaningless except the one that none of us wanted to discuss for fear of adding to the others' anguish.

My grandfather still prayed every morning, without benefit

of tallis or tefillin. He had abandoned those items when we
fled from Teleki Tér. He had no prayer book, either. He prayed
from the memory of his heart. When I listened carefully to his
murmurs, I could occasionally make out the words "Moshe"
and "Simcha" in the otherwise unintelligible monologue.
Well, God, I thought, here is Your chance. It is a good man,
not I, beseeching You.

The lower we sank, the more rumor-logged we became.
They were going to execute us all tomorrow, or some other
tomorrow. The Americans were sending in paratroopers to
land in the courtyard to rescue us. The water main just outside
the building had been poisoned; that was why we were all
fading. The Russians had surrounded Budapest.

What upset me was not the recurrently false news but the
feverish breathlessness with which the adults whispered it.
There was something very frightening about that. It was sickly.
It was mad. If only Iván were here. He would agree with me,
I was positive. And possibly he could stop them. Perhaps.

A few days later—in a manner of speaking, because in the
darkness it was very hard to hold on to time—two elder committee members appeared at the door. They looked stern and
determined.

The older one, with white hair and a beard, said, "Now
listen to me carefully. I know you have heard many rumors.
We are here to give you the facts as best we know them. Budapest is surrounded by the Russians. Some of the suburbs have
already been taken. Sections of the city have also fallen, but
we don't know which they are, how close or how far from us.
We know this: The Nyilas are trying to exterminate all witnesses against them. On the streets they shoot anyone they
catch. They have been emptying the ghetto. We don't know
to where. Perhaps those Jews are all dead by now. We just

don't know. It is, however, our considered opinion that they will attack us. We are a large enclave. It makes sense for them to kill us.

"If anyone wants to leave, now is the time. We would, however, not advise it. We think the street is certain death. Here we might be able to get through to the consul by telephone, although we have not been successful for the past several hours. Still, it could happen. We might bluff the Nyilas. We are also mounting resistance. We have no guns to speak of, of course, but some of our young men are athletes, and all our young men are very brave.

"Your situation in this basement is special. We all think the false wall is perfect. It will hold and not be discovered—provided you all remain silent as a tomb.

"We will hand out bricks to each of you in case the ruse of the false doors fails. Hurl them. Who knows? Chance might become your avenger." He was close to tears. "And remember," he added, "those who survive must bear witness." He turned abruptly and left. His silent partner followed him.

In a little while, some Hashomer boys brought the bricks and distributed them one to a person, with no discriminatory restrictions. My grandmother and I both counted as full-powered brick-throwing citizens.

The announced official assessment was correct. A few hours later, the Nyilas did attack. The false wall was snapped into place and we sat in the dark, clutching our bricks. "Isn't it wonderful," my mother whispered to me, "that the boys at least are safe away from here?"

My brother had educated into me something that was unable to take a reality tilt of this degree. "No," I whispered back. "Our dying has nothing to do with the boys. They may be alive or dead. But that is independent of our situation. Can't you see that?"

"No," my mother answered. "What I can clearly see is how mean you are."

As if by way of punctuation, something very loud exploded outside. We also heard barked orders. Faint wails. The rat-tat-tat of a machine gun. We are going to die, I thought. And to my utter surprise, I broke into a cold sweat and started to tremble. Don't you want to die? I asked myself. No, for shame I don't, I answered. I want to go on living.

How peculiar, I thought. What an impractical idiot this other me is.

For distraction, I placed my brick on my lap and gave it a thorough checkup. Doctorlike, I slid my fingertips quadrant by quadrant over its upper surface, its sides and its back. I noted that it had some all-around mortar attached to it, which was scratchy. It had a ridged back, and it seemed porous. Otherwise, it appeared completely normal. I knocked on it once, but before I could proceed with the protocol, my mother shushed me. "Not to worry, Mrs. Dénes," I replied. "The brick is hale, hearty, and entirely fit." I sensed her thinking that I had gone mad. Perhaps I had.

More intermittent rat-a-tat, more screaming. No whoosh of air from the door being forced. We sat.

I wanted to think of other things, but I had noticed lately that my mind had become a country of mines, of trenches, of barbed-wire checkpoints. I started out in a direction and I was almost immediately stopped by signs of No Entry, *Verboten für Juden,* Proceed at Your Own Risk, and suchlike. I turned back, and turned to the side, and turned again, and always encountered the same obstacles.

Think of poetry.

—No, that is Ivan.

Think of hot chocolate with whipped cream.

—No, that is the long lost past.

Think of Mendelssohn's violin concerto.

—No, that is Ervin.

Think of being together, safe and happy.

—No, that is depressingly hopeless.

Think of God.

—Let him think of me.

A long while later, the raid ended abruptly. A Hashomer boy younger than my brother entered. He made a trumpet of his hands and yelled through them, "It is over. Come on out. They are gone. You are safe. Saaaafe! Saaaafe!" In the doing, he acquired a taste for his work. "Redeeeemed!" he yelled. "Redeeeeemed!" He fell apart laughing. All of us laughed with him. What a joyous thing it was to be redeeeemed!

"And for God's sake get out of here!" he yelled through his cupped hands. "The air in here is foul. Fooouuul! I don't know how you could have breathed, or how come you're still alive. Come on, come on!" He started to dance out, shaking himself as he went. I missed him when he disappeared from my sight. Where was my brother?

The courtyard was full of people. They jumped up and down; they hugged and kissed each other. We, the privileged Hashomer of the undiscovered cave, felt a little like outsiders. "You don't know anything," people shouted, waving in our direction. True, although all of us were extremely interested.

We learned that the Nyilas had discovered everyone except us. Only the Hashomer hideout had held. The others were herded to the street and made to stand with their hands up for hours on end. Some got hysterical, some fainted. Their friends picked them up and covered for them. To everyone's utter surprise, as they were about to be marched toward the Danube to be shot, the Swiss consul arrived. He negotiated. The Nyilas left. The people returned from the street to the courtyard. No lives were lost.

Mr. Arthur Weisz got up on a chair to be better heard. "We did this trick twice," he said. "There will be no third time. We are finished. There is no more money, there are no chits left to call in. The consul has been recalled. If they attack us again, we will be lost. Let us all pray that the Russians reach us first. Please return to your original hiding places. It is the only way. Good luck to us all."

The next day, a Nazi detachment arrived. The senior officer asked to speak to Mr. Weisz. They met on the sidewalk outside the annex. In the presence of a dozen witnesses, the German colonel said, "Come with us, Mr. Weisz. We need to talk. It is, of course, entirely your choice. I give you my word of honor as an officer of the Reich that you will be back here in two hours."

He wasn't back in two hours. He wasn't back in two days. As we learned much later, he never came back.

On the afternoon of January 6, 1945, seven days after my brother's departure, three days after Mr. Weisz's nonreappearance, we were liberated by the Russian army. Our heroes. Our yearned-for allies. Our long-awaited saviors. The news of our survival came to us through the unlikely personage of Mr. Fehér. Mr. Fehér was very old. He was totally bald, hunched, and so thin that every time I saw him, I wondered at the miracle of the skin's elasticity. How could it be so taut and twisted and not tear?

Mr. Fehér stood at the entrance and, in a lesser tone than if he were announcing "Dinner is served," said, "The Germans are gone. The Russians have occupied our street. We are liberated." He stopped, a look of extreme puzzlement on his face.

No one reacted. I knew I had heard him, but I lay low.

After a few seconds, our former lawyer-chef called out, "Fehér bácsi, what did you say?"

"We are liberated," Mr. Fehér repeated. "The Russian soldier I saw pointed to my wrist. He said, 'Watch,' in Hungarian. 'Watch, watch.' 'I have no watch,' I said. 'I am a Jew. Welcome, comrade, I am a Jew.' The soldier shrugged and spat in the snow. What's going on?"

While Mr. Fehér spoke, the chef climbed down from his bunk, walked over to him, and put his arms around him. "Fehér bácsi," he whispered, "things are fine. Don't worry. We have survived. The Russians are good."

To the rest of us, he yelled out, beating his breast, "Winners! Survivors! We made it! Life, food! Come on, let's go up. Come on!"

No one, not one soul, responded. Mr. Fehér started to weep. The chef went crazy. "Cowards!" he shouted. "Goddamn cowards! Brave the easy way. Brave to die. Show me your stuff and live." He, too, was near tears.

From way back in the cellar, someone started to sing loudly, in a sweet, high voice, the words of "Hatikvah": *"Kolodba levov . . ."* All joined. The effect was electrifying. Singing, everyone wanted to run out. There was no trampling, but there certainly was a rush that hinted at it. In less than five minutes, the cellar emptied.

We alone remained. "Let's wait for the boys," my grandfather said.

"Good idea," said Guba. We sat and sat.

My bones started to ache. I was trapped among lunatics. Upstairs, one courtyard away, lies food, I thought. Freedom. A bath. Words of consolation and acts of restitution. We could probably ask the Russians to raise a convoy to look for Ivàn and Ervin. These are our good friends. We should go and greet them, and be comforted by their joyous welcome.

"Shouldn't we go up like everybody else?" I asked.

"No, we are waiting for the boys," my mother said. "This is where they will find us fastest."

"Fine." We sat. We did not eat, we did not drink. We sat, we sat, and sat.

"Anyu," I said, "don't you think perhaps you should find out if there is anybody left in the building? I mean, otherwise, we could just sit here forever and turn to stone."

"Insolence! Again insolence!"

"I know. But go anyway. Please. Please find out if there is anyone left in this building."

My mother left and returned triumphant. "You were wrong, thank God."

"As usual," I muttered.

"There are people in the religious basement—people who come from towns that have not yet been liberated. Also people from other streets in Budapest that have not been liberated. People from Buda, which is still under siege. We are not the only ones here. Other people, too, have had the sense to stay."

"Yes."

"Chaim, one of the Hashomer boys, Ivàn's friend, you know, told me that we should move over to the other basement. That's where the food will be distributed and where they'll knock some bricks out and keep a fire going in a wood stove. They also have many blankets. Then he said, 'I am very sorry about Iván.' I don't know what he meant."

I remained silent. My heart was frozen. I imagined it breaking in the jagged pattern of a cracking iceberg.

Addressing Rózsi, Guba said, "You should all definitely go to the other basement. I'll start for Miskolc today. I want to find out what happened to my sister and my house. Also, perhaps Ervin will come there instead of returning to Budapest. I am very sorry, but I must leave you."

Rózsi gave him a doleful look full of reproach. He owed her his life. When she had heard rumors that he was part of a particular death march toward a labor camp, she paid a courier to find him on the road and deliver false papers ordering his release and transport back to Budapest.

"Fine," she said quietly. "Go."

By evening we had moved. Of 3,600 people, perhaps a hundred of us remained. The committee gave us each a three-person lower bunk and three blankets, and served us a poor man's *gulyás* for dinner. Luxuries like this ought to lighten the heart. But my family just sat. They were waiting for the boys. They were killing me.

I did not wait for the boys because I knew them. I knew for certain that if they were alive, they would be here. Consequently I did not wait. I mourned. And mourned. Alone.

In another two days, my mother decided to give the outside world a chance. We would surface. The envoys were to be Rozsi, Mother, and me. Zsigmond and Emma would stay to wait for the boys. We bundled up as best we could, crossed the courtyard, passed through the gates, and stepped into the street of liberation. As one, we stepped back. What lay before us was not of this world.

"Jaj Istenem!" Rózsi gasped. "Oh my God!"

The time was around noon, but we could not see the sky. Billowing gray clouds of smoke floated at the top floors of buildings, and far above them. Large pieces of ash fell everywhere. We grope in the noonday as in the night, like Job, I thought.

"Dramatic analogy," my brother whispered. "Bravo!"

"Fine," I answered. "Sarcasm is cheap, but where are you?"

A crater split the road before me. There were gashes in the asphalt. To the left, a huge crumpled Russian tank sat, its metal twisted in a thousand tortured angles. To the right lay a dead horse, a snowdrift growing on its bloated belly. Its four rigid legs looked like exclamation points. Dirty frozen snow covered everything. Hypnotized by despair, we walked a block, and encountered uprooted tramway tracks, perpendicular to their normal position. A tramcar lay on its side about ten yards away from the tracks.

On the corner, a building burned wildly; the flames stretched toward the sky like praying arms. No firemen appeared, and no victims yelled for help. A few steps further, my mother said, "Don't look!" and tried to encircle my head to cover my eyes.

I wriggled free. I saw a Russian soldier in uniform sprawled on a mound of snow, his right arm stretched long. His hand was extended, the ring finger missing. The snow under it was bright red, like strawberry ice. "I am going to throw up," Rózsi said.

"No you aren't," said my mother. "We will turn back." Exactly then, a six-story building on our left sustained a cannon hit and began to disintegrate in slow motion. An oddly clownish collapse.

I knew it was wrong, it was worse than wrong, it was truly sinful, but I could not contain my laughter. I rolled, I cackled, I wept, I held my aching belly. I lost my breath and laughed and laughed and laughed. I lowered myself to the frozen ground and laughed some more.

"Please! Did you see that? Oh, please!" I shook. I yelled.

"There has always been something wrong with this child," my mother said, turning to face Rózsi, who was not there. At some point, Rózsi had lowered herself onto the snow and begun laughing with me.

"Did you see those windows go, one after the other, down, down? Hahahaha. Did you see it, Rózsi néni? Hahahaha."

"And the doors," Rózsi said. "Hahahaha. They wobbled back and forth. They were almost airborne! Then they fell. Did you see that? Hahahaha."

"Yes, yes, hahahaha."

"That building could have been us, the three of us," my mother said bitterly.

Rózsi and I laughed harder, and, without any caution at all, we stretched straight out on the dirty snow. "That's just the point, Margit," Rózsi said, and we laughed again.

"It must be the liquor," my mother said.

Rózsi sat up. "What liquor? I could use a drink."

"Haven't you noticed the stench?" my mother asked, arching an eyebrow. Now that she said it, we both nodded. The air was saturated with the fumes of alcohol. "The rules of war," said my mother. "I remember it from the Great War. The conquering Russian army had three days of looting and free liquor. They terrified our town. When they took Miskolc, Mother hid us. You don't remember that because you're three years younger. But let me tell you, the Russians pillaged and raped."

A truck almost passed us by, then backed up next to us. The drunken Russian soldiers filling it hooted and yelled, "Missy, *barishnya, mademoiselle, kislàny!* Come on the truck. Pengö, pengö." We stood still.

"No child," an officer said in broken Hungarian. "Ladies, money, yes?"

No, no, Rózsi and mother gestured in unison. "Home, please, home," Rózsi said.

The officer laughed. "We will walk you home."

They did. The truck paced itself behind us until we reached the safe entrance of Vadász Utca. Then, out of nowhere, unseen snipers tossed several grenades at the truck. Two or three exploded on target. Some of the soldiers were hit and hurt.

The officer became enraged. "Whores! Collaborator whores!" he screamed, and he ordered one of his soldiers to turn his machine gun on us. Rat-a-tat went the Russian's gun. I suppose my mother's faith in a universal language was finally substantiated. All guns shoot in Esperanto.

FIVE

T HE HASHOMER BOYS WERE STILL STANDING GUARD. THEY
pulled us in fast, then pushed us roughly toward the courtyard, away from the doors. "What's the matter with you?" a
red-haired young man yelled at us. "Don't you know what's
happening?"

Before we could answer, a ruckus started at the entrance.
The Russians were breaking some of the glass bricks of the
gates with their rifle butts. The officer pushed through, followed by a few of his men, guns at the ready. "Give us the
collaborator whores!" he shouted to the redheaded young
man. "Surrender them at once!"

"Sir," said the young man in broken Russian, "you are making a mistake. This is a hideout for Jews persecuted by the
Nazis. We have barely survived. We have prayed for you to
liberate us. We welcome you. We are your friends. There are
no collaborators here. All of us here are Jews."

The officer, rocking on the balls of his boots, exactly as a
Nazi officer would, thought for a few seconds, then said, "Surrender the whores, or I will attack the building."

The men locked eyes. The few of us Jews around locked our breaths. "With all due respect, sir," said our redhead, his voice steady, although he was putting his life on the line, "I must remind you that this place is still an annex of the Swiss consulate. It is protected neutral territory. Attacking it would cause, I believe, a major international incident. But in any case, we are not enemies, Sir. We have prayed for your arrival, whatever silly thing the women might have done, it was not collaborationist. We welcome you. We are Jews."

During this entire speech, not a muscle moved on the Russian officer's face. At the end of it, he slowly looked around the courtyard, noting everything flawed, dirty, and destroyed. Finally he nodded. "Yes," he said, "I believe you are Jews. The stench has been attacking my nostrils for a while." He turned and left with his men.

Everyone around ran up to the redheaded young man. Some called him by name. "János, Jánoska! How brave you were! How smart! That stupid Russian." They tried to touch him, as if physical contact with the redeemer would turn into a protective spell.

"I was lucky." He shrugged. "He could just as soon have shot me. And then shot all of you. We are in trouble. The Russians don't like us. Nobody likes us." He shrugged again, and walked away. Cheers and whistles of approval followed him.

I think he walked away just in time to hide his weeping.

Chastened but not deterred, we braved the streets again the next day. If possible, conditions had worsened. There were more burning buildings, more bomb-created craters, more enraged Mongolian combat soldiers seeking revenge. The streets were in total chaos. From time to time, the skies fell and made the earth rise into rubble.

The three-day looting permit in effect again at this Russian victory had made the city into a mud-covered mad market of discarded goods. Hats by the dozen were ground into the vodka-laced dirt. Shoes, mateless, and boots, cut off at the ankles for the leather above, stuck out from mounds of frozen snow. The gutters flowed freely, on and on, from tapped barrels and broken bottles and split casks of alcohol.

Everyone in the city appeared to be drunk, with liquor and with survival. Only the three of us stayed close to the side of buildings. "Come on, come on," people yelled at us. "Come join the party. The war is over."

We all nodded and continued to hug the buildings' bricks. A few blocks later, further into the former shopping district, we found the cause of the scattered discards of the previous streets. Crowds were looting the main shops. The Russians were inside taking their pick. They piled their goods onto armored trucks and carts and motorcycles with sidecars, guarded by their buddies with machine guns. What they didn't want they tossed among the screaming, scrambling population. Fistfights broke out, spit flew, hair was yanked. I didn't understand half the language that was screamed. I recognized one sentence, though, that seemed to recur, yelled in a frenzy over and over by various people. I had learned the sentence a long time before from a girl at the Szani, who had heard it once muttered by her parents' chauffeur. After making me swear that I would not tell anyone, she kept repeating it: "A horse's prick up your ass, my friend." Neither of us could make anything of it. Now, everyone seemed to repeat it compulsively.

"Let's go home," my mother whispered. For a moment I was confused. Then I realized she meant the new basement at Vadász Utca.

"Yes," Rózsi replied. "Yes. Let's go wait for the boys."

As we retreated, a soldier stopped us. "Here, *anyuska*," he said to my mother, pointing. "Take this." He offered an enormous bolt of herringbone wool fabric, the likes of which had not been obtainable in Hungary since before the war. "Take it."

My mother looked at Rózsi. Rózsi shrugged. My mother shook her head. "Thank you, but it's too heavy to carry," she said. The soldier looked totally astonished and a little offended at the refusal.

"I'll carry it," I said. I was a child of war. I knew one should not refuse anything usable. By now I also knew one should not offend a Russian soldier. "I will carry it," I said again, gesturing toward my shoulder. There were seconds of silence.

The Russian burst out laughing. *"Da, da, horasho,"* he said. He lifted the bolt and gently lowered it onto my shoulder, then let it go enough that I began to buckle. My mother screamed. The soldier laughed so well that I had to laugh with him. That made him laugh harder, and me too. I looked at my mother's and Rózsi's bewildered faces and laughed some more. The soldier was delivering a long Russian monologue of obvious approval, because he kept patting my head. Abruptly he stopped, blew me a kiss, and left. He took with him our badly needed and foolishly forfeited fortune.

We settled into the routine of the new basement and behaved as if history had stood still. Somehow we had remained under siege, imprisoned by invisible Nazi guards at the gates, unable to surface for fresh air.

My family did nothing but sit, motionless and mostly mute. From time to time, one or another, inexplicably roused from stupor, would say, "When the boys return . . ." then trail off. I thought this to be a hopeless hope, and therefore I felt obliged to step into Iván's shoes and take care of us.

I stood in the food line three times a day, with five mess kits in my hands. The actual delivery took me two trips. One evening, a man in the line yelled at me, "Hey, girlie! No hoarding. One person, one dish. Damn pushy kid."

My brother's Hashomer friends manned the ladling table. One of them, Gábor, shouted back, "You imbecile! That girl is Iván Dénes's little sister. Simcha's cousin. They are both missing. The family is stuck here. She's trying to feed them, idiot."

The magnitude of my misfortune had just been unwittingly confirmed. To me, Gábor said, "Come, dear. I will fill the five kits for you. Baruch here will help you carry them. You can also come back for seconds. Don't ever stand in line again. Come straight to me." He winked, and produced a cookie from some hidden store. "For you," he said, with a flourish of his arm.

"Thank you."

I had no trouble being yelled at. What undid my bolted heart was kindness. Perhaps under certain circumstances, kindness ought to be regarded as a corrosive. It eats away at the heart and dissolves delicate, necessary scabs.

After this meal, I felt forced to confront my mother again. "We have to leave here," I said. "Now, before the boys come back. We have to leave here or we will die."

"We will leave," she said. "We will. I promise."

Mother and Rózsi left to scout. After far too long a wait, they returned pale and shaken. The apartment at Teleki Tér had sustained a full aerial hit, they told us. The building still stood, but our former home was now just empty space. Air on air, with some twisted beams jutting into the void.

"Margitka," said my grandfather very quietly, "you must

find another place. We have to leave here. The child cannot survive." I agreed. Rózsi and Margit scouted again, and came back with triumphant news. They had been assured by the superintendent that the Bergers, second floor front, would definitely not return. They were dead. We could safely occupy their apartment. Who else from the building was gone we didn't know and we were afraid to care.

On the day we left Vadász Utca to move back to Teleki Tér, my mother heard a dreadful tale. A friend of hers told her that she had heard from a friend who heard it from someone else that Iván had been seen late in the afternoon of the 31st of December among a group of Jews, their hands tied behind their backs, all of them hatless and coatless in the snowy, sub-zero weather, being herded by a Nyilas detachment toward the Danube. The "witness" did not stay around long enough to see whether they veered off toward a nearby detention center or continued to walk straight.

As my mother told us the story, she became more and more hysterically indignant. "The malice of people!" she yelled. "The sheer nastiness of their inventions. It boils the blood and defies the imagination. The woman always envied me my son. She has only daughters. Now she wants to see me scared. The whore, the dirty whore! What ugly lies the witch spits from her snake mouth. Let's forget it. Just let's forget it."

We all sat in stunned silence as we looked up at my gesticulating mother, whom I expected to foam at the mouth any second.

My grandmother was the first to speak. "It is well known that she's a whore. She has made her living on the streets for years." I knew my mother had not mentioned the woman's name.

"Whatever she does, she's a liar for certain," my grandfather said.

Rózsi got up and hugged my mother. "Forget it," she said. "It's a stupid lie. We would have heard if it were true. The woman invented the story to torture you."

"Yes." My mother nodded. "Definitely. Let's just go, and leave this hellhole behind."

"I have to go to the bathroom," I said.

"When don't you?" my mother yelled at me. "Is there a time when you don't have to go to the bathroom?" I shrugged.

Sitting on the toilet, I decided that it was most important to evaluate the evidence. Weeping, feeling crazy, I tried very hard to think as I thought Iván would. One: The story is obviously not a malice-dictated lie. Two: Coming as it does thirdhand, it qualifies as rumor. Therefore, three: It may or may not be factual. Four: The ignored crux is in the veering off. If they turned the corner, he is not dead.

What then had happened? Where was he? I deep-plumbed my insides first, then the universe beyond the lavatory walls, but no answer came back. All right, I thought, all right. Alive or dead is as yet unfathomable, therefore undecided. I must wait.

Rejoining my family, who were all set to go, I realized, to my utter despair, that we had at least two hours of walking ahead of us, and I had forgotten to urinate.

ON CROSSING THE Berger threshold, we all wept a little. Who knows why? They were an aged, childless couple, and none of us could recall their faces. Perhaps that is why we wept.

At bottom, we felt like squatters. The impression was reinforced as we furnished the apartment through scavenging. We took dishes from this dead family's place, and a bed from another's, until we acquired the bare essentials. We felt no guilt. We kept our inner eyes fixed on the hidden sun, and we beseeched it to rise the next day. When we were done, we had three daybeds pushed together, on which the five of us slept in descending order of former importance. Grandfather, Grandmother, Rózsi, Mother, and I. We had a table and five chairs. Naturally the chairs didn't match, and one had a broken leg. Nevertheless, it was usable if one was careful. We had some pots and pans, a few pieces of cutlery, and assorted china. I gathered most of the china. Some I took from the Nussbaum place and some from the Berkovicses'. After the Nazi and then the Russian lootings, there wasn't much left, but we made do. We shared four blankets, each somewhat torn. We used small rolled towels for pillows.

Most important of all, we had a stove. That was my grandfather's acquisition. He traded for it the last personal item he owned—his Doxa pocket watch. Actually, it was a lucky bargain, because not long after, the Russian soldiers accelerated their appropriation of watches. Strapped to their arms they wore six, seven in a row, like heathen phylacteries.

The stove was potbellied, made of gray metal, and it burned wood. We stoked it with broken furniture, splintered beams, uprooted floorboards, and other combustible debris that littered the empty apartments. Well fired, it turned maroon. It became the center of our existence, like a long-awaited newborn around which the family hovers.

The stove stood in front of the windows. The windows were boarded, creating a permanent twilight. The Bergers had done that according to blackout regulations and against shock

waves. My grandfather had to saw a hole in one of the boards
through which to conduct to the outside the chimney of the
stove. That was now standard practice in the city. One could
observe it walking on every street, no matter how formerly
fancy. The fronts of the buildings were dotted with scattered
chimney ends, from which black smoke rose. The smell they
emitted recalled horrifying scenes of corrupt ceremonies and
murderous acts whispered to us recently by returnees from the
concentration camps. None who spoke to us were close
friends, so we didn't know for sure whether what they
reported was true or not. We hoped they were exaggerating,
although we could see that they all looked ghostly and very
ill, and much more wasted than we were.

Still, for us, the next urgent order of business was to bid
farewell to our ever-faithful companions and loyal comrades in
filth: the lice.

My mother boiled water on the stove and immersed in the
pot all clothing that she hoped would not shrink. The rest of
our garments she put in the kitchen, which was the farthest
place from our heated room. She cracked the window open so
that the temperature fell well below freezing. Whatever clothing was not boiled was now frozen for four days. By fire or by
ice, the lice were done in.

My head was a special case. Mother spent almost an entire
day on the streets begging Russian soldiers for gasoline. After
many rebuffs, she finally returned by nightfall with a liter con-
tainer. I sat in a chair, a towel around my shoulders, bent over
a bucket, as my mother soaked my hair in the gasoline and
then poured the extra all over my head. She then covered my
hair tightly with newspapers. Over the paper she tied two kerchiefs, one on top of the other. The insulation was so perfect

that not a single drop of gasoline escaped. She thought that in twenty-four hours both the lice and their larvae should be dead.

The next evening she unswathed me. I leaned forward again, this time over a white towel, as my mother systematically pulled a lice comb through segments of my hair from my neck forward. Dozens of very dead things fell to the white towel. The ordeal is over, I thought. I am again a lice-free citizen of the human race, possible to kiss without danger or sacrifice.

There was a snag, though. The comb seemed to be stripping my skin as well. Long, thin, semibloody bands of epidermis rained onto the towel. My mother screamed. "I left it on too long! I killed her! She will die! I am stupid and ignorant, and, and . . ."

Three pairs of terrified eyes shifted to her in total silence. I knew it was again I who had to put an end to this. "You are not the heroine," I said, at my driest. "It is not your doing, or your head." I knew that she would get furious, which is what I meant her to be. I had learned over the years that anger was the best antidote to her hysteria.

To my despair, she stepped out of character. She started to weep bitterly in true remorse. I patted her arm. It was the most I could do for now. "Stop it, Anyu," I said. "I hated the lice, and this barely hurts. It's all right."

I was not lying. It did barely hurt. I guess the gasoline acted as temporary anesthetic, because the agony didn't start until the following day. I complained in whispers only to Rózsi.

Outside, the horrifying disorder of the liberation increased. The Nyilas still mounted a resistance, and occasionally managed to recapture a street. The Russians would take it back, and, enraged, shoot everyone they caught, including the pleading Jews who, in their habituated dread, had not yet dared to remove the yellow stars sewn above their hearts.

Aside from Ivàn and Ervin, this was the puzzle of my life. How could we have hoped for so much, and gotten nothing? Where did promises come from, and where did they go? Was there any room left for us in the world? How could a life be shaped from rubble and no favors? Where do you start? Many nights, kept awake by my growling, hungry stomach, I worried about these questions. If only I had someone to talk with. If only I had Ivàn.

What I had was a private home, a place to wait and to plan, a fire, and hot thin soup made by my grandmother from caraway seeds. At the end of the fourth day of our idiosyncratic independence, I stood in the doorway of our apartment house waiting for my mother.

The landscape before me was beautiful. Mounds of debris composed of charred wood, pieces of glass, broken tiles, pulverized bricks, and torn sheets of tar, fused and snow-covered, rose from the ground like white monuments.

Meanwhile, dark and curfew approached. My mother was late, my nose ran, my frostbitten toes throbbed, and I worried. She had gone to view corpses. Somehow, I don't know how, the citizenry of Budapest had learned that in the last days of the war the army had gathered, at certain locations, rows of corpses that could be viewed by family members for purposes of identification and private burial. The unidentified would go to mass graves. Perhaps in the Kerepesi, where all major dead heroes rest.

What if my mother does not return? I thought. What will happen to me? Not much. I will walk up to the fifth floor instead of the second. At the end of the stairs I will turn right, then turn again, left. I will reach our old apartment. On the jutting beams I will walk into the air with my arms raised upward and wide. I will ascend.

"I told you not to wait for me," my mother said breathlessly when she suddenly appeared. "They are still shelling. You could have been hit."

"I know. Did you find . . . I mean, did you see . . . I . . ." I could not survive this question. I lowered myself to the cold stone floor of the entrance and put my hands over my face to sob in privacy.

My mother's voice towered over me. "No, little missy," she said, "it's not for you to cry. It is I who looked at the corpses. It is I who smelled death's stink. It is I who did not find my son. It is not your grief. It is I who should weep tears of blood."

With every ornate sentence, I became more panicked. Had she gone crazy? Had Iván given her, too, lessons in literature? Was the tongue of madness always Greek in style?

"Why don't we go upstairs," I said, standing up, as I gave her a little forward push.

Miraculously, she became my mother again. "You can't imagine the stink," she said, weeping. "Or the quantity of them. There are hundreds. Jews, Hungarians, Germans, Russians, all mixed. The men in charge grab them by the hair and flip their necks back to show their faces. I cannot do it again. God forgive me, I cannot go again tomorrow."

"Oh, Anyu," I said, "you shouldn't. You mustn't. There is no reason. He will be back. Iván will be back very soon."

Upstairs, we were awaited with unusual tenderness. None of the anti-Russian furniture had been placed to barricade the front door. We were admitted at our first knock.

"Nothing," Rózsi said as we walked in. "Right? Nothing. You found nothing. Margit, I tell you, both our boys are alive. And they are better off than we are. A lot better off. That's why we don't hear from them. They are having fun, as they should."

She was unmistakably very drunk. In one of his rare instances of assertiveness, my grandfather turned to her. "Enough, Rózsi. You've said enough. Lie down now. Go to sleep." To my astonishment, she obeyed.

Turning to my mother, my grandfather said, "Here, Margitka. Have a bit of vodka." He offered her a bottle, from which she took a slug. "The strangest thing happened today at the market," he said to her. "I got to talking with this Russian boy, this soldier. He can't be more than twenty. It turns out his grandfather was a prisoner of war in Hungary during the time I was a prisoner of war in Russia. I didn't remember that I remember how to speak a little Russian. He knows a few words in Hungarian that he learned from his *zayde*. So we spoke and got along. He gave me two bottles of vodka. I gave him our address. He promised to come tomorrow with food and other things. I think he will."

He stopped. There was silence. After a long while, my grandfather said, "You did not find Iván."

"No," said my mother. "He was not among the corpses I saw."

"That is good," said my grandfather. "Then we still have hope." The last word turned him toward me. "Ah, you, too, can have a drink," he said. "A little one for the little one." He handed me the bottle. With my head thrust back, I tilted it toward my lips and poured the burning liquid through my gullet, straight into my dead heart. It didn't help.

We had no food left. We huddled around the stove to keep warm, and we pretended that we were not dying of hunger. A charitable neighbor who liked children gave us an apple. We divided it into five equal pieces, and we each ate our portion in one bite. I thought it was a mistake to do this. A teased stomach is a vengeful organ. It clamors for more, a lot more, and when it is frustrated, it punishes with cramps.

In a day or two, Irma arrived at our door. She had been our old cook at Személynök Utca since well before I was born. The gift she brought was a dozen rolls, dried for grating into bread crumbs, hard as gravestones.

"*Küss die Hand,* Madame Dénes," she said, attempting to grab my mother's hands.

"All right, Irma," my mother said, not at all warmly. "All right." She snatched her hands out of reach. I agreed with her. Iván loved Irma; I never did. I thought she was a snake. "Thank you for the rolls," my mother said.

"Oh, no, madame," said Irma, "it is the least I could do. Actually, they are the only thing I had."

Before my mother could thank her again, Rózsi interrupted. "Well, in reality, Irma," she said, "you could have done a little more. You could have brought with you the pieces of jewelry and the little cash Madame Dénes gave you to safeguard. Where are they?"

"Oh, Madame Rózsi," Irma said, bursting into tears, "there is nothing left. The Russians took it all."

"Irma," Rózsi said, barely containing her rage, "actually, where you live was one of the few districts that didn't resist. There was no house-to-house combat, and therefore there was no looting."

"Oh, Madame Rózsi," Irma said through thin lips, filtering

big gulps of air as if she were a dying fish, "don't accuse me! Don't blame me! The stuff is gone. I didn't do it."

"Who, then?"

"Stop it," said my mother to Rózsi. Turning to Irma, she said, "Your husband or your son took it. Not you. I know."

Irma started to cry in earnest. "Oh, Madame Dénes," she sobbed, "you have always been so good to me. So generous. Different from the Mr. Editor. You . . . I would never . . ."

"I know, Irma," my mother said. "Go now."

By this time, four of us stood in an ushering-out attitude. Irma caught on. After a few steps forward, however, she veered back. "And Ivánka? where is he? What has happened to him?"

After a moment's hesitation, my mother said, "He has disappeared." It was the first time I had heard this formulation.

Irma left, prodded gently by my grandfather. I sat down on the floor. I had always been told that the great advantage of being on the ground is that you cannot fall further than the bottom. What a naive assessment! There is no place on earth where you can stand, sit, or lie that does not contain, hidden in itself, an incipient descent.

Each evening, Mother gave me one of Irma's dry rolls. I gnawed on it ferociously, even though it made my gums bleed. At night, I woke often. "Why aren't you asleep?" my mother whispered.

"I am too hungry," I whispered back. She started to weep. What could I do?

At dawn, every dawn, Russian soldiers marched by, five abreast. I watched them through a crack in the boards of the window. They wore big fur hats and heavy black boots. The leader whistled a tune. The rest of them hummed it. The tune sounded weightless and sad, like a soul departing. I always heard them before they arrived, and long, long after they were gone.

The best thing those days was that my scalp had stopped ejecting strips of itself. My head was clean, lice-free, and without scabs. My hair could be combed in any style, if only my mother felt like combing it.

At one of my early awakenings, I realized that before the miracle of Iván or Ervin returning, another, lesser miracle had to happen, or else we would be found as five starved corpses worshiping a fireless stove.

I wasn't the only one who thought this, because next morning Rózsi said to my mother, "We have to go out today. We have to get some food. If we don't, we will all die."

"What about the Russians?" my mother asked. "Haven't you heard the rumors? What Mrs. Deutsch said? How the women are rounded up to peel potatoes? Then three days later, they bleed to death, and their dead bodies are thrown on a mound of snow in the nearest park? What about that?"

"I heard it," Rózsi said, nodding, "and it is probably true. But we have no choice. We will put kerchiefs on our heads and smudge our faces with coal from the fire. I will wear my pants and you will wear Apuka's."

"What?" my mother and grandfather exclaimed in horrified unison.

"Yes," Rózsi said. "It is the only way. We have to get to Pista at the nursery. He has my several thousand pengős, and the antique lace, and the other stuff I gave him."

We all stared at her in utter shock. My grandfather's pants, worn by my mother, and thousands of pengős with which to buy food? She must be mad! Insane. This had to be one of her bizarre jokes, for which she was famous. I started to giggle.

"Quiet," my grandfather said, clearing his throat. "Rózsi, do you really have pengös at Pista's, or is this a dream?"

"No, Apuka, it is not a dream. I have many thousands of pengös. I gave them to him for safekeeping in the summer of 1944, before Szálasi came to power."

No one spoke, although there was a question that had to be asked. My grandfather dared it. "Why have you allowed us to starve?"

"I was waiting for Ervin to return," Rózsi replied, without any hint of shame or guilt in her voice.

No one commented. I understood Rózsi perfectly. Profligate spending at this end might have delayed Ervin's departure from elsewhere. There exist in the universe unarticulated laws which are most dangerous to defy and which must be obeyed by instinct.

Watching my mother and Rózsi get ready for their outing was like being behind the scenes at the circus. My grandfather wrapped a towel around his waist and dropped his pants. My mother put them on. The bottoms hit her legs just a bit above the ankles, making me hope to see a clown being built. She had to wrap his belt twice around her waist and then tie it. Margit and Rózsi put everybody's spareable clothing on their upper bodies in layers, until they resembled misshapen, puffed-up pigeons. They lifted some soot from the embers of the stove with their thumbs and, in mirrored gestures, painted each other's circled eyes to deeper dark and engraved each other's gray wrinkles into black wounds. The job done, they linked arms, kicked their heels high, then started to weep. We all hugged each other in breathless denial of what the future might hold. They left, and I thought that I could not endure the recurrent disarray of my life. Up, down, disappear, laughter, pengö, hunger, come, stay, go, worry. Please! Enough!

By nightfall, when they returned, having, thanks to their disguises, escaped potato-peeling abduction, we all had news for each other. "You first." "No you," we yelled in relieved, liberated spirits. Who cares about hunger when you can behold again loved, imperiled, returned faces? We felt very happy.

We told our news first. The soldier boy befriended by Grandfather had come. He brought a little food: a cup of sugar, a bar of chicory, two cups of flour, four eggs, one apple. He also brought a fortune: two very large bolts of prime-quality wool fabric for gentlemen's suits, double the quantity that my mother had let go two weeks ago. He said he would not return; it was dangerous for ambitious young Russian Orthodox soldiers to be caught helping Jews. Grandfather and I thanked him profusely, over and over. On his way out, his hand, in atavistic, unconscious habit, shot to his lips, and then to the Bergers' mezuzah, which somehow still hung on the doorframe, undisturbed and unnoticed by everyone, including us, until now.

"You next," we said to Rózsi and Mother. But their story was less cheerful. Yes, they had found Pista, who, thank God, had survived. He took them around his property to show them the antique lace, the hand-embroidered tablecloths, Rózsi's long-saved-for and triumphantly purchased fur coat, all trampled by the Russians, along with his own belongings, into the mud of melting snow. The pengös were also mostly gone. Pista had misjudged several people to whom he gave money for safekeeping. He had also invested unwisely. "Or so he claims," Rózsi said.

"Please, I trust him absolutely," my mother said.

"Naturally, my dear. It wasn't your money."

"The bastard!" my grandmother said, to my relief, because she had not uttered a word in days.

"How much is left?" I asked.

"We don't know yet. Some of it is still outstanding and possible to recover," my mother said.

"I don't mean that. I mean how much do you actually have to buy food?"

"A few hundred," Rózsi said. She looked very sad and very feeble.

"Rózsikám, just think . . . how your coat . . . um." I could not continue. I had no joke to make.

"Never mind, my dear," Rózsi said. "The truth is I took that fur away from some animal. And now another animal took it away from me. The world is ruled by justice." I threw my arms around her. She squeezed me back, hard. "Don't worry, darling," she said. "Pista gave us a loaf of bread, a yard of bacon, an onion, and six hard-boiled eggs. Tonight we feast."

We all protested. There should be rationing, thought of the morrow, moderation, caution, parsimony. "Yes," Rózsi said, "there should be. But for now, to hell with it all. It is my fur coat, my pengős, my decision. I will eat like a queen. You are invited to join me. But I won't cry if you don't. I'll just eat more." In instant regret, she added, "Please join me?"

My Aunt Rózsi was a big-hearted woman with a mouth that often went awry. I was the first to volunteer. My grandfather was next. He put his hand up like a schoolboy waiting to be called on. "Yes sir, please!" Rózsi said. My mother and grandmother pulled their chairs to the table in wordless disapproval. We ate and ate and ate to bursting.

A few days later, all of us watched breathlessly as my grandfather cut a length of the cherished wool, sized for a gentleman's suit. The violated bolt was replaced, tilted against the wall and covered with dirty sheets. A pathetic, pretend precaution against potential looters.

My mother and Rózsi walked downtown to trade the cloth for food. They returned far too late by our worried expectations. We didn't question them, because they both looked ashen and exhausted. We helped them drag and pull bags and satchels and loose items of food into the apartment. A big haul, I thought. It looked as if we could live on all this for at least two weeks.

Abruptly, without saying anything, Rózsi and Mother kicked their shoes off and went to bed fully clothed. What had happened?

My grandfather motioned to my grandmother and me to come to the table, away from the beds. "Don't worry," he whispered. "It must have been a long, hard day for them. They are very tired. But by morning, they will be all right. I am sure of it."

"What about the food?" my grandmother asked.

"You will cook for the three of us, Emma. We have not eaten all day. The rest we will put away."

"It is their food," I said, from some raging, wanton, unfair expression of fairness.

"No, Magduska," my grandfather said quietly. "The food belongs to all of us. When we have it, we all eat. When we don't, we all starve together."

For some reason that I do not fully understand, my grandfather was the only person to whom I didn't talk back. Were he anyone else, I would instantly have replied, Well, now, I have some other complicated little memories about Grandmother tucked here in my rhinitis. No, I am wrong. That's a disease of the nose. In my, in my—dammit—cerebrum. That's it. I dismissed myself with a downward wave. Why do I have to get it right when I don't even want to say it? My mother is correct. I am very difficult.

"Come on, little girl," my grandfather said. "Help me put the food in the other room." His arm shot out and his fingers jabbed my ribs lightly in fast little tickles. Seeing my face, he added, "Quickly, before the oil lamp breaks." I had not heard that expression since I was three. People say it just as a little child is about to burst into capricious, unjustifiable tears. I did exactly that.

"Come help me," my grandfather said. Together we dragged a bag of potatoes into the stoveless other room. "Look around. Did you ever imagine that we would be so rich as to have a whole room as an icebox?"

I kept crying.

"We will eat something," my grandfather said. "Tomorrow will be better." He pressed his lips together, then drew them back to produce his special trick noise, the single chirp of a single cricket.

I laughed, and went on crying.

Next morning, the news was bad. Only a fraction of the food came from trading. The rest had been bought with Rózsi's money. The whole city was starving. One had to trade in the provinces. The roads were dangerous, but there was no other solution. Because of the repeated looting, Budapest was finished.

"Not an altogether undeserved fate," said my grandmother.

"No, damn them," Rózsi said, "but we're caught in the middle of it."

There was other news, too. Ilonka and Miszlai néni, although crippled, were all right. The Fischer brothers survived. Mother and Rózsi ran into Gyula Fischer on the Körút. He gave Rózsi the address of a former client, a pro-Jewish rich Christian man who lived in Békéscsaba. If he was still there, he would probably know the neighboring peasants and be glad to help with the trading of the wool cloth for food.

And one more neglible fragment of news. A rumor, really. Most probably a malicious lie. An evil invention born of envy, nothing more. Mother was recognized by a classmate of Iván's on Váci Utca. He expressed his condolences. He had heard that Iván and his group had been marched toward the Danube and shot into it. No one had survived.

"You should have seen Margit act the duchess," Rózsi said. "She looked straight at him and said, 'That must have been the other Iván in the class. My son, Iván Dénes, has disappeared.' The boy blushed, his eyes lowered to his shoes, and he couldn't walk away fast enough. The lying little bastard."

"What a pig," my grandmother said.

"A very bad boy," said my grandfather.

I looked at the four of them, each in turn. I nodded. Yes, a malicious bad bastard pig-boy. Yes.

What a sad, frightened fool my mother was. "My son, Iván Dénes, has disappeared." She made it sound as if Iván had become the victim of his own conjuring trick. I wished he had. Then perhaps he could conjure me to his side.

The family decided that Mother, Rózsi, and I must travel to the provinces to trade one of the bolts of cloth for food. The adults calculated that by multiplying yesterday's haul by an unknown factor of x, we would probably be able to return with enough food to last for six weeks. "At the very least!" my grandmother exclaimed. With enormous restraint, I refrained from pointing out that x must have a numerical value for their calculations to make any sense. I also failed to mention what I perhaps erroneously assumed we all knew: that in this process of trading, one, two, or all three of us might be looted, crippled, murdered, or done in by some other unspeakable means.

We departed two days later. The date of our return was left blank.

We packed a blanket for each of us, changes of underwear, six hard-boiled eggs, some bacon, bread, and a small onion. We wore all our clothing, in layers. Anyu lugged an old, beat-up suitcase we found at the Bergers', kept closed with a rope. The bolt, unwound from its cardboard tube, was hidden in there, folded, covered by our underwear. Rózsi hugged to her chest the paper bag filled with food. I was empty-handed.

Grandfather embraced us in descending order of importance to him. Margit, Rózsi, me. "Come back safely," he said, then turned away weeping.

Grandmother wailed, "You have to go, I know. But oh, God, *shema Yisrael*, what will become of me? How can I lose everyone again?"

I looked at her with renewed interest. Does she really think she loses people? Doesn't she know she poisons them and that's why they disappear? Looking at her clutching at Rózsi's coat sleeve, I decided that she really didn't know. To my surprise, I suddenly felt very sorry for her.

We set out on foot toward the Eastern Railway Station. We might as well have been traveling to Mars for all we knew of what the journey held. What mutants are out there, we wondered, and of what intent? Does the atmosphere contain oxygen, and is it safe for Jews to breathe?

The walk was long, and we got tired. Mother's suitcase was heavy, so we took turns carrying it. Finally we just slid it along the pavement, worrying that its cheap bottom would fall apart. This was the best we could do. We came upon a woman who sat on a cart pulled by three young men.

Rózsi began to beg, "Please, could I rest our luggage against your cart?" she asked. "Just half of it, and I could push. That would make up for the load. We need some help, please."

The woman looked at the sky and said, "You must be crazy. I don't know you. Why would my sons pull your luggage?"

"Because," Rózsi said, and burst into tears. The woman's caravan proceeded. I had known, probably since second grade, that the wheel is considered one of the major revolutionary instruments of mankind. It was invented over 3,500 years ago, and altered the course of history. This was one of those clusters of facts you had to absorb in school, just in case, in adulthood, someone at a distinguished dinner table turned and looking straight at you asked, "So what do you know about the wheel?" I was now overprepared to answer this question. The wheel eases burdens, accelerates locomotion, promotes trade, and divides the haves from the have-nots. The possession of even a lowly single-wheeled barrow enables you to carry the sick to hospital, luggage to trains, food to your home, wood to the stove, caskets to the grave. Owning a wheel attached to anything makes you independent and free. Without a wheel, you are stuck and trapped.

"All right. We need to get something with a wheel," I said.

"Don't be stupid," my mother replied. "We don't have that kind of money. Besides, if we just keep pushing, we'll get to the railway station soon. The trains will have wheels."

When we arrived, the Eastern Railway Station was in a state

of catastrophic disarray. Half of it was bombed out. The other half looked in obvious danger of immediate collapse. Soldiers shouted instructions through handheld megaphones in alien languages. After I listened for a while, I realized that one of the alien languages was Hungarian.

"Let me find a railroad official," Rózsi said.

Anyu and I both laughed. What official? We were in the lap of anarchy.

"You sit on the luggage," my mother said to me. "I will go find out what to do."

"Wait," Rózsi said. "Perhaps we should go back home. It is safer there. I am tired. I want to go home."

"Snap out of it," my mother said to Rózsi, as if Rózsi were four years old. "I will go inquire. You just sit. Magda will take care of you."

I patted Rózsi's hand until my mother returned, about an hour later. "This is the situation," my mother told us. "There is a troop train going toward Békéscsaba. The two front cars are under the protection of the Hungarians, meaning the Russians have been bribed. The charge is fifty pengős a head. They guarantee safe passage in those two cars, but only up to the second station away from Budapest. After that, it is on the *qui vive*."

"Let's go home," Rózsi said. "To die of hunger is better than this. And anyway, at home someone might rescue us. The boys might come home."

"No one will rescue us," I said. This I knew. I had no opinion about our direction. Going away seemed terrible. Going back home seemed terrible.

"No," my mother said. "We have to go. It is the only chance we have. If we don't, we will all starve to death. Let's go forward."

How wrong we had been to laugh at Rózsi for wanting to find a railroad official! There was a stationmaster, dressed in his prewar uniform, thereby masking his more recent political affiliations. Mother paid him three times fifty pengős. He put it into the already bulging pocket over his heart. "Go," he said. "Run to the left. Get into the car, quickly."

The "car" turned out to be a flatbed on which a disabled Russian tank had been placed upside down. We had to enter it by climbing through a large circular hole. Inside, it was crowded, but we found an upwardly curving corner where we settled. How cozy, I thought. What stupid fears we had. No bullet can penetrate this armor. No one dangerous can enter here. Two brawny Hungarian fellows had placed themselves at the climb-in circle, and they rejected everyone attempting to board who did not speak perfect Hungarian. We filled up beyond capacity. The train sat. Two hours, three, four.

"We should each have an egg," Rózsi said.

"No," said my mother. "Not yet. We ate about seven hours ago. We have to pace ourselves."

"You are a demon," Rózsi said.

"Probably," said my mother, not caring at all what she was called when she thought she was right, which, lately, was always.

Surprisingly, I fell asleep. I woke to pandemonium. The Hungarian stalwarts at the door were sitting handcuffed. Everyone else was being kicked and slapped awake by Russian soldiers. "Out, out!" they kept yelling. *"Davay! Davay!"* They also kept everyone's belongings.

"Go," my mother whispered to me. "Go around the soldiers. Get to the big hole and lower yourself. I'll throw you the suitcase. Then run fast. I'll find you later."

"I can't do it," I whispered back.

"Yes you can, yes," my mother hissed. "You can. You will. Our lives depend on it. Go."

On hands and knees, I crawled around the soldiers' legs. My mother, in cautious, almost imperceptible movements, pushed the suitcase right behind me, as if it and I were one long segmented worm. I made sure to reach the entrance hole with my backside toward it. With both hands I grabbed the bottom rim of the hole and quickly lowered myself to the ground. In a flash, my mother kicked the suitcase after me. I picked it up and ran like the devil. Some of the soldiers cursed after me, but none bothered with pursuit. One kid, one suitcase. To hell with both.

When I reached the end of the platform, and more or less hid behind a small mound of snow, I realized the recklessness of my mother's scheme. Here I was, a kid alone, sitting on a battered suitcase with a fortune inside. I couldn't take care of it. I couldn't even take care of myself. If we didn't meet up, the suitcase would be stolen and I would be dead. What was it with her? We should have let the suitcase go and stayed together. Yes, that was the principal thing. To stay together.

I almost burst into tears, but then I heard Iván in my head. "Don't be so mad at Anyu," he said. "It's just a little literary misunderstanding. She read Julius Caesar and thought the motto 'Divide and conquer" meant 'Divide the family, conquer the enemy.' "

"Not funny," I replied.

"Actually, I think it's a pretty good joke," Iván said. "Certainly not bad enough to be criticized by a snippet."

"Iváááán!" I was about to answer, when I came back to myself. My ears and toes were numb. I was dizzy. Iván was dead.

From afar, amidst the noise of a fired-up, moving-off train, I vaguely heard my mother calling, "Magda!" I considered not answering. I had heard that freezing is a good death. You drift, you smile, you float to heaven on the wings of your shimmering wishes.

I climbed out from behind the mound, dragging the suitcase. I saw them walking toward me slowly, Rózsi clutching the paper bag of food. When they reached hearing distance, I asked, "What happened?"

"A Russian officer arrived," Rózsi said. "He yelled at the soldiers. He made them give back everything they took. Except for the two handcuffed men, he let us go. No civilian was allowed on the train. It has now left."

"I know. I heard it. By the way, have any other children rescued suitcases?"

My mother turned red. "You insolent little . . ." She couldn't find the word.

"Ingrate?" I offered solicitously.

"Oh, Margit," Rózsi said, angered. "Stop it. Just stop it. Go find us another train."

As soon as my mother left, Rózsi laughed. "How about those eggs," she said, "now that the dragon duchess is gone? Aren't you hungry?"

"Yes, of course."

"Let's eat, then."

"All right." I took two eggs from Rózsi's bag. "Here," I said, handing her one. We peeled the eggs in silence and ate them in two bites each.

"How about the second one?" Rózsi asked. I nodded. We ate those also. "Margit is not here," Rózsi said. "She may never return. There are two more eggs in the bag."

I put my foot down. "She will be back," I said. Until then

it had not occurred to me that she, too, could disappear. I got frightened. "Rózsi néni," I said, "do you really think she might not come back?"

"Of course she will," Rózsi said. "Come cuddle with me. I am cold and you are hot, like a bag of smoldering coals."

"She will return, won't she?" I asked again. But my unpredictable aunt was fast asleep.

Shaking us awake at dawn the next day, my mother said the situation was this. There were still only two trains. An ordinance had been issued forbidding Hungarians to travel, but this might be just a rumor. I interrupted, "But we are Jews, not Hungarians, aren't we?"

"It depends. According to the Hungarians, we are Jews. According to the Russians, we are Hungarians. Whichever, we are always shuffled to the losing side."

"No," I said, "no. We have to be something definite and be treated as such. In ancient Greece—"

"No!" my mother yelled. "No! I cannot stand another lesson. We have a problem here. Number one is, how do we avoid being robbed? Number two is, we are stuck. We cannot retreat or proceed. What do we do?"

"Ask the Russians to take us on," Rózsi said. "They are men."

"Yes," my mother said. "That's just why we can't ask them." Sharp whistles shrilled through our argument. A voice announced, "Those with paid tickets from Budapest may board the third car." We ran. The third car was so full that a flea couldn't jump on. Fistfights broke out on the platform. The Russian soldiers fired. As it turned out, after all of us hit the deck, they shot at the sky.

Another car full of baggage was opened to the paying customers. We boarded, stumbling over rucksacks, bags of wheat, ruined machine guns awaiting repair. Again we settled in a corner. Slowly the train brought itself to life. It coughed, spat, spluttered, spurted forward for a yard or two, then stopped.

The Russians banged on the side of the cars. "Everybody out. The train has to be repaired. Out, out, everybody!"

A cold heavy rain had started. There was no shelter anywhere. We sat exposed on the platform, Rózsi and Mother on the suitcase, I on the ground. We covered ourselves with threadbare blankets. Within ten minutes, the blankets were soaking wet. More and more people gathered. A rumor circulated that a passenger train was about to arrive, sanctioned to carry Hungarians. Throngs, hordes, multitudes seemed to want to board it. Luckily we were sitting in the middle of the platform, because people kept screaming that they were being pushed and were about to drop onto the tracks.

And still the rain fell. Periodically my mother stood up. She took my blanket and methodically wrung it out in sections. Our neighbors yelled at us. "Hey, lady! We have enough rain. Don't make more!" said the witty fellow to the left.

The angry woman on our right complained, "You are getting me wet!"—eliciting a riot of laughter.

My mother, indifferent to criticism, wrung out Rózsi's blanket and her own as well. The maneuver helped a little, I guess. A wrung-out wet blanket was probably better protection against the elements than a soaking-wet blanket. I wasn't altogether sure. Disloyally, I thought that saturation might be a shield in itself.

Finally, after many hours, the awaited train arrived. It was definitely not a passenger train, although Hungarians were allowed to board it. We nearly got trampled in the stampede.

One person, a young girl, did fall onto the tracks. She was hurt, but rescued. By the time the three of us made it to boarding, we were alone on the platform, and there was no place left for us. Everything was full, barred and guarded. "No more! no room!" the people on the cars shouted as they waved us away.

We kept on walking and pleading. At last, at the end of the train, we reached three open cars piled high with coal, on top of which were piled many loud, colorfully dressed, despised gypsy women. "Join up, join up," they shouted down to us, in their weirdly accented, fractured Hungarian.

"Up, up!" one said.

"In speed," said another.

"Gypsies good luck," called a third.

"No," my mother said to us quietly. "We cannot travel with gypsies."

"Why not? I asked. "They look friendly enough, and they have room up there."

"No," my mother said. "They are filthy and they steal children."

"They do what?"

"They steal children."

"Oh, I get it," Rózsi said, in a total loss of temper. "They are better than we Jews. We eat children. Haven't you read that in the newspaper? I have. At Passover the paschal lamb is really the limb of a Christian child. They lie about us. Also about the gypsies. The gypsies don't steal children, and we don't eat children. And as for filth, I don't think a person could be dirtier than we are."

"Ours is new dirt, the dirt of war," my mother said lamely.

"It stinks the same," I yelled.

"Enough," Rózsi said. "I'm climbing up." That task, hard

as it was to intend, was even harder to accomplish. The open car had handholds meant for climbing, but at the moment they were wet and slippery. Handing her paper bag to my mother, Rózsi grabbed hold and attempted to swing her right foot onto the first rung, which was too high up. She slipped and fell to the ground. The women above us shrieked. We rushed to Rózsi, but she got up unhurt. "I will try again," she said gamely, and succeeded. The gypsy women hooted and clapped. One started to beat her tambourine.

"You go next," my mother said. She followed me, dragging the suitcase. Miraculously, we made it. I learned a new thing: It is possible to be soaked, then, sweating, get wetter yet.

The view from the ground had been deceptive. The coal pile was more crowded and the seating arrangement more precarious than it had appeared from below. No wonder the Russians allowed gypsies to occupy the space, I thought, although as I looked around I could see Hungarians as well, including some men.

The coal was piled into a steeple. On each side of the decline, in four tiers, people had made little seating indentations for themselves and cut into the coal with their heels to support their feet. These maneuvers notwithstanding, the steeple kept shifting. Rogue coals rolled and fell to the ground, hinting of an avalanche.

"This is terrible," Rózsi whispered. "I am very sorry I insisted."

"You didn't," I said.

"Please," my mother said. "It was the only way. We would have been stuck back there for days and died of hunger." Hand over hand, the gypsy women helped us to occupy the second tier of the decline. It was clear we were getting special consideration. Why, I did not know.

Our wet blankets began to weigh a ton as the unceasing rain saturated them more and more. If we drown here, Grandfather will say Kaddish for us, I thought. I was comforted by the idea, even though I was not at all religious.

The rain fell and fell. The train did not and did not move.

"Let's eat our eggs," my mother said. "Now is the right time."

"Actually, you have to eat yours first," Rózsi said, "because we have devised a little puzzle."

"No, we eat together," my mother said.

"No," Rózsi and I replied in alarmed unison.

"You have to do this, Margit," Rózsi said reprovingly. "It is a little game. Something to cheer us up. You have to go along."

"All right," my mother said. She peeled and ate her first egg, then rebelled again. "No, I won't do this. You have to eat with me."

"Margit, stop being a spoilsport," Rózsi said. "Eat your second egg and we'll tell you the puzzle."

Anyu complied. Finishing, she asked, "What is the puzzle?"

"The puzzle is for you to figure out when we ate our eggs," Rózsi said.

My mother got very angry. "You are both so stupid," she yelled. "I could have had one egg, and the two of you could have shared the other. We must economize! Now none of us can eat anything for hours!"

We remained silent under her rebuke. I didn't know what Rózsi was thinking, but I thought that my mother was right in the first place.

At last the train started. I heard its rhythmic whoosh whoosh whoosh whoosh with mixed emotions—afraid to leave, glad to depart. And as always, with everything, I heard memories. "Isn't it exciting?" Iván asked as we watched trains come and go at the Eastern Railway Station. He sounded sad, not excited. He had brought me there for our afternoon of entertainment. It was what we did on Sundays after Éva Hirsch left for Sárbogárd on a train.

The pressure of my bladder woke me. I nudged my mother with my elbow. "I have to peepee."

"Oh, God," my mother said. "I don't know what to do. The child has to urinate," she said to Rózsi.

"The child has to urinate," Rózsi yelled to the world.

Instant committees formed. One group advised letting me pee into my pants, since I was thoroughly wet anyway. Another foolish group said we should stop the train. The gypsy lady at the apex of the coal pile said, "Pull her pants down, hang her over the side, and let the poor child pee in peace." I applauded her decision, although I was chagrined at having my private needs so blatantly broadcast.

We slid down to the edge. Mother and Rózsi each grabbed one of my arms, and, with my pants pulled down, hung me over the rim of the railroad car. I knew I was in danger, but I didn't care. I joined nature and gladly wet the world.

Rózsi and Mother pulled me back and adjusted my underpants. Laboriously we regained our seats. The train chugged on; I nodded and weaved and fell asleep over its mirthless uneven rhythm. When I woke again, we were at a stop across from a Russian troop train. Soldiers hung on the cars like grapes on a stem. They were yelling and hooting in a frightening way, and so were the gypsy women. On each side, some soldiers and some of the women were making circles with their left forefinger and thumb as they jabbed into the encircled space with their right index finger. It was sign language, I knew, but what did it mean? And why did it elicit ever wilder guffaws from everyone but us?

"What are they doing?" I asked my mother.

"Nothing," she said. "Hide your face in my lap now. Instantly."

"No," I said. "Tell me what this means." I imitated their gesture.

"Noooo!" my mother screamed, and pulled me down. "For God's sake, don't do that. Oh, my God."

She was getting hysterical. "Stop it," Rózsi said to her. "She has to learn if she is to protect herself. You have to—"

She was interrupted midsentence by the train's lurching forward. A great cry went up from among the Russian soldiers. The gypsy women replied with their taunting tambourines. Everyone seemed to be energized except us three.

"What were you going to say?" I asked Rózsi.

"Go to sleep," she said.

"Go to sleep," my mother said.

I went to sleep. I dreamed. We are on holiday in Zirkveniza. We are on a sailboat. A storm comes up. My brother loses hold of the mainsail. We overturn. He yells for help. I see him bobbing up and down in the water. I am three years old and my arms are made of lead. He drowns. I wake screaming for help. "It's all right, it's all right," my mother said, hugging me. "Wake up. Let me wring out your blanket. If only this rain would stop, you would feel better."

"Anyu, do you remember Zirkveniza?" I asked.

"Of course I remember," she answered. "Why?"

"Nothing. I just dreamt of it."

I couldn't go back to sleep, because insidiously I had now turned cold in layers, which was colder than anything I had ever imagined possible. The blanket above me was covered with brittle ice patches that crackled and broke every time I shifted my weight. My clothing was wet and felt frozen to the touch. My skin steamed cold sweat, fueled by my ice-box-cooled flesh. Below all this, what I used to call my soul had become a block of ice, unmelting and impenetrable.

Worse yet, my paralyzed brain was unable to conjure anything warm. I wanted to visualize a volcano, but all I saw was frozen tundra. Instead of a forest fire, tumbling mountains of snow appeared. December beaches, Swiss Christmases, Siberian storms, and the one Alaska postcard I had ever seen danced before my tearing eyes.

"Anyu." I looked at my mother and started to laugh. Overnight, the soot from the engine smoke had streaked her face black. She looked like a funereal clown.

"What's so funny?" she asked, annoyed.

"Look at my face." She did and laughed. "You look like a chimney sweep." There's a hot thought for you! We asked Rózsi to look at us, and told her she looked the same. She laughed. We laughed. We nudged each other and pointed rudely, and kept on laughing. After a while, the joke thinned. It turned to a mere streak, so to speak, but we laughed on, because it felt good, and because it warmed us.

The train slowed. An incomprehensible word bounced from car to car. It sounded like Daradem. When at last it reached us, it acquired meaning: Debrecen. Debrecen?

"Anyu, this is Debrecen!" I said in disbelieving shock. "Debrecen, not Békéscsaba."

My mother shrugged. "So what's in Békéscsaba? We had to get out of that station. This train was leaving. So it's Debrecen."

I turned toward Rózsi. "This is Debrecen," I said.

Rózsi also shrugged. "What's the difference? You know the rabbi in Békéscsaba?"

What a question. I didn't know any rabbis anywhere. They were right, of course. There was no difference. Still, I continued to feel deeply betrayed.

The train stopped. Two young men who had kept themselves barely visible through the journey stood and offered to climb down and help the "ladies." The descent was tricky. The shifting bodies and the rain had loosened the coals so that now they fell to the ground in a steady stream.

Wet, the coals had also become slippery. Rózsi failed twice in her attempt to stand. Each time, the coals skipped from under her heels, and to avoid falling, she sat down hard on her behind. I won't laugh, I thought. It's not funny. It is *not* funny. Humiliation is never funny. Disability is never funny. Misfortune is never funny. All right, Iván, all right. I said it wasn't funny.

Finally all three of us stood on terra firma. Even as we walked away, I kept feeling the rocking of the train. Ah, at last I could walk on waves. That grace notwithstanding, I felt bleary-eyed, filthy, and frightened.

"Look," Anyu said to Rózsi and me. "Look." We saw a united crowd within the crowd and someone standing on a chair in the middle of them speaking through a megaphone.

"Oh, God," Rózsi whispered. "A roundup!"

"We have papers," mother whispered back.

"Yes," Rózsi said, "but which ones should we show?"

"You are carrying the Jewish papers. I am carrying the Christian papers. Right?"

"I don't remember. Should I check them?"

"No," my mother snapped. "No, not now. I'm pretty sure I'm right." After seconds of thought, she said, "I am positive."

"You are right," I said with total confidence, not because I remembered the distribution, but because it made sense. The Jewish papers were real. Rózsi could handle those fine. The Christian papers were false. She couldn't possibly manage them. We all knew that. They must have divided them by that logic. So yes, Anyu was right.

"You remember for sure?" my mother asked.

I took a deep breath. If my reasoning were false, we might get killed. "Yes," I said. "I remember for sure."

"All right," Mother said. "Let's mingle, then. We'll judge by the situation. Rózsi, you watch me. If Christian papers are called for, I'll whip them out fast. If I do nothing, you bring out the Jewish papers."

"All right," Rózsi said. We proceeded forward, ears cocked, trying to assess the political direction of the crowd.

Suddenly, from a platform we had not seen, a voice boomed through the megaphone. "Madame Dénes and Madame, Madame, Madame Rózsi, beg pardon, come up here." It's over, I thought. Whatever papers are whipped or flogged, we are done for.

"What now?" Rózsi asked, her voice cracking.

"We'll face it down," Mother replied. "Let's just go forward."

We reached the platform. People parted to let us mount its steps. "Madame Dénes," said a rotund, bald little man, bowing from his nonexistent waist. "What a pleasure to see you. And you, Madame Rózsi. Forgive me, but although I remember your beautiful face, I don't recall your surname."

"Rózsi will do," Rózsi said flirtatiously. Most likely, she had forgotten for the moment which name her Christian papers carried. "I remember you very well," she said to the man. "You used to buy mirrors from the Fischer Brothers."

"Yes, madame, and you were always very kind. Discounts, and delivery on time. It makes me very happy that you are joining my campaign."

Rózsi's eyes darted to Mother, who barely nodded. "Thank you," Rózsi said, not committing herself.

"Well, let's go to the carts," the man said. As if out of nowhere, two peasant carriages had appeared at the bottom of the platform. Each was drawn by two horses, a forgotten sight.

All in all, about twenty-five people mounted them, including us. The first carriage had a metal arch up front adorned with posters and small Hungarian and Communist flags. The flags flapped in the cold morning wind. They sounded like long-ago kites I had known.

Our host, benefactor—and possible murderer, I thought—got into the first cart and seated himself under the flags. "What are we doing?" I whispered to my mother.

She shrugged. "How should I know? Is there another place for us to go? It's seven a.m. We don't know the town. These people aren't overtly Nyilas, and they're not Russian soldiers. So we go with them."

"Then what?"

"We'll see," she said. "I don't plan very far ahead."

"I have noticed."

"What are you whispering?" Rózsi whispered.

"She doesn't plan far ahead," I said in a normal voice.

"I have noticed," Rózsi replied, and we both burst out laughing. My mother tightened her haw jaw and hiked her nose five degrees higher. She looked hurt just the same.

"I am sorry," I said, suddenly sorry. "You have done very well."

"Yes," Rózsi said. "Pardon us."

My mother made a deprecating gesture with her right hand. "This is no life for human beings," she said. "It's not between us. It's between the world and us, and I am getting very tired."

She was scaring me. "Oh, Anyu," I said, kissing her and hugging her sideways. "Please don't get tired."

"No, please, please don't get tired," Rózsi said, imitating me, but also scared, I could tell.

The carriages pulled up in front of a farm. A piss-poor gypsy band consisting of an accordion, a violin, and a tambourine approached us. They played an upbeat, kick-your-heels-high number. Our rotund host jumped off the cart and, dancing, entered the front portals. We, along with his legitimate entourage, followed him. Inside, breakfast tables were set to buckling with food. Chicken, ham, goose, pork, bread, beans, onions, potatoes, pickles. I hadn't seen anything like this since my father left. There was enough for ten times the number of guests. I was incredulous.

"We, too, can eat? I asked my mother, awe and doubt warring within me.

"Why do you think we came?" she asked back, assuming her fun-haughty manner, years lighter than she had been minutes ago. "So," she said to Rózsi, "was it worth the game?"

"You are a grand and major vizier and I will henceforth always unquestioningly obey your commands," Rózsi said, bowing.

I had, however, a small nagging thought. "What will this cost, and whom?"

"Don't worry," my mother said "I don't think it will cost anything. I think we will be able to exit graciously. Anyway, our bellies will be full. That is worth something."

Rotund Baldy gave a speech. All applauded. We were invited to dig in. "And a healthy appetite. Honor to the hosts. Long live Hungary. *Proszit.* Bottoms up." That's blessing for the wine. The candidate announced, "Each district supporting me, please identify yourselves so our hosts can know whom they have treated to this exceptional feast."

A man stood up from a three-person committee. "Mr. Candidate, honored hosts," he began. I didn't hear the rest from the pounding of my temples. A woman was up now, then a man again. Pop-up-johnnies out for our lives.

Finally only one committee of three had not been heard from. All eyes were on us. "Madame Dénes," said the candidate, "stand up, please. You speak for Budapest."

My mother stood up. Her cheeks were crimson. Her voice was steady. "No, Mr. Candidate," she said. "We do not represent anyone. We are your personal guests. You invited us to join your party on the platform of the Debrecen railroad station, and we accepted gladly. We have known you as an honorable man since before the war. We feel . . ." She hesitated.

"Esteemed," I whispered.

"Esteemed to be chosen as the guests who demonstrate that you are not only a political star but are also committed to real life and friendship."

Thunderous applause. One more such speech, and they will elect her, not him, I thought. Anyway, my mother was wonderful. She had saved us again.

"Comrade Dénes," he said. "I had hoped you would say exactly what you said. The truth—the reality of my concern for the welfare of everyone. I thank you very much. I thank you for your time and effort. And as I promised, a carriage will take you back to Debrecen at once, because I know your time is limited, and you have a train to catch."

"Right," said my mother, nodding vigorously. "At once. Thank you very much. Goodbye. Goodbye."

The carriage driver slapped the horses to a trot. "To the railroad station," he said. It was not exactly a question.

At the station, the driver told us pointedly, "Take a train. Today."

We all nodded, thanked him, and wished him good day. Inside, we giggled and pushed each other like schoolgirls. Amazing what a full stomach and a little body warmth will do. We were postively giddy. For once, we had taken advantage instead of always, always being the patsies.

Rózsi twirled around and asked, "So what's for tonight, Margit? The queen's ball?"

"Let's sober up," Mother said. "It is late afternoon. I don't think we should travel at night. It's harder and much more dangerous. We cannot stay here at the station. The Russians regularly round up stations. Bad things happen, particularly to women. I think we should find shelter here in town."

"How?" Rózsi asked. Her good mood vanished like exhaled smoke.

"Magda," my mother said to me, "You should sit on the luggage. If anyone suspicious approaches, scream and cry and yell for help." She turned toward my aunt. "You, Rózsi, should go in one direction, I in the other. We have to find some Jews to tell us what's what in Debrecen."

"Are you crazy?" Rózsi said. "How am I going to find Jews? I can't ask for their papers!"

"Find the obvious ones. Big noses. The shadow of ripped-off stars. Curly red hair. You know. Find Jews."

"You are insane. I will not find Jews. I don't know how," Rózsi yelled. We were attracting attention, a cardinal no for the endangered.

A thin young woman with curly red hair and a young man in army boots approached us. Behind them lingered another young man. He had bandages over his head and all around his ears. Some loose gauze was tied in a bow under his chin.

"You want Jews?" the young man in army boots, really a boy, asked belligerently. "You've found them. You want to arrest us? Hurt us? Kill us? No more, no more. Nyilas Nazi scum. We have been liberated. Now we kick in your dirty faces." He looked apoplectic.

A crowd gathered around us. Murmurs surfaced as factions formed. "The filthy Jew! Insulting our patriotic sisters," came from one end. "Let him kill the Nazi bitches!" came from somewhere else.

Suddenly Rózsi stepped in front of the young man, close enough for their noses to nearly touch. "Pipe down, son," she whispered. "You are causing a riot. We are Jews, too. You misunderstood. When the melée starts, you and we will be knifed first. So calm down and let's try to survive."

The boy looked dazed, but somehow listened to her and stopped yelling. The young man with the bandages came closer.

"All right, Sándor?" he asked his friend. The boy nodded. "All right, everyone," said the bandaged man. "It's over. Nothing to see. A family fight. Nothing to gawk at. Disperse. Go home; your stew is burning." Slowly the crowd drifted away.

"Are you really Jewish?" asked the redheaded girl, who until now had been silent.

"Of course, my dear," Rózsi replied, patting her cheek. "We are looking for shelter for the night among Jews. We are strangers here." She trailed off without saying that we were also very scared.

They did know of a Jewish shelter for children, but no housing for adults. Anyu asked for the address and for directions on how to get there. I could see what was coming, so I began to beg. "Please, let's not go there. What's the point? They won't take us in. Let's find some other place. We can ask other people. These three don't know everything. Please, please, let's not go there."

"Just to see, just for information," my mother said. But I knew she was lying. Again she wanted me to be "safe," which in her vocabulary meant I was to be deposited, left behind, put on a shelf, out of danger and out of her care.

I am the child, I thought, I am the headache, the limp, the stutter, the extra, the yoke and hardship of her burdened life. If only I could walk to Amerika, or disappear. If only I could say with feeling, "I don't want you, either."

When we located it, the shelter turned out to be two large connected rooms on the ground floor of a dilapidated, bullet-pocked building.

A woman who reminded me of Dora néni from TB times greeted us. Her smile flashed with large, threatening teeth, as she said, without preamble, "The child can stay. You must go."

"But," said my mother, "but—"

"There are no buts here," the woman interrupted. "These are the rules. We shelter children. No adults, ever. No exceptions."

"But—" Rózsi repeated loudly.

I blessed the lady. She just might irritate them enough so they wouldn't leave me here.

"What but now? I told you the rules," she said, wagging a forefinger at Rózsi.

Rózsi was the only redhead I have ever known who lived up to their mythic reputation. When she lost her temper, it was worse than God's worst thunderstorm, after which even He sends a repentant rainbow. *"Kuss,"* she said to the woman, rising on tiptoe. *"Kuss." Shut up* does not translate it. The word is more aggressive, and much more vulgar.

To my despair, the woman turned out to be a true bully; meeting with superior opposition, she folded. I knew I was done for. "What exactly would you like to know?" she asked Rózsi in a somewhat shaky voice. I stopped listening.

The room seemed to be filled to top capacity with children of my age and younger. There were bunk beds—what else?— cribs, baby carriages, infant baskets, and blankets on the floor. Everywhere children slept, wept, sucked, peed, ate. I tugged at my mother's arm. She didn't respond. I tugged again.

"Stop tugging," she said. "It's rude! You can see I am talking."

I was without recourse in the custody of an insane person. She spoke of manners; I thought of dying. "Well, whenever you're free," I said, and lowered myself to the floor.

"Get up," she said. "Get up. You are mishbehaving. Say thank you to the lady. She will give you supper and take care of you for the night."

I did nothing.

"Get up," she yelled. I sat. She started to yank me by the arm.

"Don't yank," I said. "It's very rude."

She lowered herself to my ear level. "You have gone mad," she whispered in a rage. "You are inconsiderate and selfish and mean. You are your father Gyula. You don't care how you would endanger Rózsi and me if you stayed with us. You don't care about anybody."

The yoke rebelled. With a scream the sound of which would make angels tremble, she took a machine gun out of her battered suitcase and, cocking it, shot Mother, Rózsi, the woman, all the children, two or three people in the distance making soup, and the four bare bulbs that illuminated the rooms, and, in the ensuing darkness, crashed through the window and flew to the moon to meet her brother, risen from black waves.

"Yes, Mother," I said. "I am sorry I was bad. I will stay." I wondered what Rózsi's altercation with the woman would cost me.

It didn't cost anything. The lady was fair. She offered me pea soup, which I declined. She showed me a corner with a blanket, where I could sleep, for which I was very grateful, particularly because it was a corner. During the night I woke often, with one recurring nightmare. I am running away. I stumble. I fall into mud. As I am about to get up, someone pushes my head down and forward. I try to scream for help, but no sound comes. I woke. I slept. Again I dreamt, and again and again. By morning, I wished there were no nights. Perhaps I wished something worse, but I could not face that knowledge.

I barely expected them, but they arrived at six. I was ready. I had been up since four. My face was washed, my hair combed, my teeth clean, rubbed with a forefinger dipped in soapy water. "*Szervusz*, Mother; *szervusz*, Rózsi," I said. "I am so glad you came for me. I thank you. Thank you very much."

"Well," said my mother. Oh, I knew that "well" so well! It rang disaster. "Actually, you have to stay here for the morning. We must find a train out of here, and many trains are not suitable for children. I have to see what I can do. You must stay until I find a solution."

"You are leaving me again?" I asked.

"For a little while." She patted my head. "Eat breakfast. We will be back."

"Rózsi!" I screamed.

Rózsi looked away, then looked back at me. "Margit is running things," she said, shrugging.

Right. What my life needs is disclaimers.

For breakfast the lady offered me pea soup. I declined. Actually, I did feel nauseated. I yearned to lie down on my feather bed, in my old home of strife and plenty, where the servants outnumbered us.

The next train we boarded toward Békéscsaba was an ordinary freight car with fairly clean straw strewn on its floor. It was not crowded, which caused fresh worry. Were there enough of us to be safe? Would the Hungarians in the car feel free to attack two women and a child? Would marauding Russian soldiers kill all of us? What was the balance point? Does safety always twirl on a pin where uncountable angels dance?

Nothing happened. Rain kept falling, but this car had a roof. We were dry, not too hungry, and not very cold. Straw is a good insulator. It even smelled good.

On arriving at the Békéscsaba station, we headed directly for a Jewish organization, the name and address of which had been given to my mother at the Debrecen shelter.

I did about seventeen mental shrugs of I don't care, I'll run away, I'll just die, I don't care, before I dared to ask, "Is this another children's shelter?

"No," my mother said. "It's a way station. They will give us information and hot soup. They will tell us where to go for the night, and where we can best trade our goods."

As we walked, we got soaked again, blankets and all.

The "way station" *was* a shelter, crowded to capacity. People were sitting, standing, crouching, lying down. They breathed, sweated, sneezed, sighed, coughed, farted. The air was heavy with exudate that in concentration almost acquired color, green as bile to my eyes.

"Stop this whining," my mother replied to nothing I had said. "Of course I won't leave you. I never have. I have always kept my children stuck to me. Perhaps that was my big mistake."

I craned my neck to look at her face. Was this the expression of a newly acquired sense of black humor, or had she gone mad overnight? I couldn't tell, but my blood froze. What if her lying was from now on to be taken as fact? What if she could grind the truth, as she did me, under her thumb? What if truth was just the power of one person over another, or of many over one? What if what I knew was nothing without a witness? All my witnesses were dead. How is truth preserved? In a blown-out eggshell? In a casket? In the flame of a torch? Secretly down in a grave? Where do you hide truth to make it safe? And when does it spread its everlasting golden wings for all to see?

"What's the program?" I asked my mother.

"Well, these people say there is a farmer some miles away, a gentleman farmer, or at least a big owner of acres and acres of land. He has many tenant farmers who would probably trade food for cloth. The farmer and his wife are said to be charitable. They are devout Catholics. They might take us in for a day or two. There is one little snag, though. No one has been sent there before, because no one has had valid Christian papers."

I looked at Rózsi in shock. "It's all the same," she said, shrugging.

By the time we set out, it was five o'clock in the afternoon. They had told us that walking over the fields as the crow flies, we would arrive at the main house in two hours. This was perhaps an accurate estimate for foot soldiers in top shape. We got bogged down thirty minutes into the walk. The ground was so muddy that with every step, our feet were sucked ankle-deep. The fields darkened as the rain began again.

"I cannot do it," my mother said. "I will sit down to rest. You come back for me in the morning."

"No grandstanding," Rózsi yelled at her. "No duchess shit. Lift your feet. One, two three."

"I can't!"

"Look at her," I said to Rózsi. "Her tongue is hanging out."

"Rózsi averted her eyes. "I don't care what she looks like," she said. "She has to walk. One two three, one two three, walk, walk." My mother dragged herself forward at turtle speed.

We reached the farm at Pusztaótlaka after midnight. The house was locked and dark. We didn't dare to knock, so we made as much noise as we dared. A light went on in one room, then in another. We heard clatter, murmurs, and heavy steps. The main door opened an inch. A man, who turned out to be

Mr. Zsiros, the farmer, stuck his nose out. "Who are you at this hour? Are you the police?"

"No sir," Rózsi answered. "We are fugitives from Budapest. We are cold and hungry. We have a ten-year-old child with us. We need food and shelter. We heard in town that you are a good Christian, charitable and kind, as all we Christians ought to be. Only at this moment, we are the supplicants."

My mother meant to kick Rózsi, to tone her down, I assumed, but she got me at mid-shin. "Oh, God!" I cried out.

Mr. Zsiros misunderstood. "Come in, come in," he said, opening the door. "I have heard of people like you. Good families, roaming the countryside starving. This insane war, that sinful Budapest. Come in."

We thanked him from the depths of our sinful Jewish Budapest hearts.

Inside, more lights came on. He ushered us into a very large country kitchen. In the middle of it stood a stocky, handsome woman, older than my mother, dressed in a thick flannel robe. Her face was square-jawed and kind. She had miss-nothing cornflower-colored eyes.

"Please come in," she said. "You must be wetter than fish. Take off your coats and things and put them in that corner."

She pointed to her left, where a large camel-humped clay oven stood. I had never seen one before in real life, although it was a standard item in children's picture books dealing with peasant life. I recognized it immediately. It was sand-colored, with a rosy cast caused by the ebullient crackling fire inside. What my picture books had not conveyed was the enormous amount of heat it generated. Oh, venerable oven, I salute you.

"This is Mrs. Zsiros," Mr. Zsiros said lamely, after she paused. I curtsied without hesitation. It was a combination curtsy, directed as much at the oven as at Mrs. Zsiros.

"Good evening, good evening," Rózsi and Anyu said in turn. "I am Mrs. Dénes, and this is my sister, Mrs. Balázs." Aha! the Christian papers! "And my little daughter Magduska." I felt obliged to curtsy again.

"Get your shoes and socks off, too," Mrs. Zsiros said, turning to me. "They will dry in no time at the side of the oven." I did as I was told. To my embarrassment, I started to shiver violently. I didn't know why. "This child is exhausted," Mrs. Zsiros said. "She needs a hot bath, food, and sleep. Mr. Zsiros," she said, turning to her husband, "let's drag the wooden tub to the center and fill it with hot water."

I was amazed at this attention and the priority I was given. My mother was the one whose tongue hung out of her mouth. Why should I bathe first? "My mother," I said involuntarily. Mrs. Zsiros caught my drift. "Your mother can wait," she said. "She is an adult. We take care of children first. Don't we now?" she asked.

"Of course, always," said my mother.

"Always," Rózsi echoed.

Yep, always. I was being unfair; sometimes they did put me first. *In extremis.*

Mrs. Zsiros exiled her husband from the kitchen, and the women bathed me in hot, soapy, scented water. It was like being home again with my Fräuli. It was like being pampered, powdered, and called my little darling by everyone. I started to weep.

"Is something hurting you?" Mrs. Zsiros asked. "Did you pull something during that long walk?"

I shook my head. "It's the steam," I answered. "The steam makes my eyes water." I knew that what I said sounded stupid.

"It happens to me, too," Mrs. Zsiros said. "Particularly when I am very tired."

I wept some more and still tried to hide it. Mrs. Zsiros put me to bed, taking over from my mother, who was too tired to do it. Everything around me was clean, dry, fluffy, and stuffed with homegrown goose down. Why then did every turn into softness pierce my heart?

When I woke late the next morning, the kitchen bustled. Rózsi, Mother, and Mr. Zsiros were eating at the table; Mrs. Zsiros was cooking at the stove.

"Good morning, lazy little miss," Mrs. Zsiros said. "Do you know what a *lángos* is?"

"Oh, yes," I said. "Our old cook, Irma, used to make it. But she always said that a real *lángos* should be baked in a humped oven." I stopped abruptly. I had forgotten myself. Could Irma be made part of the Christian papers story? I couldn't remember. Had I given us away? I glanced at my mother.

"Yes," she said. "Irma always complained of that. How odd of you to recall it."

"So you had a cook before the war?" Mr. Zsiros asked. "What did your husband do?"

"You misunderstand," my mother said, laughing. "I had a friend who was a cook for some rich people. On her days off she stayed with us and cooked, because she did it better than I. In the family, as a joke, we referred to her as 'our cook, Irma.'"

"Ah," Mr. Zsiros said, losing interest. I looked at Mrs. Zsiros. I saw her shrewd blue eyes adding information like a cash register.

How to explain *lángos*? It was a medium-sized covered

pizza filled with goat cheese and dill in a pizzaless country, at a pizzaless time. I ate two, and I was waiting for a third when Mrs. Zsiros burned herself at the oven and yelled, "Jesus Savior!"

"Jesus Savior our Father who art in heaven bless us," Rózsi said, crossing herself. All of us in the room picked up our heads in surprise.

"You are good Catholics then, are you, my dears?" asked Mrs. Zsiros as she put butter on her hand.

"Indeed," said Rózsi.

"Not at all," said my mother. It took all my underground training to keep from laughing out loud. "Well," said my mother, taking a deep breath, "our mother was Protestant, our father Catholic. They divided the children. I went my mother's way. Rózsi was Father's. We get along, though."

My mother is brilliant, I thought, she is the best. But oh, God, what am I supposed to be? Never mind, I'm sure she will invent something when we come to it.

"Not to worry," Mrs. Zsiros said. "We are all God's children."

Jews, too? I yearned to ask.

Days passed. We were well fed, warm, and very clean. They gave us toothbrushes and toothpaste. We acquired a nailbrush. We could live like our former selves, provided we pretended to be someone else. What a puzzle. What a degradation. Mother and Rózsi went bartering. I stayed in the kitchen with Zsiros néni. She cooked. I read to her from her favorite books, popular novels from before the war. At first I was hesitant, but then I got into the swing of it—not meanly, as I had with my grandparents centuries ago. "You are a remarkable little girl," Zsiros néni said.

"Because I can read well?"

"For that, and other reasons. I have a little granddaughter your age. She's still putty. You are already iron. You will stay iron. I don't know what she will become."

Yup, that's me, iron. You've got me to a T, Zsiros néni.

I never again spoke to her for real, upset that she hadn't seen through to my shattered heart.

Rózsi and Mother had traded all the cloth for dozens of eggs, lengths of bacon and salami, kilos of sugar and flour and tea. It was time to go home. My mother took me aside. "You will have to understand this," she said. "Listen carefully. It is in your best interest that—"

"Stop," I interrupted. "How long are you leaving me? A year? A month? Forever? It doesn't really matter to me. I just want to know."

"You misunderstand. I am not leaving you—"

I interrupted again. "Great. You are not leaving me. Then I should go pack, right?"

"Well, now, I'm not leaving you, it's just that—"

"Wait a second. Am I to go with you and Rózsi? Yes or no?"

"Well, it is a complicated situation. I am thinking of you and—"

"Yes or no?"

"No. You know, you are just like your father. Mean and unreasonable. Little Gyula. Gyuluska. I am doing this for you. You have probably gained five pounds since we got here. I want you to gain another five. You are tubercular. It is essential that—"

"I am recovered."

"You are tubercular and—"

"I am recovered."

"You are—"

I walked away. When they were all packed, loaded, and ready to march, my mother yelled to me, "Aren't you going to kiss me goodbye?"

"What?" I yelled back. She repeated herself. "What?" I yelled again. We would probably have gone several rounds this way except that Zsiros néni intervened.

"Children not used to being left get offended," she said to my mother. "Accept it and just go."

Thank you, Mrs. Putty-iron Zsiros. Great assessment. Terrific insight. Idiot. Your knowing eyes are blind. We are lying to you. Nothing about us is real. We are shady prestidigitators, we are sharks at life's roulette.

Days passed, perhaps weeks or years. I had no calendar and no watch. I measured time in units of pain.

A pale sun appeared in the sky, the sign of sick heavens slowly on the mend. Zsiros néni encouraged me to play outside. Obediently, I sat on a rock and contemplated the ground. She called me in for meals. I sat on a chair and contemplated my plate. At night, I contemplated the ceiling. Zsiros néni said I looked peaked. She also told me not to worry. My mother would come to fetch me soon. My former self would have asked, "How can you know? Have you traveled on a railroad train lately?" I said nothing. I felt stuffed with cotton. Its density clogged my brain, dried my tongue, and soured the taste in my mouth.

One of the Zsiroses' daughters arrived with her husband and child. They hadn't seen each other in months, and everyone was jubilant. I contemplated their happiness.

The daughter and son-in-law looked very different from Mr. and Mrs. Zsiros, let alone me. The Zsiroses were rich peasants, with manure still stuck to their boots. They were kindly, and down-to-earth. Birthing, dying, soil, blood, spit, and sweat were as close to them as their nearest cow. Not so with this next generation.

Clearly, the couple were educated. They spoke French to each other in my presence. Rude, but effective. They were tall, well dressed, clean, and carefree. They were impressively slim, in contrast to me, who was sickly skinny. They teased each other and laughed as if there had been no war.

Their child was a son, age seven, treated by the four adults as a priceless, radiant jewel that brought light and meaning to their lives.

What about me? I screamed silently through my cotton stuffing. What about me? In 1937, when I was three, we were vacationing in Zirkveniza, Mother, Iván, and I. I won the children's beauty contest. All the newspapers and all the photo studios in town exhibited my picture. Everyone wanted to talk with me, and I gladly wanted to talk with everyone, in languages I did speak. In Zirkveniza, I was a pearl of a girl. How had I become so disposable? A put-here, put-there, left-at-a-whim nothing. A less than nothing. A dull, swollen-bellied beggar child.

Suddenly, half a dozen Russian soldiers arrived at the estate on two horse-drawn carriages. The soldiers were very drunk. They shot their pistols into the air as they yelled, *"Barishnya! Barishnya!"*

Mr. and Mrs. Elegance trembled like leaves. The little jewel hid himself with a scream under his grandparents' bed. Dangerous as I knew it to be, I could not stop grinning. What do you know? Evidently superiority is a mutable posture. Status is context-bound. What do you know? There may be hope for me yet. I may still have a future.

The Russians continued to race their carriages in circles.

They kept shooting and yelling as they took big swigs from their bottles of vodka. I was not in the least afraid. If they had wanted to shoot us, they would have done so by now. They continued to yell for women, but so what? I was not a woman, and neither was Zsiros néni, in the way I thought they meant it. That left Miss Priss, who had disappeared into the house. Her husband was also out of sight. Zsiros néni watched from the doorway for a while, then was gone. Mr. Zsiros and I stood our ground at the edge of the road.

"Go inside," he said, turning to me. "You can climb out the back window and disappear into the fields. You may even catch up with my daughter and the rest of them."

I shook my head no thank you. "I am tired of hiding," I said. As soon as I uttered the words, I realized their absolute truth. Yes, I was tired of hiding. I didn't want to run anymore. I had had enough. To hell with it. I suddenly remembered Spanish Red Cross Ervin, how indifferent he was to danger, to choice of hiding places, to everything, and how free it made him—free and loose. "Besides," I said to Mr. Zsiros, "I don't think they mean us harm. They are just being rowdy."

"Rowdy?" he repeated, with great indignation. "Rowdy? They are rotten, stinking, murderous Russian scum. They are the invading enemy. You'd better be sure, my girl, they mean us harm."

I shrugged. To you, not to me, I thought. But of course to me, too. I was tired of that, also—tired of keeping my enemies straight. Everyone was my enemy, even Mr. Zsiros, were it not for my fake, mother-manufactured Christian birth certificate.

One of the carriages stopped in front of us just as I saw two distant figures on the road walking slowly toward the house.

Judging by his ribbons, the soldier who got off was an officer of rank. This fact did not in any way influence the earthquake proportions of his stagger. He could barely speak. Still, through sign language and pidgin Hungarian, he conveyed to us that he wanted something to drink, and that he was offering me a ride around the circle. Since the carriage was piled high with unopened bottles of vodka, we surmised that he wanted water.

"Go to the kitchen, find a pitcher, and bring it filled with water," Mr. Zsiros said to me. "Never mind the glasses." There went my ride.

When I got back, Mr. Zsiros was busily explaining that I couldn't go for a ride because I was retarded. My eternal disguise. Did these people know something that had so far eluded me? The Russian shrugged. He emptied the pitcher in almost one gulp. Mr. Zsiros sent me to fetch more water for him, then for his men. The officer yelled toward the other contingent, but they waved no to him. As he stumbled back into the carriage, he handed me a bottle. Mr. Zsiros said firmly, "No, thank you."

I said, *"Spasibo!"* and grabbed the bottle. The officer laughed. The soldiers fired another round of shots into the sky and urged the horses into a trot.

Mr. Zsiros glared at me. "How do you know Russian?" he asked suspiciously.

"I don't," I said. "I know five words. Thank you, *spasibo*. Good, *horosho*. Woman, *barishnya*. Police, *politsya*, and *davai*, which they say when they take things from you. They have been in Budapest since January."

He looked unconvinced. "I speak pretty fair German," I said. Then I wanted to cut my throat. I *am* a retard, I thought.

How could I have volunteered information? Stupid careless idiot! What if he asks me where I learned German? Can I mention my Fräuli? Is my father a newspaperman or a factory worker? Oh God, what is my story? I can't remember, I can't remember.

The two distant walking figures reached us. They were Rózsi and Mother, looking much worse than when they left. Their eyes had grown larger and their lips thinned into slits like fading scars. Rózsi had developed a little tremor of the head, as if she were a slightly bobbing doll. Something bad had happened again. I knew it.

We all greeted each other with muted enthusiasm. "So you are back," Mr. Zsiros said. "Good. I have to rescue my family from the fields. The girl can explain what went on here. Meanwhile, go to the kitchen and eat whatever you want. Not the goose, of course, or its liver. That's for my children." He started to leave, then turned. "How come the little girl speaks German?" he asked my mother.

"My father's people are Sváb, from the border country. He taught the child German. It was pretty much his mother tongue," my mother said, without missing a beat. Mr. Zsiros looked almost reassured.

Anyu, Rózsi, and I sat at the kitchen table, too polite to eat without Zsiros néni serving the food to us. I remembered my bottle of vodka, which I was still clutching to my chest. "Look," I said, lifting it. "A gift for Grandfather."

They burst into tears. "Grandfather is dead," my mother said.

"Grandfather is dead," Rózsi echoed.

I started to cry. "How did it happen?" I asked, as if that made a difference. Dead is dead. Knowledge of the method does not alter the outcome. Nor does it restore. Poor Grandfather. "How did it happen?" I asked again.

"He got an infection," Rózsi said. "Under his right armpit. They went to the hospital. A doctor cut it open. That made it worse. His whole arm swelled up and turned red, like ripe tomatoes. The doctor said he needed sulfa. Grandma traded the last of their flour on the black market for one tablet. It didn't help. He died at home during the night, just before the morning, when they were going to amputate his arm. Grandma says he kept crying and saying, 'Emmuska, don't let them cut off my arm. I am a tailor.' Then he just died."

"What did she do then?"

"When?"

"When he died. How did she manage? He was dead."

"Well, she asked a neighbor to help. They washed him, then wrapped him in some sheets and put him in the maid's cupboard."

"*Where* did they put him?"

"You know, that narrow wooden cupboard in the hall that used to be the maid's closet. It always looked a little like a coffin. They put him in there."

"How?"

"I don't know. You are asking too many questions. It is unseemly. Anyway, I wasn't there," Rózsi said, blinking hard.

"No, please, I want to know. I have to know." So much for my earlier penny-candy pragmatism. "You must tell me how it happened." I was crying hard, almost out of control.

"Calm down. They placed the closet on the floor. They opened the door, put grandfather in, then they closed the door. They nailed it shut. Pretty much what they do with regular coffins."

"I didn't know that. None of us ever had a coffin before."

"I know," Rózsi said, sobbing. "I wish I had been there."

"What happened next?"

"Grandma hired some boys with a cart. She gave them her wedding ring in exchange. They wheeled grandfather to the Korvin Department Store. They let her sit on the cart. This way she could accompany him. The bargain included their bringing her back home."

"I am sorry," I said. "I know I am not being polite. But why did Grandmother want to take Grandfather to Korvin's in his coffin? Anyway, I thought it was bombed out."

"It is. But that's where they are gathering the identified, coffined dead. The government takes them from there to bury them in proper graveyards. The Jews in Jewish cemeteries—"

"Quiet!" my mother whispered sharply. "None of this to the Zsiroses." As one, we snorted our snot and wiped our eyes and noses with the backs of our hands.

As the Zsiros entered the kitchen, Rózsi began, "So then Mrs. Schwartz said . . ." as an inspired cover-up. My mother kicked her. But we were all too sad to think of a suitable subterfuge to rescue the slip. Fortunately the Zsiroses were too busy with themselves to have noticed.

The child and his parents looked a mess. They were covered with mud, cow manure, wet clumps of earth, and other unidentifiable filth. They no longer trembled, but they still seemed shaken. Zsiros néni was also messy, but on her the dirt looked dignified.

"Out of here with all of you, for the love of Jesus," said Mr. Zsiros. "I cannot stand the smell. Clean up, for heaven's sake. Go, go."

Obviously Zsiros bácsi felt taken down in front of us by

quite a few notches. I felt bad about that, but I didn't know how to help him.

Turning to us, he said gruffly, "Why haven't you eaten? I told you to eat. This little girl had lunch at noon. It is now eight o'clock. What kind of a . . ." He checked himself. "Please. I am not myself. Madame Dénes, would you be kind enough to set the table?"

"With pleasure," my mother replied, in full fake royalty.

The next morning was Sunday, and breakfast didn't go well. Except for the food, of course. There were *lángos*-heavens filled with dill-sprinkled *brinza* cheese and unchickoried coffee with whipped heavy cream and plenty of sugar, and a lot of heat from the hearth. Otherwise, the members of each family fought intermittently. Naturally our arguments were more muted than theirs, as befitted our lower station. Also as befitted our hidden fugitive status. The first church bells rang midway through these grotesqueries. By the second set, Rózsi was asked to go to mass. After all, she was the Catholic. Mother and I took a walk outside. We tried to find cows to pet. A small early sunshine promised spring. The first spring without Iván, I thought, and lost all interest in cow petting.

"What is the matter with you?" my mother asked. "Why are you so unpredictable? Why are you so moody? What is wrong with you?"

Dear Mother. Maid's-closet coffins are wrong with me. Being left behind at any opportunity, over and over, is wrong with me. Watery graves are wrong with me. "I don't know what you mean," I said. "Losing a taste for cow-petting is not exactly a crime, is it?"

She spluttered. I knew the routine. I always won by words. I never won her heart.

A while later, Rózsi and the Zsiroses returned from church. Rózsi looked sick. The Zsiroses, all five of them, looked angry. "Perhaps we should go to our room," Rózsi said with eyes downcast, addressing Mother and me.

"Yes," said Mrs. Zsiros. "You'd better tell your sister how you have betrayed her. Because if you don't, I will."

Locked safely in our room, Mother glared at Rózsi. "What in God's name did you do now?"

"I crossed myself with the wrong hand," she said miserably. "I forgot which hand was proper. I figured it must be the one nearest the heart. So I crossed myself with my left hand. They noticed. That was the end."

Mother and I both started to laugh. "Please, Rózsi néni," I said. "Don't look so sad. So you are an ambidextrous Catholic. So what?" The three of us became uncontainable, even though my mother kept shushing us.

"Ha, ha, ha. That's not the worst," Rózsi said.

"Ha, ha ha. What's the worst?" my mother asked, continuing to laugh.

"I told them our mother and I have been fooling you all these years. Father was not a Catholic at all. He was really a Jew. But you didn't know that to this day." She stopped in the face of our silence. "I was trying to save Magda and you," she added lamely. Anyu and I stared at Rózsi and at each other.

"Well, that's that," my mother said, standing up. "We'd better tell them we are leaving in the morning."

Just then, a knock sounded at our door. Mr. Zsiros stood at the threshold. He looked withdrawn and uncomfortable. He cleared his throat. "You must understand," he said. "To my wife and me, religion, class, status, don't matter. We saw the little girl and we wanted to fatten her up. That was all. Well.

. . ." He hesitated. "Perhaps it was not all. We still have not heard from our other daughter, her husband, and her children. She has two little girls. God knows where they are. Perhaps I hoped that people like you, who will now be in power, might help them, directly or by chance."

Rózsi stepped forward. "People like us?" she asked, her voice arching toward hysteria. "People like us who will be in power? What exactly are you saying, Mr. Zsiros?"

"I meant nothing. I meant I don't care if you are Jews. I help you today, and perhaps you will help mine tomorrow. That's all. I knew you were Israelites the moment you stepped on my land. My wife argued with me, but I knew."

The gifts of food they packed for us in silence lasted all the way to Budapest and even a few days beyond. When we arrived home at Teleki Tér, the pockmarked mirrors were still covered with sheets. In my family, we didn't honor prescribed lengths of mourning.

SIX

No ONE MADE A FIRE, OR COFFEE, OR CONVERSATION. IN
the apartment's shuttered twilight, I gnawed on dry bread
until my gums bled again, and then I went to sleep. I woke to
silence and slept again.

We are waiting for the boys, they said. Stupid, stupid
women. I hated them. And I hated to hate them, because they
were my only loves left. Fine, fine, I told myself between
nightmares. If they want me to die, I will.

Then one morning I woke murderously angry. "No!" I
yelled, standing up on my bed. "No! Life is for the living. I
am alive. You have to keep me alive. I am the child. You have
to take care of me. I am not Iván, I am not Ervin, I am not
dead!"

"*Shema Yisrael,*" my grandmother said, and covered her
ears. "The child has lost her mind."

"No!" I screamed. "The child has not lost her mind. All of
you have gone insane. And I'm not going with you." I was
beside myself. I had meant to bring them to life but the

attempt had jumped some boundary and careened out of control on a track I did not recognize. Despite myself, I continued. "You should have left Ervin and Shosha alone. They would be with us today. You should have cut up Iván's coat with scissors. He would be with us today. You did the wrong thing all the time. All the time. You will not do it again. I will not let you."

There was silence. I felt a heartbeat away from convulsing. When I recovered a little, I looked at them. Whom was I accusing, and from whom was I expecting help? Three specters. Thin, sad, broken, mute. What had I done? I started to sob.

"No," Rózsi said, "don't cry. You are right. About everything. But most of all about our duty to you. Go get the wood for the fire. I will cook some food."

I began to weep again, but now I wept the tender tears of the understood. "Cruel and insolent as always," my mother said. "I'm used to it. From Gyula to her in a straight line."

"Margit," my aunt said hoarsely, "keep your mouth shut. Just peel those two potatoes."

"Both?" my mother asked.

"Yes," said Rózsi. "We are celebrating."

"Is it over?" my grandmother asked, lifting her hands from her ears and opening her eyes. What a new, sad way for her to be. To run away into herself instead of fueling the fires.

"Oh, God," I prayed, "dear God, please help me. I can't cope, I don't know how to survive. Send a sign, please."

"Come on, the soup is ready," Rózsi said in a little while. "Soup?" I said, looking at the ceiling. "Soup? That's it? That's your big message?"

"Yes," Rózsi said, sounding a little offended. "What more

do you want? It is good soup. It has bits of sausage and vegetables, and two whole potatoes. It is very good soup."

"Of course, Rózsi néni, thank you," I said. "Thank you very much. I didn't mean to criticize. I was actually talking of something else. I don't know what I'm saying."

In the days that followed, Grandmother cooked until our food supplies became near-starvation low. Mother and Rózsi decided to hit the road again. As they were about to leave, a woman knocked on the front door.

"Open up!" she yelled through the layers of barricades. "If you are related to Ervin Guttman, open up." We removed all obstacles in seconds.

The woman who stepped through the doorway looked compressed, as if the aftershock of a bomb had reduced her and then she had risen again to half height. She was blond and very blue-eyed, clearly Christian. "I bring bad news," she said without ceremony. "Who is the mother?"

"I am the mother," Rózsi gasped.

"Come inside, please," my mother said, her voice breaking.

"No," said the woman firmly. "Bad news should stay at the threshold." She turned to Rózsi. "Your son is dead."

None of us screamed. Not my family. In times of catastrophe, we break inside. We bleed inside. We turn black inside. The veins in our eyes pop. Our tongues swell and we stay silent. After what seemed like years, my mother asked, "How do you know?"

"I was their landlady," the woman said, shrugging. "I took care of the young couple. They were beautiful."

"*Kommen sie herein, bitte,*" my grandmother said. "*Nehmen sie Platz.*" Grandmother suffered from the delusion that if you spoke good German, all bad news would go away.

"I don't speak German," the woman said belligerently. "I am a Hungarian patriot."

"Yes, yes," my mother said. "We can tell by your coming here. Please tell us what happened to Ervin."

"A short story," the woman said, so heartlessly that I wondered why she'd come. Just to hurt us? "Well, they moved into our community, into a room of my house, in fact, as man and wife. The police checked their papers, which seemed in order. We welcomed them. They were so much in love, and their story was so sad. To tell you the truth, madam, I am more than a little resentful over that," the woman said, looking at Rózsi.

"You resent them for wanting to survive?" my mother asked bitterly.

The woman shifted her gaze. "No, madam. I resent their lying to me."

"Would you have—"my mother began.

At the same time Rózsi said, "Please continue."

"Well, they told us that her parents had died in an air raid in Pest. She had no other relatives. Only her sweetheart young husband. They said he came from Herend, and knew nothing of the fate of his family. He had been in the army, but was wounded in an unmentionable part of his body. They said that so that no one would dare to ask him to drop his pants. It was clever. Once, when a party member who didn't like strangers in the neighborhood asked him to do just that, we nearly stoned the man in protest. Your son fooled us good," she said, sounding sad.

This had never occurred to me before: the people we fool feel fooled. They feel as hurt and angry as I would. How interesting. But what would they have done had they known the truth? Do they ask themselves that? Is that question ever pushed all the way to the answer: If you had not lied, I would have killed you. Do they then decide that the lies were justified after all? Or do they believe murder is a lesser sin than lying? How interesting.

"Wouldn't you like to come in?" my mother asked.

The woman shook her head. "I liked them very much until . . ." My mother opened her mouth and closed it.

"Please continue," Rózsi said again.

"Well, my neighbors and I took care of them until the final Russian push. Then we all ran blindly. The Russians won their victory hard. They had to fight for it house by house, door by door. There were bullets flying everywhere. Mortar fire. Grenades. Streams of blood, and men fell like summer flies. They won. To our shame, we were marched to the nearest square.

"Your son, your Ervin, shouted at them, 'Jude, jude,' surrendering not even in his mother tongue. They ignored him. The Russian officer told us all the restrictions, all the punishments, all the shame we would have to endure as a conquered nation. When he stopped, he said, 'Those who speak good German, put up your hands.' Ervin put up his hand. Among others, he was chosen. Special envoys to go behind German lines. Carriers of the message: Surrender. On hearing what the task was, the boy broke down in tears. He told them he was fourteen years old and Jewish. He could not possibly go. The Nazis would shoot him on sight. The Russian officer shrugged and assured him that if he did not go, he would be shot on the spot. He went and never returned. Naturally. The Russians are like that." The woman stopped again.

"How did you get to me?" Rózsi asked, barely audible.

"Through his wife. I guess I mean his girlfriend. After waiting two weeks for his return, when it became obvious that he would not come because he couldn't, she said, 'I have to get away from here. From you. From everyone and from everywhere.' She gave me your address. She begged me to come and tell you the news. She offered me all of Ervin's clothes, but I didn't take them. I couldn't. Although some I had given him, from my dead husband."

After a while, when no one spoke, I said, "Please come in. We can offer you coffee."

"No," the woman said, starting to weep and shaking her head. "I loved them, and they fooled me."

When she left, she left a desert.

The next morning, Rózsi and Mother departed as planned. Goodbye, goodbye, kiss kiss. And to whom will you report your death, or we ours?

Grandmother and I circled and eyed each other for a while. We realized almost at the same instant that we were alone, needy, and dependent on each other. "Would you like me to make *nokedli?*" she asked. "It used to be your favorite when you were little."

"Yes, please. It is still my favorite. And cucumber salad with it."

"I will make that too. Go read. I will call you for supper."

"Thank you, Grandmother. Thank you very much."

Her attempt to pretend that we were still a family and to normalize our lives tore my heart to shreds. The Old Hen spreading her wings to protect me. Oh, my dear Old Hen. I almost love you.

After a very good supper, I said, "Would you like me to read to you? Not scary like before. Just plain."

"I would enjoy that very much," she said. We settled in. I started a water-damaged, crumbling first chapter of Mark Twain's *The Prince and the Pauper.* We escaped our lives for hours, and barely wanted to return.

This sun burned out in less than a fortnight. We started bickering, then escalated to bitter accusations and finally reached relentless verbal murder. In a day or two, after much mutual suffering, we made up. In still another few days, our irresistible tango began again.

We, and all Budapest, had filthy water in the house, and my disgust with it was such that I stopped washing myself. Then I got so disgusted with myself that I washed twice a day. I slept too much, until I couldn't sleep at all. I ate. I didn't eat. I cried for a while, then I spit for days, at least mentally. My life had become an out-of-control seesaw. We waited for Margit and Rózsi to return, and they were late. Conservatively, one week late. Hysterically, at least two.

In that time of waiting, it was as if all things had become imitations of themselves. The air thinned until breathing became a hardship. Colors faded. Absence was sucking away my soul. I yearned to die.

When they finally arrived, they seemed to be receding, as if the universe were reabsorbing them in barely perceptible increments. We kissed, hugged, exchanged news, didn't mention the boys, cooked, ate, drank Grandfather's vodka, and generally behaved as if we were alive. I was, however, in full possession of our secret. We were ghosts.

Mother and Rózsi left again to trade food in the provinces. I no longer cared. Occasionally I thought of jumping out the window, but when I looked out, the distance between the pavement and the second floor seemed no higher than a broken ankle. I shrugged and felt sorry for myself. Thwarted once more. It didn't occur to me that this building had a fifth floor. Mostly I lay on my bed, gazing at the ceiling. I was aware of the irony that at Ilonka's, this had seemed a hardship, and now it seemed a relief. What was that about? The exact same act, its meaning tilted by context. Iván could explain it. Yes . . . well . . .

I lay in silence and allowed Grandmother's gambits to fly over me like poorly aimed rockets. That worried her. She liked a fighting partner. But I could also tell she was concerned that there might be something wrong with me. One midmorning she sat down on my bed. "Isn't *madártej* your favorite desert?" she asked.

I became breathless. Yes, floating island was the most favorite food of my life. But also, more important, I had never, ever, been offered a truce of this magnitude. "Yes, Grandmother," I said, sitting up and kissing her with a very full heart. "It is my most, my very most favorite."

"Well," she said, "I have all the ingredients. Why don't we have it for supper?"

"Oh yes, please."

She shooed me out of the kitchen when I offered to help, and served the dish with unusual care and ceremony. It was wonderful. The best I had ever eaten. The egg-white islands were pale and fluffy. The yolk sauce, laced with wine, was thick and sweet, with a hint of nutmeg. "Perfect," I said. "Perfect." After the fourth spoonful, I started to vomit in an arc. There was no nausea, no warning rise in the gullet. In two seconds, I moved from zero to full fountainhood. We both watched in paralyzed amazement as my vomit piled up about five feet away to the right of the table.

Eventually I stopped. I didn't dare look at my grandmother. I just stood.

"Go to the bathroom," she said. "Wash your face and brush your teeth. Do it thoroughly. Vomiting is bad for you."

"Yes." I didn't understand what had happened. I felt sick in body and sicker at heart. I barely dared to leave the bathroom. "I will clean up now," I said when I came out. "I have done it," she said. "Go to bed."

"Thank you."

I didn't wake until noon. Grandmother had made coffee, and served it to me as if nothing had happened. For once, her capriciousness was a blessing.

"You will have to go into the market," she said. "You will have to buy some eggs"—I wanted to die—"and some flour if that is possible. Rózsi left some money. We need to use it now. Can you do that?"

"Of course I can. I'll do anything you want," I said, still feeling utterly penitent. "I'll get dressed and go."

On the landing I met Ibolya, the oldest of the Kornitzer girls, of lye-drinking fame. *"Szervusz,"* we said, and shook hands.

"How is everyone?" I asked.

"Fine," she said. "And you?"

"Fine."

"Any news of Iván?" she asked. I shook my head. "I've been meaning to ask you this," she said. "Have you ever thought that maybe my brother survived because he prayed to God in tallis and tefillin every day, and Iván died because he never prayed?"

"No," I said. "I never thought that. I thought your brother survived because he is a sniveling coward who hid under your mother's skirts while my brother was out saving people's lives. I thought that when your brother shat in his pants out of fear he stank so much that even the Nyilas couldn't take it. Drop dead, both of you."

That is what I said on my way down the stairs. On the landing, I said nothing. I did glare at her, though, until she lowered her eyes and pulled in her neck.

In the market I got lucky. In addition to eggs, I was able to buy both flour and bread. On returning, I met Mrs. Eisler, my friend Ági's grandmother, at the entrance to the building. "Oh my God, child," she said when she saw me. "You are very sick."

"No, Eisler neni, thank you very much," I said. "I am fine. My family is fine. Everything is wonderful. We are prosperous and happy. All right?"

"Cut it out, Magda," she said sternly. "You are ill. Who is at home?"

"My grandmother."

"I thought so. She can't see very well. That's why she doesn't know. I will come with you and talk to her."

We knocked, and because she heard two voices, my grandmother panicked. "Who is with you? Who wants to get in?" She screamed.

"Eisler neni. Ági's grandmother. Open up, please, for heaven's sake." The door clicked open.

"Come outside," Eisler neni said.

My grandmother stepped out to the walkway. "You lost the money, or you have been robbed," she said to me.

"It's not about that," said Mrs. Eisler. "This child is very sick. Her skin looks like a Chinaman's. The whites of her eyes are the color of ripe lemons. She needs a doctor. Come out farther. Look at her. Hold your arm against hers. Can't you see how yellow she is?"

"I can," said my grandmother. "Even my blind stupid eyes can see that." She started to weep.

"Stop that," Eisler néni said. "It doesn't help. Do you have a doctor?"

"My doctor practices far away," I said. "And I don't know whether he is alive or how to get to him."

"We have no doctor," my grandmother said.

"I know of one," said Mrs. Eisler. "He's in the neighborhood. Come upstairs, Magda. I will give you his name and address."

"Excuse me," said my grandmother. "How much does a doctor cost?"

"That is not a question," Mrs. Eisler replied. "This child needs a doctor. Now."

"Madam," said my grandmother, and I had never felt for her more, "the question was, do I have enough cash, or do I have to go to the market to sell something?"

The doctor's office was very full, and I waited for hours. When I finally entered the consulting room, the doctor seemed angry and distracted. "Sit, sit," he said. "Where is your mother?"

"I don't know exactly," I said. "She's somewhere in the provinces. She's trading cloth for food. She will be back soon, but I am sick now. At least Mrs. Eisler thinks I'm sick. Probably she's right, because I vomited badly the other day. On the other hand, that may have been an anomalous event due to other reasons. Mostly I'm a healthy person, except for the tuberculosis, and I have recovered from that. I think I'm fine."

"Just a minute now," he said. "How old are you?"

"Ten and a half."

"Ten and a half, and you are here all alone?"

This was what I hated the most, this well-meaning pity. I hated it when my abandonment, my solitariness, my deprivations became public. "Well, my mother will be back soon, but my friend Ági's grandmother said I ought to come at once. She thinks I look the color of a Chinaman. Do I have yellow fever?"

The doctor started to laugh. "No, my dear," he said, "you are jaundiced. Bad water, bad food, the war. You don't have yellow fever."

"Will I recover?"

"I wouldn't be surprised if in time you came back from the grave," he said. "Yes, you will recover. I will give you some pills to take twice a day for two weeks. Can you remember that?" I looked at him. "Yes, you can remember that," he said, and laughed again. "One thing, though. Don't drink wine, and don't eat eggs. They are terrible for this condition. They induce projectile vomiting. But I don't suppose that will be a big problem for you." I froze. "What is it?" he asked.

"Mr. Doctor, I made a mistake," I said. "My memory is very bad. I am ashamed of it. Please write it all down. The pills and all. And what wine and eggs do to a person. The vomiting, you know?"

This time he looked at *me*. "With whom do you live, exactly?" he asked, full of suspicion. "My grandma," I said. "She made me *madártej*."

He laughed, totally out of control. When he recovered, he asked, "As a treat, because you were sick?" and laughed again.

"Yes, a very big treat," I said, a little offended. "It was terrible."

"I bet it was," he said. "Go on home now. Come back in two weeks if you don't turn white." He went on laughing. "But don't eat *madártej*. Not for a year."

"Mr. Doctor," I said. "The fee?"

"Zero," he said. "For you, zero."

"Thank you. And the note, please."

He shook his head. "I would like to meet the person who brought you up," he said, handing me the note and the prescription.

"He was murdered," I said, and left the room.

Once home, I presented the note to Grandmother in breathless triumph. "You see? You see?" I said. "I was not bad or mean! The doctor says the *madártej* made me throw up."

Grandmother was too blind to decipher the doctor's scrawl, so she asked me to read her the note. When I finished, she said, "You think I poisoned you."

"No," I moaned, "no. That is not the point. This is not an accusation. This is an explanation. An apology. A way of saying I meant no offense."

She was silent. After a while, she said, "You told the doctor I poisoned you."

How had this happened? I could have left it alone. I meant to exonerate myself from the possible suspicion of a spiteful upchuck, the kind I used to perform at the Szani when I was three. I wanted to tell her I harbored no malice. Now she was hurt. And she was accusing me of having accused her of intent to murder. How could talking get so tangled? How could meaning go so awry?

"I am going to bed," I said. "The doctor told me to sleep a lot." Note to self: Henceforth use words as a cloak. Use them as a three-card monte: Now you see the meaning, now you don't. Put your money where your meaning is! Meaning wouldn't melt in her mouth. I drifted off.

It was late afternoon when my grandmother woke me. "Ági is knocking at the front door," she said. "She wants to play with you, but I have already set up the barricade."

"We could undo it," I said.

"No," she said. "It is past four. The Russians start marauding at around this time. It would be too dangerous to leave the door undefended."

"All right."

I walked to the front. Ági was two years younger than I, a child. I played with her only as a last resort. I found her drumming on the door impatiently while she peered through the undersized, loosely barred window to the left of the door. "Let me in, let me in," she whispered. "I don't want to play. I have to go to the bathroom. Now. Immediately."

"Go home," I said. "We are barricaded for the night."

"I can't," she wailed. "There is no one home. The door is locked. I have to go, quick!"

"All right." I opened the window. "Squeeze through here."

"Through the bars?"

"Yes. You are small enough."

She hesitated, then her bladder overrode her caution. She pushed herself up from the window ledge and squeezed her head and shoulders through the two widest-set bars.

"Come inside," I said, as I started walking toward the bedroom. When I didn't hear footsteps behind me, I turned. Ági looked like someone taking a swimming lesson with a lifebelt around her waist. At the far end, she kicked her legs. Up front, she moved her arms in opposing outward circles. I laughed.

"Very funny," I said. "Actually, you are funnier than I ever thought. That is very good."

"Help me!" she croaked.

"All right, all right," I said. "I got the joke. Don't push it. Come on."

"I can't," she said. "I am stuck."

In a shower of ice, I realized she wasn't lying. I ran to her. "You can't be stuck, Ági," I said. "Your shoulders are the widest part of you, and they are in. Come on, push."

"I'm pushing," she said. "Maybe my hips are the widest part of me."

I considered the proposition. "Perhaps," I said, "but they would be mostly flesh, and that gives. Shall I try to pull you?"

"You'd better," she said. "My parents will be home soon."

"Oh, my God," I said. I pushed, I pulled, I squeezed. We prayed, we cursed, we laughed. She peed in her pants, and still nothing happened. "I must call my grandmother to help," I said.

"She's a witch," Ági said.

"Less of a witch lately," I said. "I must call her."

Grandmother went through all the routines Ági and I had just completed, but Ági remained stuck. She started to weep. "Don't cry, Ági," Grandmother said. "I will remove the barricade and we'll get you out."

Pushed hard by me from the walkway, and simultaneously pulled inside by Grandmother, Ági was freed in an instant. I didn't know what had gotten her stuck. Had she been stuck?

Unlike my family, who sought isolation as if the deaths we sustained were a shameful *faux pas*, I thought we needed neighbors, and I was worried about losing any. "What now?" I asked Ági. "What will you tell your parents?"

"What is there to tell?" Ági shrugged. "They locked me out and I peed in my pants."

Two days later, we had another visitor—Uncle Dávid, my grandfather's youngest brother, now his own wandering ghost. "Dávid!" my grandmother said in shock. "Dávid! What has happened to you?"

"They took us, my son Bandi and me, to Mauthausen," Dávid said. "Don't ask me about it, Emma. I can't, I don't want to speak of it. Where is Zéligel?" he asked, using the diminutive of my grandfather's Jewish name.

Grandmother started to sob. "Dávid bácsi," I said, "Grandfather is dead. He died of an infection."

"I see," Dávid said, without moving a muscle in his emaciated face. From his sickened dark eyes two large tears slowly rolled. "I see." His sorrow was wordless, and weighty as all the earth piled on all the graves of the world.

"Dávid bácsi," I said, "my brother, Iván, is also dead." It was the first time I had dared to utter this sentence.

Dávid nodded, then started to shake. "Is there anyone else left besides the two of you?"

"Anyu and Rózsi are traveling in the provinces to trade cloth for food. They should be back home in a few days."

"And Ervinke?"

"Dead," I said. This admission out loud was also new. The Bible came back to me: "Love as strong as death." Yes. And I will set you both as a seal upon my heart for eternity.

"I'll make you something to eat," Grandmother said to Dávid.

"Don't, thank you. You probably don't have enough."

"We do," I said, much too loudly in my fear that Grandmother might allow herself to be talked out of the offer. Because, of course, we didn't have enough.

We watched Dávid eat. It had never before occurred to me that any act, even mastication, can become a ritual of mourning. Dávid was obviously very hungry. Still, instead of enjoying his food, he made it his medium for praying Kaddish. He chewed precisely, and swallowed in pain, hardly able to push the food beyond the tight knot of his unshed tears. Perhaps all the Indig brothers were expressive this way, I thought. By mouth, not speech.

Rózsi and Anyu returned, satisfied with the results of their trip. They got a lot of food for each yard of cloth. But a few days later, when they tried to exchange the food for new cloth, the picture had changed. The food price of cloth had gone up. There were many competitors. Able men and large families with trucks and cars had gone into the business. Also the peasants, now that the fighting had stopped, felt easier about parting with their excess food for badly needed clothing. The exchange Mother and Rózsi made was too low to allow them to buy back the same amount of cloth as they had traded. This happened for two more trips. Finally, when their stock had dwindled to almost nothing, they caught on.

Meanwhile, currency kept inflating. In the morning, a loaf of bread cost x pengős. By night it cost x plus five hundred. Negative numbers became a lived event. We started with zero; then we had less.

"We can't survive this way," Rózsi said one evening. "My savings are almost gone. We have to find jobs. We know shit about business."

"No need to be rude," Grandmother said.

"Sshhh," my mother said to Rózsi, reminding her to curb her temper.

Within the week, Rózsi landed a job. She was to be a sales-lady at Imre Garbovitcs's bombed-out store, formerly a palace, now a hole in the wall, where he had, in peacetime, gotten very rich. Imre Garbovitcs was a distant cousin on my grandmother's side. He was also the man who, in 1942, when my mother asked him to lend her a thousand pengös with which she might have had a chance to take her children to Amerika, had said, "You are not a good risk, Margit. Besides, I can't go to Amerika. Why should you and yours? Let Gyula help you. The Mr. Editor was always a big shot. Too big to say even hello to me."

My mother paled at the name of Rózsi's employer. "You didn't!" she said.

"I did indeed," Rózsi replied. "The money I make will feed all of us, including Magda."

There was no arguing with facts. Rózsi went to work, and Mother went on yet another bartering trip, teaming up with Mrs. Gold, formerly our neighbor on the fifth floor. I was at loose ends alone.

Loneliness is always spoken of as a matter of lack. But loneliness is also a condition of surfeit. It is too many runaway thoughts, too great a pull of gravity, too much attraction to the grave, too many shadows that turn into shades, too full a moon on which to wish in vain. Loneliness is the tombstone hung around your neck, to carry until the day when at last it can be laid to rest above you.

As soon as Mother crossed the threshold upon arriving home, she announced breathlessly, "The business is bust."

"Astonishing," said Rózsi dryly. She and I knew there was no other possible outcome.

"How did it happen?" I asked. "Tell us."

Rózsi waved at me a most threatening forefinger, so I stopped. Poor Anyu.

The food Mother had brought, although not very much, was fresh and fine. It was, therefore, a total puzzle why the bean soup that grandmother made the following day was as foul as Beelzebub's breath. The damn thing stank.

"We can't eat this," Rózsi said in disgust. "What have you done, Anyuka?" she asked, turning to my grandmother.

My grandmother burst into tears. "I don't know," she said, sobbing. "I am turning into an old fool. That's it. That's all. I have wasted all these good ingredients. What are we to do now?" She kept on crying.

"Don't cry," we each said in our own way, but she remained inconsolable.

"I have an idea," Rózsi said. We all looked at her, lit with hope. "Magduska should go downstairs and sell the soup."

"A good idea," my mother said.

"What? Me? I don't know how to sell soup. I am lodging an official diplomatic protest."

Grandmother stopped weeping. Rather than removing her eyeglasses, she lifted them with one hand toward her forehead and with the other hand, holding a handkerchief, she wiped her eyes, one after the other. Those lifted and held glasses, those reddened eyes, the wiping motion, lacerated my heart almost beyond repair.

"Yes, I will sell the soup," I said. "I will."

I went down to the street and, armed with two deep plates, two spoons, a ladle, and a bucket of murky water in which to rinse after each customer, I started hawking. "Soup, soup, good soup for sale! Hot soup, bean soup, good soup for sale, hot!" I sold quite a few platefuls. Some customers ate it without complaint. Others yelled and grimaced in disgust. I stopped before the pot was empty.

I was not exactly aware of the immorality of my doings, except for a little sour feeling of indigestion in the pit of my stomach. Still, the scene became like a shrapnel fragment lodged in the body which, unremoved, circulates, causing periodic pain. Those poor duped people, their squandered money, that inedible soup. And I the vendor.

In the eyes of a hypothetical stranger, our lives would have seemed almost normal. Mother went back to work for Pista Papp. Rózsi worked for Garbovitcs. Grandmother cooked. I pretended to be a child. There were paydays and Sundays and Mondays. But below this visible world a deep rot ate away at everything we were. Both Mother and Rózsi lost chunks of their hair. They each needed to have some teeth pulled. Mother developed boils. Rózsi couldn't contain her temper. Grandmother hid in corners and wept. As for me, I endlessly fell out of endless windows. I was hit by buses. At the backfire of every car, bullets pierced my body. I was repeatedly broken and bled. It wasn't just me. Without notice, my mother was suddenly in a coffin, carried to a graveyard on a sunless day, in a seasonless year. My brother, pale and water-bloated, floated on the ceiling. The teeth of my grandfather, one by one, like tilted dominoes, fell into the soup plate in front of him.

I was not starving anymore, so that wasn't the explanation. Evidently I had gone mad. It is of the utmost importance, I thought, that I keep this a secret for as long as I can. How long is that?

Official notices appeared on building walls and in the newspaper. "All persons between the ages of six and fourteen must be registered for school. Failure to comply carries the penalty of . . ." Ah, official threats. Normalcy restored!

Ever since first grade, I had thought of September as a month of magic. The hot sun in retreat acquires a hint of silver in its shine. The morning air turns crisp. The melting summer asphalt becomes firm again, and stepping on it bouncily, my mother and I made our yearly pilgrimage to the stationery store, a holy place, the last station before entering Nirvana, school itself.

The store was located on Népszinház Utca. Inside, it resembled a long tunnel. Tall glass counters rose on each side of its narrow aisle. Although business was most brisk in autumn, it was a timeless store. The merchandise was always the same. The men behind the counters always wore green eyeshades pushed high on their foreheads, and fancy black cloth sleeve-protectors to spare their French cuffs.

In all the sameness, the most outstanding constant was the smell of the store. Every type of paper had an encoded odor of its own, ranging from musty to insolent, spiked with the smell of graphite, glue, ink, chalk, crayon, and the shreds of rubber erasers. In conglomerate, they formed the world of September, the world of fresh starts, of revived hopes.

But not that year. First, it was the month of May. And again first, there was no good paper anywhere in Budapest. And that store had been bombed to bits.

"Where do I go to register?" I asked my mother.

"You have finished fourth grade; you go to the old Jewish *gimnázium*, I assume," my mother said. "To Abonyi Utca."

"Really?" My heart leapt, then flattened just as fast. To Abonyi Utca. For four years, I had dreamt of that trip. Iván in the eighth year, Ervin in the fifth, and I a freshman, going with them to the same school, to the girls' section, abutting their building on the next street. No longer a lowly elementary-school child. A grown-up with an ID stuck into a pocket-size metal frame, my picture showing in the oval center, and my transportation ticket tucked behind the ID with the punchable part hanging loose in casual elegance. Not this year.

As it turned out, the school building at Abonyi Utca was ruined. I had to go to another address. It didn't feel like a *gimnázium*. I secured my ID laboriously through hours of red tape and waiting. I decided to keep my transportation ticket separate. I mostly held it in my sweaty palm, because I couldn't think of a less elegant way to carry it.

On the first day of school, I was late for class. As I walked in, the professor, whose name, I later learned, was Dr. Magda Timár, was reading the first two lines of a poem by Dezsö Kosztolányi: "The little dog is still the most beautiful animal / He reigns from high upon the cushion." When she finished, she glared at me as I stood on the threshold. "Excuse?" she asked, arching her voice and her right eyebrow.

Excuse? Is she crazy? I need an excuse to be five minutes late? I daydreamed, lady. I watched the sky. It was not the same as when my brother lived. I thought of different poetry. I wondered where are the snows of Abonyi Utca's yesterdays. "No excuse," I said. "Sorry," I added, with utmost reluctance.

"Well, you missed learning the first thing taught," she said. "Now you may never know about the little dog."

"Kosztolányi's stupid poem, where he measures the heartbeat of a dog? I hate that poem. I don't much like Kosztolányi. But he certainly wrote better poems than that. His love poems are far superior." A silence fell. I knew I should carry a razor, so on these occasions I could cut my throat. "I am very sorry," I said, and I meant it. Then another tongue, unowned by me, spoke out again. "However, my critique of Kosztolányi is correct. It is not exactly my critique. But I'm convinced of its validity. My brother, Iván, taught me this, and he was always right about poetry."

"Report to my office at the end of class," Dr. Timár said. I was unable to read her face.

I reported. She told me to sit and got to the point at once. "Your brother Iván is dead?"

"No," I said. "He was murdered, shot into the Danube."

"Who else was murdered?" she asked.

"It varies. My grandfather just died, mostly of hunger."

"You are a very difficult child," she said.

"I am not a child," I said. "I am a first-year *gimnázium* student with an ID and a transportation pass."

She threw up her hands. "We are all hurt," she said. "Don't let it get the best of you."

"Don't worry," I said. "There is no best of me left."

During the four months of classes, which the government decreed to be worth a full year, Dr. Timár and I jousted and sparred over many a poem. I continued to be late every morning, and because it was an offense meriting expulsion, she made a deal with me in front of the whole class. If I could identify the poem being read as I entered late, and supply the next line, I would be marked present. The class applauded in derisive triumph, aimed at me. Ha! The end of Dénes! Not quite. I got about 80 percent of them right, which was enough to pass and reenter school in September.

Then there was Mr. Rausch. He was a slim, redheaded, thin-lipped old maid who taught math. He was repetitious and boring. I started conversations, I read poetry. When I was most immersed, he would pounce. "Yes, Dénes? The answer?"

"Sorry, sir, I have not heard the question," I would say.

"Aha! No answer! I am marking you five." Meaning F.

"But sir. I could most probably answer the question if you asked it again."

"You should have listened the first time, Dénes. You should have listened. Five for you."

And for you too, jackass. Who cares?

I was upset all the time from within, but from without, nothing bothered me. What could they do to me? Shoot me into the Danube? What else was there? Nothing. There was nothing threatening short of that. Conversely, what could they do *for* me? Restore my brother? Return Ervin? Crossbar-ride me on a bicycle to Amerika?

As it happened, Mr. Rausch did in fact succeed in doing something to me. However, only half the credit was his. The other half belonged to my friend from first grade at Bezerédi Utca, Jutka Schwartz. Jutka, like Ági, was not exactly well-read, or very swift. But she was an excellent friend, and I had loved her. We were overjoyed at meeting again in *gimnázium*. On exchanging news, we learned that we'd each lost the person we most loved. Her mother had been murdered by gassing at Auschwitz. We sat next to each other in the second row, and we talked, I more than she. Her grief remained, somehow, without sharp edges. She mourned as if her mother had died of pneumonia, or in a car accident. I couldn't understand it. "They murdered her!" I would say. "They murdered her. Don't you understand that?"

"You are upsetting me," she'd reply. "Don't do that."

"But Jutka, the point is—"

Mr. Rausch interrupted us. "This cozy duo will now be separated for three weeks," he said. "Dénes, who is clearly the more condemnable culprit, will move to the last row. If a lesson is learned by both Schwartz and Dénes, Dénes may move back up in three weeks."

"Thank you, sir," I said, gathering my books and moving back.

I counted the days. My life was too silent to lose a friend with whom I could speak. On the twenty-first day, I dutifully raised my hand. That was another thing for which Rausch kept after me. If someone missed an answer while I happened to be listening, I would supply it without asking for permission. I was too soul-weary to explain to him, or to anyone, that raising my hand reminded me of the Nazi salute, and I just didn't want to do it. After many minutes of pretending, like a fool, that he hadn't seen me, he called on me. I stood and said, most respectfully, "Mr. Rausch, the time of punishment is up. I have behaved. You have not had to reprimand me for three weeks. I can sit up with Jutka again, right?"

Mr. Rausch cleared his throat. Before he could answer, Jutka's hand shot up. He called on her. Jutka stood. She wrung her hands. "Actually, she said, "actually. . . ." She stopped.

"Out with it, Schwartz," Rausch said.

"Actually, my father thinks I would go further in life if I did not sit next to Dénes."

The shame at her words, like death-dealing lightning, hit every organ in my body and left me breathless and burnt. Oh, Jutka, my friend. I sat down.

Mr. Rausch looked shocked. "Well, whatever you young ladies have decided is fine with me," he said, trying, to his credit, to dilute the blow. No one was fooled. I became a pariah in the math class. Thereafter, I made no pretense of being present. I read poetry books, I looked at the ceiling, I sucked on my teeth. I never put up my hand, or spoke to anyone. Mr. Rausch stayed away from me. Even his general class-assessing glance skipped over my chair.

The class outcast, short, redheaded, and dull-eyed, was Edit Müller. I didn't know why. She seemed no worse to me than everybody else. Still, she was a loner, as I had now become. She approached me in the bathroom one day, when we happened to find ourselves alone. "Have you ever touched the inside of your vagina?" she asked.

"What?" I couldn't believe my ears. "What did you ask?" She repeated the question. There was a sick urgency about her that made me unable to walk away, as I knew I should.

"Of course not," I said. "You know perfectly well you're not supposed to, except with a washcloth, when you're bathing. To clean yourself. Why are you asking me this?"

"Try it," she said. "It feels very good."

I was not averse to feeling good. On the other hand, I knew deep inside that this was the road to perdition. I couldn't consult Iván. My curiosity won. "How?" I asked.

"Go back in the stall, lower your panties, and tickle your vagina."

I proceeded as instructed. Nothing happened. I felt stupid, not good. "This doesn't work!" I yelled to her.

"Come on out," she said, exasperated. "You are too inexperienced."

I came out, feeling a little embarrassed. "What do you mean?" I asked.

"Well, it takes time to learn," she said. "You see, my mother is living with this man, and—"

"She's doing what?" I interrupted. Now I was on familiar territory. I knew living with a man was wrong. It was immoral.

"She's living with this man," Edit continued, oblivious to

my disapproval. "He's being very nice to me. He tickles my vagina every night. Actually, you know, there's a canal up there. He puts in one finger. In a while, he will put in two fingers. He's trying not to hurt me. He's preparing me for his penis, from which I will get more pleasure than I have ever had in my life." She stopped, looking lost.

"Oh, my God," I said. "I think I hear the bell for class. We should go."

"I hear no bell," Edit said.

"I do, I do," I said, as I ran out. For the rest of the day, I was preoccupied with Edit's story. I knew there was something very wrong with it. I just knew.

That night, I confided in my mother. Not about my experimentation in the bathroom, which I thought it better to skip, but about the rest. "Isn't there something wrong?" I asked.

"Yes, very wrong," my mother said. "And you are never, ever, ever again to speak to Edit or to have anything to do with her. Never."

"All right. I don't want to. But what about Edit? Shouldn't something be done?"

"Not by us," my mother said. "I know of the man who lives with Edit's mother. He's a high official in the Communist Party. If this got out, he would have all of us shot in about twenty seconds. Rózsi and Grandmother, too. Make sure you keep your mouth shut tight."

"Yes, of course, but what about Edit?"

"Not our concern," my mother said. "Another casualty of the war."

I stopped speaking altogether. Mr. Rausch could be proud of me now.

One day, at a long, silent, solitary recess, a sixth-year

approached me. "I hear you are quite a cutup, Dénes," she said. I looked away. "I am Katz. Malvina Katz. I knew your brother."

I snapped to attention. "Yes?"

"Yes. He was very handsome. I liked him. You seem much dumber than he was."

"I know," I said grinning. "I am dumber."

"Well, do you know the word 'fuck'?"

"I, I, I have heard it said," I fumbled.

"Well, learn it. Shit, piss, cunt, prick. Up your ass and down your throat. Fuck your grandmother on her deathbed in her mouth. A horse's prick up everybody's ass. If you can learn the vocabulary, we've decided that you can join us while we eat our elevenses. You must understand, this is a great honor. It is rendered in respect to your brother. Not to your stupid little self. There is no one below fourth year in our group."

"Shit piss fuck shit piss piss," I said.

She laughed. "You really are dumb," she said. "Come along."

They changed my life. They looked after me, and they cheered me up, even before I knew that I was about to burst into tears. Still, the rides from home to school and back again, whether by bus or train, remained long and lonely. Each jolt and the sight of each corner revived another hurt. To combat it, I silently recited poetry, stanza after stanza, to no avail. I added columns of figures. I tried to remember or invent the details of the Battle of Waterloo and other high points of history. Nothing helped. In minutes, without noticing the switch, I was back to the pictures of Iván being marched toward the Danube. We had heard that his hands were tied behind his back. With what? His belt? String? A rope? Metal cuffs? Whatever it was, did it cut into his wrists? Did his wrists bleed?

I didn't want to, but my possessed mind made me walk along with him in lockstep. It was very cold that day, and a light snow fell. Did he shiver? Did we sweat? Did the beads on our foreheads turn to instant icicles or did the fever of our fear melt them?

No, no, I yelled at myself. This is an insult, a travesty, an outrage. You are sitting here. Alive. Almost safe. He is walking this road alone.

Yes. Seventeen plus fifteen equals thirty-two. One hundred and five plus three hundred and seven equals four hundred and twelve.

What was he thinking about? Good times? They were so meager. . . . His girlfriend? The miracle rabbi, whom he forgot to ask to pray for him to be reunited with our father? Me? Anyu? The dentist? What? Did he know it was the end, or did he hope? Could he have, in an act of desperate daring, lagged or run? He saved so many. Could he have saved himself? Or us, if I had been with him?

Napoleon's place of exile was called Elba. Freed, he regained power for a hundred days. His fatal enemy was the English duke Wellington.

They continued walking. Were the Nyilas taunting them? Probably. The Nyilas always spat at and jeered and mocked the captive Jews. "Big-nose! Killer of Jesus! Curl-head!" What could they say to Iván? Outwardly, he looked so much like them. Except nobler. That could have gotten them angry. I had noticed it before: Some people got angry with Iván just for his looks. They seemed to wish him ugly.

All right. So they reached the turning point. They veered toward the Danube, not the detention center. Did he know what that meant? Suppose he knew. Suppose he could visualize his fate. The end of his life in five minutes.

He would have been prevented by his restraints from raising a hand to put it protectively on the back of his neck. How did that feel? Did he try to pull in his neck, like a turtle? Did he, with raised head, stretch his neck tall in a final act of defiance? Or did he just weep, as I would have, terrified and heartbroken at being forced to leave forever everyone and everything? Once upon a midnight dreary while I pondered weak and weary over many a quaint and curious volume of forgotten lore, while I nodded nearly napping . . .

Then they reached the steps leading down to the frozen surface of the Danube.

What a fool I was. To distract myself, I had chosen a poem that we had read to each other over and over on those very steps. In the summers, on lazy lemonade Sundays.

Along with the other prisoners, he was ordered to kneel. A person pressed a gun into his neck, at the base of his skull.

What happened to my brother at that second? How can I ever know? Who will tell me that?

Five times four thousand seven hundred and nine equals . . .

ONE FRIDAY, WHEN when I arrived home from school after one of these harrowing trips, I found Éva Hirsch and her younger sister Babi, my brother's age, sitting on my bed. "You remember Éva," my mother said by way of introduction. I nodded, of course. "They are passing through," my mother said. "They are back from the camps. All of their family is dead. Gassed. They are going back to Sárbogárd to reclaim their home."

I looked at my mother. I thought she should invite them to stay. She avoided my eyes.

"I think you should go home," my mother said to them.

"Reclaim your house and all the lands your parents had. Get back everything you can. Then come back and stay with us," she said, looking at me straight. I smiled. Perhaps my mother knew me better than I thought.

The days and weeks went on, uniformly dull, because our hearts were dead. Revive, revive, I said to the three women of my life, but they didn't. Revive, revive, I said to my heart, but it did not respond.

On such a deadheart Sunday, Dávid bácsi arrived. "I am taking you to the movies," he said to me, full of pep. "Don't say no, Margit," he said to my mother. "I will ride her on the crossbar of my bicycle."

"No," my mother said.

"Yes!" I shouted. "Yes! I'm leaving this cemetery with Dávid. Yes! Now!"

"Let the child go," Rózsi said to my mother.

"Let her come with me," said Dávid. "Please, Margit. Enough is enough."

Sitting on David's bicycle crossbar, I was transported to another world. A pre-mourning world of Iván and Ervin and breezes. "Where are we going?" I asked.

"To the movies," Dávid said.

"There are no movie houses left in Budapest," I said.

"That's where you are wrong, Miss Know-it-all," he said. "One opened yesterday, downtown, for children. We are headed there."

"Oh my," I said, "Oh my. Thank you, Dávid bácsi."

Dávid and I watched and laughed with equal fervor. At Stan and Pan; at Latabár, although his film was a little smoky. We marveled at the Giant of Baghdad. Then it was over.

"I never thought this could happen to me again," Dávid

bácsi said on our way out. "To watch a child laugh. Don't mind me," he said. "Did you have a good time?"

Too good, I wanted to say. Too good because it makes me forget what I think I should remember every minute of my life.

"Yes," I said.

"Don't worry about it," Dávid bácsi said, as if he read my mind. "It's all right to build on the ruins. It's all right to hope. In fact, it is essential. There will be no world otherwise."

My days dragged, one after the next, in single file, exhausting and painful as a forced march.

With the exception of Mr. Rausch, the teachers thought that I was a good student. They were very wrong. I relied on my previous knowledge to get by. If one could survive by lying, one could surely pass less than half a year of *gimnázium* by faking. Anyway, the whole world was faking. The government had just declared these few months to be worth a full year's schooling. Fine with me. I didn't care.

With the cold eye of a detached observer, I noted that I cared about less and less. I missed reading novels—Dickens and Twain and Verne and whonot. Reading used to be such a fabulous flight. It was traveling, having two lives. A family sprang up around me, and cities stood with strange skies and odorous spices wafting in the air. In times of little trouble, to read is a very good vacation. In times of big trouble, it is dangerous. Looking up from the page, suddenly aching and bewildered, one needs to take new stock each time. Why am I broken into parts? What has happened while I was away in London, or rolling slowly in a boat on the lazy Mississippi?

Deaths: Iván. Ervin. Grandfather.

Lacks: Mother. Rozsi. Hope. A future. Even a present.

Ah, yes. Now I remember.

Better by far not to leave. Stick with the pain, because the shock of its rediscovery is too much to bear.

"Hey. Wasn't your brother a Hashomer?" Malvina Katz asked me one morning at recess. "Funny, you know," she said. "I didn't figure him to be a Communist. He looked too uppity."

"He was a capitalist," I said. "I mean, he believed in capitalism as the best form of government. Why?"

"Then why did he join the Hashomer? They're Commies. In funny trouble now. The Christian Commies don't think Jews can be Commies. Jews are bankers, they think. They're freezing out the Hashomer. Israelite bankers, they call them. No fucking dice, they tell them. Out, shits, that's what they say. Out, fuckers."

"I don't understand what you are saying," I said. "What's all this got to do with my brother?"

"Not much. It has to do with you. I want to invite you to a political meeting. The Hanoar Hacionim—the Hanhac for short. Far to the right of the middle. I wasn't sure whether you were of the same persuasion as your brother, who was an official Hashomer, after all."

She had it all wrong, and it would take too many words, I thought, to set her right. Iván wasn't . . . Ivan didn't . . . oh, to hell with it. "I am different from my brother," I said, for the sake of simplification. For a second the world tilted. Rivers flowed backward, the moon sucked up the oceans.

Malvina didn't notice. "Fine," she said. "I'll meet you Wednesday after classes and take you with me to the meeting. Everyone there is older than you, but I figured that was all right. Isn't it?"

I nodded, unable to speak.

"I am different from my brother," I had said. Yes, I am separate, a skin-boundaried entity on its own, all alone. I shared no arteries with him; from my heart grew no bridge whose opposite abutment grew in his. He was dead. I lived.

The following Wednesday, Malvina and I took the tram to the Hanhac meeting. We lurched along in companionable silence. It seemed to be a long ride, but I didn't care. I had told them at home that I was invited to participate in a poetry project after school. I might be as late as after supper. I lied so rarely and so well that I was never questioned. It was understood Magduska told the truth.

The meeting place was an old building on the outskirts of town, in a large room with a long row of windows facing the street. I could see the late-afternoon sun setting. About twenty-five people were standing about or lounging on chairs, on benches, and on the bare floor. All of them were at least Ervin's age, and older.

Most of those present were young men. God, why are they here instead of mine? I thought, and felt instantly ashamed. God, how could you have done this, including this last thought? What will become of me? I stared straight ahead without moving my eyelids in a colossal effort to reabsorb the moisture in my eyes before it formed into droplets.

"Come sit with us," a young man's voice said. I heard rhythmic patting of the floor. "There is plenty of room."

I hate Samaritans. He broke my concentration, and I began to tear. I waved no without turning, and stepped to the window. Its indented structure allowed me some privacy. I took a few deep breaths and wiped my eyes surreptitiously with the backs of my hands.

To recover further, I forced myself to listen. They went on and on about various boring matters. Then the discussion turned to the color of the shirts the group should wear at the next major city-wide youth march. Should it be red to conform, or blue, the color of the hoped-for state of Israel, as yet still Palestine—watched, restricted, oppressed, not ours, and dangerous?

"We have no state," someone said. "Blue is a wished-for color, behind which nothing stands. We live here. We have to march in red. Unfortunately they will still know we are Jewish."

This was more than I could bear. I whirled around and with my hand up, without waiting to be called on, yelled, "No!" All eyes in the room shifted to me.

"You must be new here," the leader of the discussion said, turning in my direction. He was much older than my brother. Between my brother's age and my mother's, I found it hard to tell how old people were. Perhaps he was twenty-six or even more. His hair was dark and curly, and his eyes were the color of coals. "We'll do the introductions later," he said. "For now, tell us why you said no."

"Because we have hidden long enough. Because there have been Green Shirts, Brown Shirts, and Black Shirts killing us. Now there are Red Shirts. They all hate us. We must say we are the Jews, the blue Jews. Because it is high time to say just because, despite, and to the contrary. Because—"

"*Dafke!*" someone yelled out from behind me. The Defiant! The general laughter did not die down for many minutes. I looked at the leader. He wasn't laughing. He nodded his head at me and gave me a little salute with his pen.

When the noise more or less quieted, he said, "I didn't

laugh, but I, too, was amused. It is always amusing to see a grown man make an idiot of himself at the expense of a child. That is truly, nobly funny. I'm not going to ask who it was. I won't even remember the voice I recognized, unless it happens again. I want to stick to the point of the discussion. It turns out I agree with our young, ill-treated guest. I think she presented my argument perfectly. I will not take a vote now. You all go home and think it over. But think of one other thing. Whatever the vote, I will march up front in blue. Good night, everyone. See you next week. *Shalom*." People stood up, and all sang "Hatikvah."

I stood stunned. Malvina walked up to me. "Come on," she said. "I'll take you home. You made quite a spectacle of yourself."

"I know," I said. "I'm sorry. I didn't mean to. I couldn't help it."

"No, she said, "it was a terrific spectacle. I am very proud I brought you. I agreed with everything you said. Maybe you aren't so dumb."

I grinned, feeling very pleased.

"Come on, I'll take you home."

"You don't have to," I said.

"Oh, yes I do," she said, sighing theatrically. "It is an enormous nuisance, but I do have to take you home. You are a child who lives far away, God help me."

We laughed. I had not felt this good for a long time. Since when? Since perhaps December 31?

Once home, all I yearned for was my bed. "It was a very long poem we worked on," I told my mother. "They fed us dinner."

"How nice of them."

"Yes, very nice. Good night."

Dávid bácsi picked me up almost every Sunday. Once we went to the proudly restored zoo. I was surprised that he, more than I, did not see what I saw. Cages. Prisoners. Nervous pacing. Skin rippling with outrage. Snorts of despair. Hoots of protest. A world of captive doom, aching to be set free. Jews. Animal Jews, exhibited and ogled.

"I don't think I want to come back here," I said. "I prefer the movies."

"So do I," Dávid said, looking very sad.

"Dávid bácsi," I said, "can I ask you something?"

"No," he said. Then he changed his mind. "What you heard is true. I know my son Bandi told your mother, and she told the rest of you. I don't mind. I would do it again."

Oh, Dávid bácsi, so would I. If that could have saved Iván, I would have done it.

Dávid started to cry, covering his eyes with four of his left fingers. "Don't cry, Dávid bácsi," I said, weeping. "Please don't cry. You did the right thing. Who would be taking me to the movies now if you hadn't?"

"You are a sweet child," he said, "but you are a child. I wanted to talk to my oldest brother, Zelig, but he was dead when I got home." We leaned into each other and sobbed in comfort for a while. The hidden topic of this conversation was cannibalism of a sort, at the Mauthausen concentration camp. The fed on were dead. The feeders survived. The fuss should be celebratory, I thought, and nothing more.

About a week later, I went to the next Hanhac meeting alone, because Malvina was busy that afternoon. When I entered, the leader greeted me quite formally. "My name is József," he said, bowing and extending his hand. "József Bálint. Jóska for short. My Hebrew name is Jehoshua."

I was a little disconcerted. I was too old to curtsy, I thought. I decided to bow also, at an ambiguous decline. I shook his hand. "I am Magda Dénes," I said. "Ivàn Dénes's sister."

"I know of him," Jóska said. "Unfortunately, I never met him. He was killed running for the Hashomer, wasn't he?" I nodded. "I want to welcome you to our group," he said. "As you know, I liked your comments very much the other night. Do you know your Jewish name?

"Gittele."

"Ah, 'the Good.' " He smiled. "You are well named. The Hebrew translation is Tova. That will be your name among us."

"Fine," I said. I didn't want a new name. He introduced me to everyone as Tova Dénes, but it was no use. The yahoo's exclamation stuck; everybody called me Dafke, the Defiant, the Oppositional, the Just Go Fuck Off. Some did it with malice, others with affection, but Dafke is what I remained.

I pretty much knew what they meant, but I didn't agree. I was argumentative, yes, but in the service of accuracy and articulated truth. I wouldn't take shit, true, but I tortured myself so much that even a straw's worth of additional pain felt like the amount that would break my back. Dafke was a narrow, abridged, shortsighted view of me. I was sure of it.

Naturally, I didn't protest the epithet. This much I had learned. In a group, if you react with hurt to a tease, you might as well move to China, or hang yourself. So yes, *dafke* to Dafke, and to all of them.

The principal players in the group, aside from Jóska, were Zsuzsa, who was sixteen and very beautiful, and her primary boyfriend, János, who was seventeen. I say "primary" because sometimes she exchanged him for Tomi, or Villi, or any number of others, all of whom wanted her, and on all of whom her interest conferred temporary player status.

Zsuzsa tossed her long dark hair and batted her long dark eyelashes which framed her violet eyes. She wore heels and no stockings. She always sat very close to the boy of the day, so that their legs touched. Generally, she kept one hand on his proximate knee. They both looked mesmerized. There were whispers in the group about whom she had and had not kissed.

I didn't get it. To me, kissing was touching those you love with your heart, through your lips. How could she love so many people unrelated to her? And how did it make her so central, when I didn't think she was even well-read or could play the piano like Éva Hirsch?

Both her popularity and the puzzle of it irked and intrigued me. At the following meeting, I sat down next to Péter. He was closest to my age, and not very tall. That's why I picked him. As the discussion got underway, I pressed my leg against his. He didn't look at me, but pressed back. I waited to get mesmerized, but nothing happened. In a while, my leg started to cramp. Then it fell asleep. I had read romantic novels, but what a swindle, I thought. People evidently do this just to conform to fiction! After what seemed like days, the meeting finally ended. We sang "Hatikvah" standing up, thank God. I was free to bolt at last, slightly limping.

Next day at school, Malvina approached me at recess. "Buzz, buzz, buzz," she said, "about what you did last night to Péter."

"What did I do?"

"Well, my dear, it was you, but if you don't remember, it must have been a total look-alike. You made a pass. You invited him to be your boyfriend. Then evidently you were not pleased and left him flat."

"I . . . but . . ." This was not a potential interpretation I had ever considered. I had made a fool of myself, yes. But of him? Absurd! But perhaps not.

To make matters worse, at the next Hanhac meeting, Jóska waved me down. "Sit, please," he said, very sternly. He remained standing, towering over me. "I saw you at the last meeting, sitting next to Péter," he said, without preamble. "I was very surprised at you. The behavior you exhibited I expect of Zsuzsa, not of you."

I turned my head away, and said nothing. What could I say? "You can't reprimand me; you are not my brother"? I would cry. "I didn't like it anyway"? I would sound like the idiot I am. "How and why did it work for Zsusza?" We didn't know each other well enough for me to ask that.

"Well," he insisted, "what do you have to say for yourself?"

I got angry. In the measured cold monotone my brother used when he wanted to put someone in his place, I said, "I am sorry. I missed something. Have you been appointed my guardian?"

Jóska was a surprising man. He burst out laughing. "You are absolutely right," he said. "It is none of my business. I just think you are a terrific little kid, and I don't want you to learn the wrong things here. You see, the group here . . ." He stopped. "You are right," he repeated, and walked away. I stayed seated, in utter misery.

Summer arrived. Through the kindness of the government and the professors, I became a second-year. By irresistible force of nature, I turned eleven.

Inexplicably, the further the past receded, the more I lived in it. I saw my grandfather, hand-rolled cigarette dangling from his lips, bent over his sewing machine, pumping away with his right foot and humming. I saw the boys and me hoisting the kitchen chairs onto our laps, the legs aimed outward, and like commanders of a tank turret, with four splattering guns each, going rat-a-tat-tat. "You are dead," we all called out. "No, you are! I shot first." Well, that argument had been settled.

I lay around. I read the ceiling. I went on family errands, but only after I was threatened with excommunication. Sundays Dávid and I went to the movies. He bought us *rizi-bizi*, little sweet-colored balls made of rice flour that faked candyhood.

"What's wrong?" Dávid asked.

"Nothing," I said.

"Magduska," he said, looking into my eyes, "you are talking to your Uncle Dávid. Tell me."

"Nothing. I don't know. Something. I just don't know."

"What would help?"

Suddenly, I blurted it out. "I want Iván!" I began to wail. "I want my brother. Ervin, too. I am lonely. I am homesick for them."

"Oh my darling, my little heart, it cannot be," Dávid said, picking me up and holding me tight in his arms. "We cannot bring back the dead. We must go on without them. For their sake, too. Did you know that no one is ever truly dead who is remembered? That is your job. Keep Iván and Ervin alive in memory. They will live as long as you live. Perhaps even beyond. You will tell your children about them, and they will tell their children. That is your job."

"I don't want it!" I said, struggling out of his arms and

sitting down on the curb. "I don't want it. Let somebody else remember *me*."

"In that case," said Dávid, in a surprising twist, "how would you like to learn to ride a bicycle?"

I looked up at him and nodded. This also could not be done. My legs were too short to reach the pedals.

In September, school started again. I got into fights with everybody—teachers, classmates, the janitors. I was possessed by a demon within me whose paw could cut through my flesh and skin and slap the world away without my consent.

I was called to the office of Dr. Timár, who had been promoted to dean. "Your behavior has been execrable," she said, getting out of her chair. She started to pace back and forth behind her small desk. After her fourth forth, she said, "Dénes, you are not the only one who has sustained losses in this war. We all have." She paused. I nodded. "Have you gone mute?" she asked. I shook my head. "But you won't deign to speak to me, is that it?"

"No, I said. "I am sorry. I don't know what's happening."

"What do you mean, you don't know?"

"I don't know. Everything is irritating to me. Everyone sounds stupid. Even you. I would like to care. I would very much like to care, but I don't. I just don't give a damn."

Dr. Timár took a deep breath. "Be that as it may, Dénes," she said, "I am putting you on probation. If you don't improve both scholastically and in attitude by January, you will be tossed out of here."

"Thank you," I said.

Suddenly she went insane with rage. "Thank you?" she screamed " 'Thank you' is all you have to say? Don't you understand what this means? No *gimnázium*? No university.

No teaching post at the university. I was certain I could help
you become a university professor. You ingrate. You idiot."

"I am sorry, Dr. Timár," I said. "I may want to become a
farmer in Palestine. You know Palestine. We're fighting for it
to become the state of Israel. The Jewish state. A country for
all of us."

"Get out of here," she yelled. "Get out of here and don't
forget you are on probation."

Oh, God. It's as hard to predict what will rub people the
wrong way as it is to predict the consequences of rubbing
them with a numb leg. What had I done again? Still, I took
her seriously. I started doing more homework, and I quarreled
less with people.

The bottoms of my shoes were in shreds. Nothing could
save them anymore. Winter was coming. I needed new sturdy
shoes. Anyu lay flat on her back, sick. Rózsi took me to the
cobbler. He measured my feet in length and width and height
and depth. Rózsi handed over the precious, dearly bought
thick black leather. "I will make you an excellent pair of
shoes," the cobbler said, and named his exorbitant price.
Rózsi haggled; they settled. There would be a fitting in a
week. Loosely cut tops fell over loosely cut bottoms. Who
could tell? Fine, I said.

In another week, we picked up the shoes. Rózsi paid the
man. After half a block of waking, I knew. The shoes, which
looked beautiful, didn't fit. They were a size too small. They
pinched, cramped, wrinkled my feet and marked them with
painful grooves. When I complained, Rózsi said, "They will
have to do. We have no more leather, and no more money."

I want to go on record. Pinching, painful shoes in the slush
of winter do not improve a person's disposition. I was forever

in search of private places to whip off my shoes and knead my toes back to life. "Where have you just disappeared to?" Malvina might ask.

"What do you mean? I was here all along."

"Oh," she would say, doubting her sanity.

In a perfect world, I thought, inept cobblers would be executed by their victims within one painfully walked block.

Aside from my David Sundays, the most acceptable parts of my life were the weekly Hanhac meetings. Somehow, mostly Jóska but also, in a way, the rest of them, seemed to be aimed. They were like arrows in a tautly pulled bow, set to fly at the slightest flicker of a hand. But whose hand?

At one meeting, Jóska approached me. "I would like to have your address," he said. "I want to go speak with your mother."

I was appalled. "What have I done?" I asked. "I've done nothing!"

"No, no," he said, smiling, "it's not like that. I want to talk with her about your future. Naturally you will be part of the discussion. Please give me your address."

"Of course. Teleki Tér 5, fifth floor, apartment five. No, I'm sorry," I said. "I got confused. That apartment is gone; it was bombed out. Now we live at Teleki Tér 5, second floor, apartment two. That is correct."

"Don't worry about it," Jóska said. "I'll come by in a day or two. Tell your mother to expect me."

I didn't. When he knocked in the evening, a few days later, he was a surprise to everyone but me.

"Who are you?" my mother yelled.

"Jehoshua Bálint," Jóska yelled back. "A friend of Magda's."

We all converged behind the door in various defensive postures, as was usual when any knock sounded after sunset. Anyu looked at me, right eyebrow raised. "What's this about?"

"He's the leader at the Hanhac group where I sometimes go to meetings. He just wants to talk with you. Please let him in." My mother hesitated.

"For heaven's sake," Rózsi said. "The child says she knows him. Let him in."

Mother opened the door. After introductions, and much hand-kissing on Jóska's part, he turned to my mother. "Could just the three of us please, you, Magda, and I, talk in private?"

Reluctantly, my mother ushered him into the kitchen. I followed. We sat at the table, and Jóska cleared his throat several times. "Well, Madame Dénes, we, I, as the head of the Hanoar Hacionim, think you have an exceptional child." He stopped. My mother said nothing. I blushed. "We understand," Jóska continued, "that she's very young. But that's just it. She shows great promise. We would like your permission to take her to Palestine. We would train her, along with a few dozen other children we have selected, to become an organizer, come back here in a few years, and do recruiting. She would be very good at that. We very much need young people in Palestine. Then, if all goes well, and the state of Israel becomes a reality, we think in time she could enter politics and represent the Hanhac in government. She could have a great career, if all goes well."

"I see," my mother said, her lips contracted into an iron band. "And if things didn't go well, there would be a state funeral, if there were a state. A flag folded over her heroic coffin, if there were a flag. She would be mourned, I know, by so many that even I might get lost in the crowd. However, it is a very interesting proposition, Mr. . . . Mr. . . . what did you say your name was?"

"Jehoshua Bálint, attorney-at-law," Jóska said, half rising from his chair.

"Well, Mr. Bálint, I am a slow deliberator. Please approach me again in about a month. I will give you my decision then. Meanwhile, I must have your word of honor that you will take no action in relation to my little daughter."

"But madame," Jóska said, utterly shocked, "of course not. I'm not a kidnapper."

"Anyu, I wouldn't go!" I said, as shocked as Jóska.

My mother stood up. "Good night, Mr. Bálint," she said, at her regal best.

"Good night, madame. I am very sorry if I have upset you." As I ushered Jóska toward the entrance door, my mother called after him, "Mr. Bálint, did you know my son, Iván?"

Jóska turned. "No, madame. I never had the honor."

"Do you know how he died?"

"Yes, madame, but that is just the reason—" He stopped as my mother turned away.

I didn't know whom to follow. I didn't know which one was more hurt. Why was I always in the middle? I would never leave my mother!

"Traitor," my mother yelled as I entered the bedroom. "Moritz Scharf!" The Hungarian Jewish Benedict Arnold. "Traitor!"

"That's me!" I screamed. "That's me!"

What I didn't know until later was that my mother contacted Iván's Hashomer friends the following day and told them that we must, *must,* most urgently leave the country, with the very next transport, and no mistake! The four of us were going to Palestine after all—but as Hashomer, not as Hanhac.

When a few days later at the dinner table she informed us

of this move, Rózsi was horrified. "You have gone mad, Margit," she said. "Leaving Hungary is illegal. It is winter. Our mother is almost blind. She's asthmatic, and she can barely walk. Magda is an eleven-year-old child. Palestine is not open to Jews. The British hunt them. They either are sent back to their own country or imprisoned on Cyprus. It is doubtful that you and I could make it. The four of us stand no chance at all. This is insane."

"No," my mother said, setting her jaw. "We must leave. I can't stand looking at these Hungarian faces. I keep asking myself, 'Is this the one who murdered my son? Or is it this one?' I can't bear to look at the Danube. Everywhere I walk, I remember. This was the street where I pushed my son in a baby carriage. And this is the street where they sent him to deliver safe papers I had just forged. I've had enough. And now the Communists. We had to join the party to be able to work. They are as oppressive as the Nazis were. Only now we've started to collaborate. I can't do it. I won't do it. We must leave."

"Can you swim?" Rózsi asked her. Mother looked nonplussed, and stayed silent.

"You can't," Rózsi said. "How will you get off the besieged boat?"

We all burst out laughing. We laughed much too hard for the weight of the joke. My mother had scared us to death.

"Well, there is another thing," Mother said, "that I haven't told you yet. I ran into Villi Weisz at the Hashomer headquarters. He's now one of the leaders. You remember him from Miskoltc. He was a few grades ahead of us in school. He told me in confidence, for old time's sake, that you declare yourself as going to Palestine here, but once you reach Germany or

France, you can redeclare yourself. You can choose Amerika, or if not that, a South Amerikan country near Amerika."

"Like what?" Rózsi asked, the little tremor of her head returning for the first time in months.

"Cuba. We have relatives there. Cousins."

"What cousins?"

"Kató, Lili, others."

"They don't know we exist."

"Of course they do, Rózsi. Of course they do," Mother said, exasperated. "We were children together. Besides, Kató was here in 1937 trying to get her little sick son cured. Don't you remember?"

"This is a pipe dream," Rózsi said. "I'm going to bed."

The discussion continued the next day, and for weeks after that. I was forbidden to attend any more Hanhac meetings. Both Grandmother and I were sworn to silence regarding these plans, under pain of death. Poor Grandmother. She had no say in anything. I kept neutral, in profound ambivalence. Finally, all the talking ended in an ultimatum.

"I am leaving with Magda on the next available transport," my mother said. "Rózsi, you do whatever you want."

There was no contest, of course.

My mother wrote asking Éva and Babi Hirsch to come to Budapest. At our kitchen table, they said yes, they wanted to go—to Palestine, to Amerika, to Cuba, anywhere that was not Sárbogárd, where they couldn't get back their properties, and where anti-Semitism, like an underground coal fire, burst into flames at unpredictable intervals and in unforeseeable places.

The moment we decided to leave, we became fugitives again—tight-lipped, furtive, isolated. Outwardly we carried on as before, but in our hearts, we had gone underground. Defection in the Communist regime was considered a capital offense. Those who aided defectors were equally punished. Therefore, Weisz told Mother, for security reasons, the transport's date of departure was not set until the last minute. We had to be prepared to leave at very short notice—a day at the most. They would also not divulge, until that time, the address of the safe house where we were to assemble. Nothing must be removed from the apartment besides personal articles and clothing. Should the police by some bad luck search the place, it must appear that we had simply gone on a short visit to friends.

Waiting was mostly dead time, a hovering between opposing spaces. The present no longer counted; the future had not yet started. Maintaining composure on this no-man's-land was not easy. As the waiting lengthened, the entire enterprise seemed to be phantasmagoric. Was there really a Villi Weisz? And Babi and Éva, who were hiding elsewhere in the city— did they exist? The strain started to show on all of us, made worse by the necessity of appearing present, involved, striving, thriving, and unafraid.

My perspective shifted. Take, for instance, my lack of caring about what Mr. Rausch had to say. I used not to care because I deemed his carping little voice insignificant compared to the death screams of my relatives. Now I also didn't care because in reality he had ceased to matter. His voice was of here. I was poised for other worlds.

Poor Mr. Rausch. I always thought that I was his scapegoat. In truth, he was also mine. After all, he, too, was only a Jew. My rage was not at him. It was not he whom I wanted to silence, but our Hungarian murderers. It was their voices that I wanted to wither and crumble and scatter to the winds. Better to leave than to harbor murder in the heart. How wise

Anyu is, I thought. Of course we must flee this country, regardless of risk or personal cost or destination.

On the evening of January 4, 1946, the long-awaited runner arrived, like the answer to a nonbeliever's prayer. He told us that the safe house was on Arányi Utca, in an abandoned school building. We were to go there by tram, tomorrow early evening, attracting as little attention as possible, carrying minimal luggage, saying goodbye to no one. After he left, we spent the night packing and fretting.

The next day was no better. Short of people, we said goodbye to our possessions. Farewell blunted knife, broken chair, crumbling book. Farewell old stove, of kind and faithful service. We will miss you and mention you in our remembrances.

It was still only noon. "How about a game of rummy?" Rózsi asked me.

"Gladly," I said.

"I can't believe it," my mother said. "You're going to play cards now? Now?"

By three in the afternoon, our churning bellies forced us to race each other to the bathroom, and there were two more hours of waiting left. "We could read the ceiling," I offered. "I do that sometimes."

Finally, it was time to leave. Grandmother started stumbling before we reached the front door. Rózsi caught hold of her shoulders and yelled at her, "Anyuka, I don't want hysterics. We have a long way to go. You must help out."

"I am nervous," my grandmother replied apologetically.

Oh, God, I thought, this trip might be a fatal mistake.

We caught a tram a block away. It was a long ride, and we had to change once. The street where we waited for the next car was dark and cold. An icy wind cut us. I kept reminding myself that we were still safe. We had not yet done anything illegal. We had our legitimate papers, a home to which we could go, neighbors, some food left behind. We could turn around and cancel being fugitives.

The bell of the arriving tram sobered me. No, no, we must stick to our resolve. This is no country for us. We rode in silence to the Arányi Utca stop. The neighborhood was unfamiliar to me. Evidently to Rózsi also, because she whispered to my mother, "Do you know where we are? Do you know which way to go?"

"Rózsi, you don't have to whisper," my mother said. "We are not illegal until we enter the safe house. So far, we are unimplicated and free. We could just go home." After a small pause, she added, "Should we?" I lost my breath at the question.

Rózsi paled. "Go back now? Just change our minds? No. Absolutely not. I didn't want to come, but now we're on our way. Just let's go. Lead on, Margduff!"

If my mouth weren't frozen, I would have laughed. Not at Rózsi's joke, but at the unbalancing absurdity of our collective ambivalence. My eyes started to tear instead, probably from the cold.

We reached the safe house, a bombed-out, abandoned building, totally dark. "This can't be the place," Rózsi said, nearly crying. "There is no one here. We made a mistake."

"It's the right address," Mother said. "I don't get it. Let's try to knock."

The door opened about two inches. "Yes?" said a man's gruff voice. "What do you want?"

"Shelter," mother replied, as instructed by Weisz.

"Enter," came the prearranged answer. The man opened

the door a few more inches and lighted our way with a hooded flashlight. We slipped into the semidarkness. The door shut behind us.

"*Shema Yisrael,* we are trapped," my grandmother whispered, unaware of the exchanged passwords. "No, madame, don't be frightened," the man said, switching on an overhead light. "You are in the right place. We are just cautious. This is a condemned, presumably uninhabited building. For safety, we observe strict blackout regulations. Follow me."

He led us along a corridor lined by a few open-doored classrooms with blackboards and bunk beds. Each room seemed crowded with people. At the end of the corridor was a small room set up as an office. A young man sat behind a desk. He stood as we entered.

"My name is Zoli," he said. "At least for today." He laughed mirthlessly. He had wine-colored curly hair. He was bent and hollow-chested. His face looked ashen, with deep circles under his eyes. Tubercular, I thought. As if on cue, he started to cough. Deep, body-racking, wrenching hacks. Each of us tactfully looked away. When his fit subsided, pocketing his handkerchief, he said, "I'm sorry. I caught a nasty cold a while back, and I just can't get rid of it." I wondered whether he was naive or lying. Or perhaps I was wrong. "Sit down, please," he said to my grandmother, as he pointed to the one chair across from his desk. "Sorry," he shrugged at the rest of us.

"This is the situation," he said. "Your forged identity papers, which in the case of displaced persons don't always require photographs, state that you are German Jewish citizens being repatriated from Poland, traveling through Hungary. You all speak German, of course."

After a long pause, Anyu said, "Well, my mother speaks it

perfectly. The rest of us are not entirely fluent." Understatement of the year.

"I see," said Zoli, frowning. He started to cough again. When he was done, he said, "That's not what Villi Weisz told me. This is a German-speaking transport." He looked disgusted and, suddenly, very tired.

None of us said anything. He can't possibly send us home now, I thought. We couldn't cope with the blow. He must have been thinking the same, because he said, "All right. We'll take the chance. Anyway, in my private opinion, if the transport gets examined that closely, we will all be done for. Nobody will make it." He caught himself. "I mean to say, we will all make it. We will sneak through, and avoid being examined at all. We have been very lucky so far, and we will continue to be lucky."

"How does it work?" I asked, although I knew I was not supposed to speak in these situations.

Zoli looked at me and decided to treat me as a person despite my age. "The border guards on Tuesdays and Thursdays are bribed. They sign the exit papers and wave our trucks through. There have been no incidents so far."

"Where are we going?" Rózsi asked. A very good question, since none of us knew.

Zoli smiled broadly. "To Vienna. The American sector. The West. To freedom." He raised an imaginary glass. *"L'chaim,"* he said. "To life," and started to cough.

When we walked out of his office, papers in hand, Babi and Eva were waiting with our original guide, whose name was Herschel. "I don't know if Zoli told you," Herschel said, "but we don't have four beds available in the same room. There is one double and two singles. You will have to sleep apart."

"Grandmother and you go to the singles," my mother said. "Rózsi and I will stay together. We have plans to make."

It has started again, I thought. Separation, exclusion.

Outside it was thirty-two degrees below zero. The room assigned to me was occupied by a young Orthodox couple and their little baby. There was a kerosene stove in the tiny room, fired to the hilt. On it, a pan of water boiled, which filled the air with moisture. The temperature must have been a hundred. I could barely breathe, and I started to sweat at once.

"Why is it so hot in here?" I asked. "Once we put the lights out, can we open the window a crack?"

"Oh no, oh no!" the woman shrieked. "The baby would die. He needs heat. He's only weeks old."

"Yes," I said, "but I don't imagine a steam bath is very good for a baby. Can he breathe? I can't. Would it be possible to keep the door open at least?

"Nooo!" she shrieked again.

"But—"

"Enough talk," the husband interrupted me. "Go to sleep, little girl." He looked ready to hit me.

This would not be happening to me if Iván were here, or Ervin. This would not be happening.

Naturally, I could not sleep. I spent the night worrying how I would smell in the morning in my sweat-soaked clothes. At last it was official wakeup time. As we stepped out of the room, the runners handed each of us a piece of bread and a mug of weak coffee. At least I could breathe again. In the corridor, I caught up with my family and Éva. Babi was in the bathroom, I was told.

My grandmother looked terrible. She had shrunk overnight. "My bones are frozen," she complained. "I couldn't sleep a wink. The stove in the room was broken. My chattering teeth kept me awake hour after hour. What a night. And none of you came to see me. I think I will die."

"Stop it!" Rózsi hissed at her.

The weirdness of my life was such that irony had ceased to be a concept to ponder. Things happen. Room assignments, the functioning of stoves. More notable than irony is the supremacy of the physical self. Stress the body hard enough, with hunger, dirt, disease, exposure, too much heat or cold, and the civilized spirit folds in on itself. Its paramount obsessive concern becomes putting an end to suffering. Nothing more.

Zoli was standing on a chair outside his office, shouting to the assembled. "Quiet!" he yelled. "Pay attention!" The din continued unabated. "Dragnet!" he yelled. Everyone froze. "Sorry," he said in a normal tone. "There is no dragnet. I just needed your very careful attention this instant. Time is getting short. You will exit by twos and threes, at five-minute intervals. If by chance you catch up, don't recognize each other. Take the tram to Buda, to the Southern Railway Station. You have your tickets. Board the train to Sopron. Sopron is the last stop on the line. Once there, go behind the station. Our trucks will be waiting for you. If anything goes wrong, don't give anyone else away. Most of all, don't give away this address, unless they torture you, in which case all cautions are off. We understand that. We have people in place and we will know. We won't be able to help, but we will know. Any questions?"

Rózsi shot up her hand. "Yes?" Zoli asked. He went into a coughing fit.

When it ended, Rózsi said, "I don't think after last night my mother can make it to Buda on a tram."

"I thought of that," Zoli said. "I think your mother and you and, given the temperature, the couple with the baby should go in a taxi. However, it costs a million pengös. We don't have it budgeted. If you can afford to pay, I can make arrangements for the car."

"I could pay half," Rózsi said. There was a long pause. Finally the baby's father spoke up. He was much younger than he'd seemed the night before. He kept his eyes glued to the floor in deep embarrassment. "We have two hundred thousand pengōs," he muttered. "That is all we have. We might need to buy things for the baby. I don't know what to say."

Rózsi looked at him. "I will pay the million," she said, very fast, before she started to cry. "I will pay and let them ride with us."

"Settled," said Zoli, emitting tight little coughs designed to delay the next big outburst. Complexly choreographed coughing was a dance I knew very well.

Anyu and I were the fifth twosome to leave. We met no one and we got on the tram with no difficulty. Other people, regular citizens, got on as well. An obese middle-aged blond woman tried to push past Mother. "Can't you move?" she asked, very rudely, giving mother a little shove.

Mother said, *"Bitte?"* I concentrated hard on the passing view, for fear that I would giggle.

"Damned Germans," the woman said. "It's high time that they went the hell home."

To our potential peril, a conscientious civic-minded soul stepped in. "Don't be so rude," she said to the blonde. "They are foreigners. *Von wo sind sie?"* she asked, turning to my mother.

"*Deutschland,*" my mother replied, at her level unfriendliest.

"*Und wo gehen sie?*"

"*Deutschland,*" my mother said.

"Come on, Klári," the busybody's friend said to her. "Stop. The woman is obviously not in a mood to chat."

"I can see that," Klári said, whining. "But I bet you they're deportees being repatriated. I would love to hear their story. Look at that child's eyes. Look how deeply sad they are. The things she could tell."

"Oh, Klári," the friend said, "your romantic notions. Really! Always a dreamer. Get ready now. Our stop is next."

"All right," Klári said, sighing, "but I know I'm right."

Drop dead and break a leg, I thought as they got off. The rest of the journey was peaceful, unruffled by rudeness or pity.

At the station, we spotted no familiar faces. "Let's board," Mother said. "We will look for everybody on the train once it's in motion."

"What if there was a hitch, and they didn't make it?" I asked.

Mother assumed her iron expression. "We have our false papers, we have our tickets, we have a little money. We are leaving."

"Just the two of us?" I asked.

"If necessary," she said. "Yes."

In about ten minutes, I saw Rózsi and a stranger half-carrying Grandmother, with the couple and the baby bringing up the panting rear. "They have arrived," I said. Mother smiled, relieved.

The couple were now all smiles and friendship, and the baby no longer needed to be kept, for his health, at blood-boiling heat.

At last, with a colossal belch, the train lurched forward and started on its way. No one had asked to see our papers. Babi and Éva came to sit with us. The car was heated just enough so I couldn't see my breath as I exhaled—a vast improvement over my last train trip. What had not changed was the lack of speed. We crawled on the old, icy tracks with the excruciating caution of a one-legged blind man crossing a busy street. We stopped in Györ. Peasant women at the station hawked boiled eggs at outrageous prices. Rózsi bought one for each of us, including the couple. After many more hours of boredom, we arrived in Sopron. "Everybody off!" the conductor yelled. "Get your passports ready. There is a dragnet for possible defectors."

"What do we do now?" Rózsi asked, petrified, as we all were.

"What we were told," Mother said. "Keep to the plan. Walk behind the stationhouse and get on the truck. But we shouldn't do it as a group. Éva, Babi," she said to them, "you lead. Walk fast, but don't run. Go now." The girls obeyed at once. Turning to the couple, she asked, "Do you want to go before or after us? We cannot go together." They hesitated. "Fine," Mother said. "Rózsi, you take Mother. We'll see you on the truck."

After they left, the husband cleared his throat. "We would like to go now," he said. "Before you. You seem to be in charge, and we wouldn't feel safe if you left."

"Go," said Mother dismissively. "Don't run. All right," she said to me, putting her arm around my shoulder. "Let's go."

"And the dragnet?" I asked. My mouth felt as dry as stale bread.

"I don't think it applies to us," Anyu said, sounding sincere.

"I think Zoli or somebody would have warned us if we were in real danger. It is a maneuver of some sort, I am almost positive."

Outside the cold hit us again. The station was barely lit, but a bright moon shone. I could see Zoli and Herschel talking with some official-looking men. The new identifying uniforms were big fur *kucsma* hats and greatcoats with heavy fur collars. Also riding boots, but that was old.

We gave them a wide berth, and walked behind the stationhouse. As promised, the truck was there, motor idling, a tall, very large vehicle, covered with a tarpaulin. Two heavy flaps hung loose at the tailgate. Inside, narrow wooden benches ran lengthwise along the sides. Despite its size, the truck was crowded. Everyone from Aranyi Utca was on it. The benches allowed enough room for only a few to sit; the rest stood. Minutes after we clambered on, we saw Zoli and Herschel running toward the cab. The driver shifted into gear, and we were on our way again.

As we squeezed onto the bench next to her and Grandmother, Rózsi asked, "How could it have been so easy? Is it a trap?"

"I don't think so," Mother whispered back. "I think the dragnet was a ruse. It allowed the secret police to make contact and collect their cash."

The truck bumped on with the soporific rocking of a cradle. Most of us dozed, even those standing.

We screeched to a halt in about two hours. For a while we just waited. Then Zoli climbed up, carefully closing the tarpaulin flaps behind him. "We have a little problem," he said quietly. "Don't panic. Don't raise your voices. The wrong men are on duty on the Austrian side. We have not done business with them before. The situation is delicate, but we are negotiating."

"What happens if you fail?" someone called out.

"We won't fail," Zoli said, starting to cough. "We never have. The important thing is that we don't want them to know exactly how many of us there are. So please, no moving, no talking. Please remain absolutely still."

We all nodded in silence. The baby let out a piercing scream and started to wail. For endless amplified seconds, nothing else was audible.

"Give him to me," Zoli said.

The mother shook her head in terror. "No," she whispered. "No."

"Give him to me," Zoli repeated urgently. "Trust me. We will say he is the driver's motherless baby. That's why he's here. That way they won't come to investigate. Hand him to me at once if you don't want to end up in Siberia, or worse."

The mother looked at her husband. He caught his breath in a near sob and nodded assent. Hand to hand, the baby was passed forward to Zoli, who disappeared with him into the darkness. I guess that in extreme situations people, however reluctantly, do give up their small, inconvenient children. I would not. Ever, for any reason.

An hour passed, perhaps two. The baby's parents prayed fervently, bowing and muttering nonstop. I began to cramp. Grandmother must be dying, I thought.

Zoli appeared at the tailgate, and some men in the truck helped him up. The baby was asleep in his arms. "It is done," Zoli said. "We can cross the border."

The truck started. In about twenty minutes, it stopped again. What now? I wondered, tired of this jerk-along journey.

Zoli opened the flaps again. Without mounting, he announced from the ground, "We have crossed the border. This is Austria."

Nothing happened. No applause, no whistles, no catcalls of victory.

Now we were truly adrift. There was no going back, and what lay ahead was darkness.

By morning we reached Vienna. It was snowing again, in small, concentrated flakes that looked like carelessly tossed confetti. Another heavenly error, because this was no Mardi Gras. We traveled for long miles through nothing but rubble. The enemy's city, I thought as consolation. But still, those fallen houses, those broken bricks, throttled my heart.

At last, we arrived at a tall gray building with bars at its windows. "Everybody off and in," our guide yelled.

He showed us to a large ward filled with rows of clean-sheeted, blanket-covered beds. Blinded by fatigue, we fell on them in silence and, fully clothed, sank into sleep.

We didn't know it yet, but we had been billeted in a former children's hospital, the only building left standing in the entire neighborhood. Hours later, when the Zionists in charge woke us, our life of being processed began.

Being processed was a protocol to which we were subjected again and again during our years of displaced personhood. First, you got deloused. DDT powder was shot into your sleeves and neck by some American soldier boy who, in every dimension, appeared to be three times the size of anyone ever born in Europe. Second, you got fed. Real food, and weird things. Something came in a tiny envelope attached to a string. You dropped it into a cup of hot water, and the brown mess it made was called tea. Similarly, a little brown cube, also dropped into hot water, was called soup. These toys didn't taste bad; it just seemed amusing to refer to them in all seriousness by the name of actual potables and edibles. Third, you got questioned, by at least three different people, sometimes four, Americans, members of the United Nations Relief and Rehabilitation Administration, who sat behind a desk covered with lots of files. To my amazement, despite the cubes and envelopes, all of them glowed with health. They asked questions about your identity, and they tried to trip you up. Naturally, there was a translator, because none of us spoke English. We assumed that none of them spoke our language, either, although sometimes they tried to trick us with their grandmother's little phrases; for instance, the Hungarian endearment "Let me eat your heart." These sayings were like the toy food, mind-bogglingly off the mark. DPs of all nationalities exchanged stories of these tricks, because at last and yet again, we had a common enemy: our rescuers.

The worst story was my grandmother's. Through the translator, the UNRRA officials informed her that she was suspected of being a non-Jewish Nazi collaborator who was trying to escape to Palestine. Grandmother was asthmatic, arthritic, and nearly blind. We thought of her as unable to survive the question "What time is it?" She entered the interrogation room alone, and four hours later, while we waited for her in total puzzlement, since most questioning lasted half an hour, she appeared, haggard but surprisingly feisty. She told us what had happened and said, "I told them, 'Get me a prayer book. I will open it to any holiday you name and pray from it.' They said, 'A spy could do that.' I said 'Fine, then shoot me.' Then I said, '*Meshugeneh. Alles sind meshugeneh.*'"

They let her go, but they didn't give her a DP card. As we

stood on the street corner discussing this development with great agitation, my mother saw a former reporter for my father's newspaper, wearing an UNRRA I.D. "Kelemen!" she yelled. "Kelemen! Come over here, please."

Kelemen, a somewhat shady character, ran across the divide and insolently embraced my mother. "Madame Dénes!" he said. "I didn't know you survived. I left Budapest before the first transport. I was the guinea pig for establishing the route. I am so happy to see you!" Remembering his manners, he bowed. To me, he said, "You must be Magduska. The last time I saw you, you were still tiny." I smiled without speaking.

Anyu told Kelemen about Grandmother's situation. "Ridiculous," he said. "You can't imagine what idiots they are. Na! But they have unbelievably healthy teeth, probably fed by brain cells."

"What are we to do about Mother?" Rózsi asked, irritated, an emotion I completely shared.

"Sorry," Kelemen said. "I do get carried away. We'll fix it right now." We all went back to the interrogation floor. Kelemen took Grandmother in. They emerged in five minutes, Grandmother holding her UNRRA passport.

"Nothing to it," Kelemen said. "No one could be stupid enough to have doubts about me. Not even the ones with the dazzling smiles." We all laughed, including Kelemen.

Fourth in the protocol was the assignment of shelter. After standing for long hours in line, we were reassigned our beds. We spent two weeks confined, because the management feared that if we were allowed to roam, we might wander away or be abducted from the American sector into another. The Russian sphere was particularly dangerous, since they were on the alert to capture Eastern European Jewish dissidents—us, if you please.

Shortly we were retrucked toward Munich, a city of solid American victory. No more sectors. As a favor to Grandmother, instead of walking, the four of us were to be taken by jeep to the Munich truck. Grandmother, feeling uncharacteristically independent, tried without help to enter the vehicle on the driver's side. She sat herself squarely on the steering wheel, setting off the horn. Pandemonium ensued. Unexpected noises set everyone on edge. People ran, screamed, froze. Not Rózsi, Anyu, or I. Cruelly, because Grandmother looked very frightened and couldn't extricate herself, we convulsed with uncontainable laughter while we intermittently yelled reassuring phrases at her. "Don't worry, it's just the horn. We'll get you off. Stay put for now. Ha ha ha ha ha." None of us could stop. We became contagious. The young American soldier who tried to help her leaned against the jeep and laughed with us. So did the worried Zionist guide who came to investigate the potentially deadly sabotage. To Grandmother's credit, seeing us, she laughed, too.

We repeated the protocol in Munich, this time housed in the Deutsches Museum. Because it was beautiful, I missed Iván more. We went through the routine again in Salzburg, in an established DP camp. Everything happened over and over, in infinite regress. Mirrors reflected in mirrors. In all the change, things also remained constant. The cold, the mud, the alien skies, the barking sounds of English. The hated, throaty hiss of German. The world kept bombarding me. I wished to be a cannon to shoot back, but I was not. So I sat instead in the rocking chair of my soul and rocked back and forth in steady rhythm.

SEVEN

GETTING OFF THE TRUCK AT THE CAMP IN POKING, A SMALL town near Munich, we were lined up by some officials for the usual routines. In the first line, holding our sleeves opened and away from our arms, we filed past an American soldier with a metal contraption. Aiming far inward, he sprayed us with white DDT powder. He did the same as we pulled our collars away, first to one side, then the other. The procedure was quick and utilitarian. Dignity was not at issue. My family and I didn't have lice anymore, but we knew that in the absence of proper precautions, we could reacquire them.

We were ushered out to form a new line in another room where a woman sat behind a desk. We each showed her our Displaced Person identity card, issued in Munich, and she handed back a week's food tickets. A translator explained that we could eat our meals at a dining barrack or take the food back to our quarters.

In the third line, we were given pillows and blankets and pieces of paper with the numbers of our barrack and room.

Luckily, they assigned only six to a room, which was exactly our number, counting Babi and Éva.

In the late afternoon we finished and headed with an assigned guide toward our barrack. The guide explained in Yiddish to Grandmother, who explained it to us, that because we were relative latecomers, our barrack was located quite far away at the edge of the camp.

As we walked, I looked around for the first time since we arrived. We were in a valley surrounded by forested mountains. The ascending fir trees were veiled in snow. In the fading light, they looked like haughty silent ghosts of menacing beauty. Ahead of me stretched many long, low gray buildings connected by paths of gray slushy mud. I saw lights here and there, but just enough to emphasize the monochrome decrepitude of the scene.

We trudged for miles, or so it felt. The guide half-carried grandmother. Periodically, Éva and Babi helped out. Finally, the guide stopped at a barrack that looked exactly like all the others. How he could tell I didn't know, but he said that this was our new home. Between dangerously breathless wheezes, Grandmother translated.

Stepping through the entrance in the center of the building, we found ourselves in a corridor. Shut doors faced us left and right. After much muttering and match-lighting, the guide finally located our room. As he threw the switch inside, two bare bulbs lit up. I saw three bunk beds in the center of the room. Pushed against the walls were six tall green metal cabinets. A large stove sat in a corner with pieces of firewood piled next to it. That was all. Everything looked dirty and dust-covered.

We had done this before in the Bergers' apartment on Teleki

Tér. We had built a home from nothing. How many times can
one start over and not die of the effort? What is the limit of
resilience? I burst into tears.

"Don't cry," my mother said. "This is a big room with many
windows. We will fix it up. Don't cry. It will be all right." I
could not imagine how.

Next morning, Babi and I were sent on a scavenge-what-
you-can errand. We needed a bucket, extra soap, rags, and a
broom, but most of all, we needed a saw. The hardest-seeming
item was the easiest and first acquired. When we walked out,
I saw a girl about my age standing in front of the door next to
us. As a joke, I walked up to her and said, 'Bzzzz, bzzzz,
bzzzz," while moving my arm back and forth.

"Tak, tak," she said, smiling broadly, and disappeared into
her room.

"So what do you think you're going to get? Some *rizi-
bizi?*" Babi asked me, rolling her eyes and dragging on her
cigarette. Babi always had cigarettes; men gave them to her all
the time, and she smoked them nonstop. She had horribly
nicotine-stained fingers. "Or perhaps a slap from her father for
making questionable gestures?"

I shrugged. "She'll bring out a saw," I said, not believing it
for a moment.

In twenty seconds, the girl appeared with her mother, carrying a trim two-person saw, both handles intact. I couldn't
get over my luck. I pumped the girl's hand with enthusiastic
gratitude and patted her shoulder. The mother spoke fast in
Polish. She told me, I gathered, that the tool was precious,
and I shouldn't break it, or steal it, or cut my throat with it.
To reassure her, I motioned her into our room. She looked
much relieved, realizing that the saw would remain within her
purview.

Babi and I set out again in search of the rest of the items. We went to the registration building, but they sent us on to the dining barrack, from which a man sent us to maintenance. It took hours of walking, waiting, pantomiming, walking. We felt frozen, and our feet were soaking wet. Finally, at the maintenance building, a young American soldier succumbed to Babi's flirting and to my childish charm and gave us a bucket, some rags, and powdered soap. On this occasion, the unfathomable language we didn't speak was English.

On our way back, Babi said, "Let's get something hot to eat. I'm starving."

"How?" I asked. "I have no money and no tickets. Do you?"

"Don't be such a hopeless loser," she said. "We'll go to the dining barrack—by the way, I think it's called a mess hall—and tell them that we left our tickets in our room."

"They'll send us back to get them," I said.

"Of course they will, dope, but not before they give us a plate of hot soup and a piece of bread. These are not the Nazis anymore. Who wouldn't pity a freezing kid and her slightly older sister?"

"Oh, is that what we are?

"You bet."

By then I was pretty good at coaxing things out of people. But not food. Babi, however, was excellent. Still, this time, it proved to be a difficult maneuver. The woman behind the counter was an SS-faced harridan. She held up a meal ticket and, waving it, kept explaining in Polish that we needed one of these to get food. Babi missed her meaning over and over. With her forefinger, she insistently pointed at her mouth, then patted her stomach in demanding, rapid-fire rhythm. The woman shook her head and waved the tickets.

"Let's go," I whispered. "It's not worth it."

"By now it's the principle," Babi said out loud, without interrupting her gestures. The impasse continued for another ten minutes.

"I'm leaving," I said, turning away to gather my bucket and things.

Evidently that was all the woman wanted. Unconditional surrender. Indisputable allocation of power to the one who held the sacred ladle. She started a fast monologue of sibilant *s*'s and throat-clearing *ch*'s. At the same time, she handed each of us a piece of bread and ladled soup into two plates. *"Spasibo,"* I said in Russian.

"Nyet po-russki, nyet po-russki," she yelled, really angry.

Babi and I sat down on long wooden benches facing each other at a long wooden table nailed together from planks. We ate our soup, which was thin and tasteless but at least was hot, and said nothing.

When we arrived home, our barrack room looked radically changed. Mother, Rózsi, and Éva had pushed the six metal cabinets together, dividing the room into two sections, two-thirds in one direction, and one-third in the other. Four of the cabinets opened toward the larger section. They had also sawed apart the connecting posts on two sets of bunk beds. They had placed two beds next to each other with heads against the main wall. These would be for Grandmother and Rózsi. Parallel to these, a few feet away, under a window, was my mother's bed. Below hers, again with a few feet of separation, under another window, was mine. The foot of my bed touched the back of the girls' cabinet.

The beds were made up with blankets and pillows, and a fire roared in the stove. I wouldn't say the room was cozy, but it definitely looked humanized.

"Well?" my mother asked eagerly. "Well? We rushed like crazy to have it ready for when you returned. It's nothing to cry about anymore, is it?"

"No," I said, "it is beautiful. Thank you." Beyond the partition, Rózsi and Éva were sawing away at the last bunk's posts. There is something elementally soothing about sawing wood. The rhythmic motion, the hypnotic sound, the pungent smell, the visible progress, all add up to a rainbow promise of renewal, most consoling even if unfounded.

I offered to help. "You'd better," Éva said, whining. "My arm is falling off. A pianist should not have to do such work. It has probably harmed me for life."

"Cut it out," Babi said. "Can't you ever not complain?"

"Come here, Éva," my mother called to her. "Sit down on a bed and rest. Don't worry. Your arm will be all right."

Babi and I sawed away. From time to time, one of us held the saw tight, preventing the other from moving. It slowed the work, but we laughed a lot.

In the evening, tickets in hand, we all went to the dining room for supper. Our preference would have been to eat at home, but we didn't have dishes in which to carry the food. After the meal, we were each handed a cardboard package with the letters C-A-R-E printed on it in bold blue capitals. The young woman handing them out punched our tickets and informed us in Romanian that we were to receive the packages periodically. (I knew that the language was Romanian only because Babi told me; she said that many of the girls with whom she had been in deportation camps were Romanian, and she had learned a little of the language. Perhaps. Babi was a very big liar. In private I had christened her the Baroness Münchhausen.) It was unclear how much time a period covered.

"Can I open it?" I asked my mother, perfectly aware that she would say no.

"No," she said.

"Why not?"

"It's not St. Nicholas Day. No is no."

Once back in our room, we all tore at our packages with equal fervor. We found: a can of Spam, a jar of Nestlé's instant coffee, a pouch of powdered milk, a can of Carnation evaporated milk, powdered eggs, packaged cheese, water crackers, miniature boxes of raisins, Crisco, a jar of peanut butter, tea bags, a chocolate bar, and cigarettes, five to a box, four boxes to a package.

"Let's pile it all up on the shelf of one of our cabinets," I said. "It will seem as if we had a pantry again."

"Not ours," Éva said. "I want to keep our stuff in our cabinet."

"Of course," my mother said. "Go ahead. Of course."

"I want to go on record here," Babi said. "Relatives are unchosen involuntary appendages."

Because I thought she was about to cry, I punched her in the arm hard. "Magda," she said very sternly, "one of these days I will have had enough of you, and you will end up dead." Then she winked at me. I had never before realized that a girl could be a brother.

Next morning, while we were still asleep, our door was almost broken down by savage banging. "Open, open," someone yelled in a funny Hungarian accent. "Open, Margit néni! Let me in!"

Mother opened the door. At the threshold stood Mendel, the son of my mother's cousin Eta, on my grandfather's side. He was from Sziget, or Mármaros, on the Romanian border.

I could never tell the two towns apart because they are geographically so close, and because they were cross-populated by everyone, including our Yiddish- and Romanian-speaking relatives.

He lifted my mother up into his arms and kissed her wildly. "Margit néni, I am so happy, so very happy to see you."

"Mendel!" we all screamed.

"Come in, you fool," my mother said, disentangling herself. "What a wonderful surprise. What are you doing here?"

"Well," said Mendel, in terrible Hungarian but bursting with pride, "I am part of the Zionist security police here. I am an officer."

"Eta's son a policemen!" my grandmother said, shaking her head. "What a shame."

"No, no, Emma néni," Mendel said, genuinely upset. "I am the Jewish police. We are the police here who guard you. We protect you from the Germans."

"What does he mean?" Grandmother asked, frightened, turning to Rózsi.

"It's all right," Rózsi said. "He's doing the right thing. I'll explain it later."

"Is there anyone else here from your family?" my mother asked.

"No," Mendel said, looking sad. "They were afraid to cross the border illegally. They stayed behind. But now all of you are here," he said, cheering up.

"Are you hungry?" my mother asked him.

"Oh, no," Mendel said. "We are the police. They feed us to bursting. But I'm sorry, I have to go."

"Mendel," Rózsi said, "could you get us a broom and some chairs to sit on? I am sick of sitting on my bed."

"No problem with the broom," Mendel said. "I am friendly with the maintenance guys. But I don't know about a chair. There may be none in this camp, except in the American officials' quarters. I'll see what I can do."

A few days later, Mendel returned with a broom, a bench, and some little shades that could be slipped onto the bare bulbs, cutting their glare. The quality of our lives improved instantly.

Still, silence settled on us again, as if we lay five fathoms deep. My mother never cried by day, but her eyes were red and swollen most of the time. I couldn't coax Rózsi out of bed. Grandmother sat facing the stove, turned away from us, reading her prayer book with a magnifying glass. Her lips moved, but no sound surfaced. When I crouched down close to her and looked through the wrong end of her magnifier, I could count her eyelashes. They reminded me of withered stalks of autumn grass.

Guiltily, I escaped behind the partition to play cards with Babi on her bed. Éva sat close by, playing the piano on a battered wooden board. She believed that this mock practicing would keep her fingers nimble.

On one of our daily treks to pick up the family's food, I asked Babi, "Do you think we live in a madhouse?"

She looked at me sadly. "No, my dear," she said. "You have never been in a concentration camp. This is normalcy. This is practically heaven."

Soon, to my immense relief, I was in school. The girl next door, who told me about it, took me with her one blustery morning. The schoolhouse looked the same as all the other barracks. Actually, it was only one room, filled with benches, and for desks, other benches raised on piled bricks. There was a blackboard and a handsome young man teacher.

Neither the teacher nor any of the children spoke Hungarian. Classes were in Yiddish. We communicated through pantomime, pointing, eye signals, and the enormous goodwill necessary to understand another without words.

The day I arrived, the class was starting a new project—learning to write the Yiddish alphabet in lowercase. I realized at once that this did not require knowledge of the language. I just had to memorize characters that corresponded to letters I knew and learn their names: a = lc = alef. b = $\mathfrak{D}$ = bays. I found it a rather entertaining game, and I played it with zest. The fact that the order of the Yiddish alphabet was somewhat out of kilter made it even more interesting. We spent two weeks on this task.

During that time, the teacher patted my back often, and sometimes shook my hand. I worried about that. In my experience, early admiration usually led to unmeetable demands. Some words of my forgotten childhood German came back to me. Listening hard to the other children, I managed to tilt those words in a Yiddish direction, and presto, I could say, more or less, that I was hungry or tired, or that I wanted to go home.

Because Yiddish, like Hungarian, is a phonetic language, I learned to take flawless dictation without understanding any of the text. On the test, I was the only one who got an A. This caused major trouble. The children were furious, and accused me of having faked my inability to speak Yiddish. To settle the matter, the teacher walked home with me one afternoon to meet my family. He was much relieved to learn that other than my grandmother, we were Yiddish-mute.

One Saturday evening, Tasha, my next-door neighbor, told

me that there was a variety show in camp, and she was on her way to see it. After much begging, my mother consented to let me go along.

Like everything else at the Poking camp, the theater was located in a barrack. White sheets that served as curtains draped a small elevated stage. Its black back wall was painted in narrow swirls of pink and white and yellow and red. Shortly after we arrived, the master of ceremonies pulled the curtains closed, adding much to everyone's sense of drama. The audience sat on rows of benches. As we waited, Tasha and I elbowed each other a little to contain and share our excitement.

At last the MC appeared again and gave us a short introductory speech in Yiddish. Two-thirds of the audience clapped enthusiastically. He switched to Hungarian and recited, I assumed, the same introduction. The minority segment of the house broke into deafening applause. I guessed all the Hungarians were as sick as I was of having to struggle constantly to understand what was going on.

The first act was a juggler. His speed was three balls in the air, one on the ground. Still, everyone was very pleased with him.

The MC came back. He told some very funny jokes in both languages. Tasha and I roared in sequence. A woman sang Romanian folk songs, accompanied by recorded music. The Romanians gave her a standing ovation. Skits in Yiddish and Hungarian made fun of camp life and of the residents. Finally, the MC announced the closing act, the highlight of the show. The star was a young cantor from Warsaw. Originally he had studied for the opera, but when the war broke out, he was forced to switch. "And here he is, ladies and gentlemen, our own personal baritone nightingale."

He did sing beautifully—sad, nostalgic songs of love and loss and death, and the death of love. The audience went wild. Tasha and I, too. My palms became red as I applauded along with the others, for encore, encore.

At the end of the show, I was lit, inspired, transfigured. Without thinking, I mounted the three steps leading to the stage. "Bácsi, bácsi," I called to the MC, "I have a collection of poems by poets who were deported or who were in forced labor camps. Also Zionist poets. Please let me recite some next week. I am very good at it."

He looked at me as if I belonged to some crawly species. Gone was the bonhomie, the jolly humor, the expansive gallantry he exuded on stage. "Girlie, get lost," he said.

"But sir—"

"Don't sir me. I am tired of amateurs. I'm tired of aspirants. I'm tired of my life. Get lost."

"Yes, sir," I said, unable not to grin. Very few adults were ever this honest. I bore him no rancor. I knew well the downward pull of dark moods, the need to be like lightning and strike at random.

The next week, I approached him again. I could tell he recognized me, although he pretended not to. Don't worry, I wanted to say to him. I know how it is.

"What do you want?" he asked curtly.

"You know. Poems from the war. I want to recite them."

"Go away. Don't bother me. We have no performers here under five feet."

I laughed.

"You think that's funny?" he asked, surprised.

"Well, I beg your pardon, but yes."

"Well, it's not," he said. "Take it as fact, and don't come around anymore."

I walked away. All right, so it hadn't worked. Why did I want to perform? What was so attractive about standing on slightly raised boards and mouthing other people's words?

Don't kid me, my other voice said.

All right, it's the applause. No, it's the resonance. Bringing to life the poet, and also the audience. Being the conduit.

Don't kid me, the voice repeated.

All right. I was trying to make Iván proud.

When I got home, I woke everyone. "You have to come and see this show," I yelled. "Next Saturday you must all come. It is real theater. I mean, the feeling of it is. It is as much fun as Latabár was in Father's . . ." I trailed off.

"We'll come," Rózsi said, and winked at me reassuringly regarding my gaffe. Father was never to be praised. I knew that rule. I believed it to be correct and fair. Nonetheless, whether my father merited it or not, I remembered myself vividly at age three, sitting next to Iván in the front seats of the author's box, listening to the deafening applause that made my then-Apuci's show a hit. I could still see the famous comedian Latabár onstage sitting on an enormous wooden trunk, at a railway station, in checkered trousers, a monocle in his left eye, tapping his feet and singing:

> *"Nem értem, nem értem,*
> *Senki sem*
> *Szaladt itt elébem*
> *Virágos kapukat reméltem."*

> "I don't get it, I don't get it,
> No one ran to greet me
> I had hoped for gates of flowers
> Standing here to meet me."

"Go to bed now," my mother said, turning to the wall. "We'll all go with you next Saturday." Then she added, "I promise."

"I promise." What a short little phrase to carry so many messages. She wasn't mad at me. She also remembered nostalgically that evening of triumph. She wanted to please me, to make up to me something we had lost forever. She was too sad that night to do anything more than promise.

We did go the next Saturday, and again and again for weeks, often joined by Éva and Babi, and by a young couple we had become friendly with, Pista Almási and Éva Váradi. I was particularly excited about Éva's presence, because her father had been an actor in Budapest. Pista was about twenty-two, Éva five years older. They seemed especially glamorous because I knew they lived together but were not married. I didn't know the technical details of living together, but I knew that to do it and not be married was forbidden and romantic, and occasionally it resulted in violent death, as in the case of my cousin Ervin, and of Anna Karenina. Éva, however, looked in no danger of dying, so I wasn't too worried.

One night, the penultimate act, before the star, fell sick, leaving a gap in sequence. I was sitting in the first row when I heard the MC say, "Where the hell is that kid who keeps nagging me about her recitations? This time I could use her."

"Sir, I am ready," I said.

"Hurry up," he said, motioning me to the stage, as irritable as ever. I was getting very tired of him.

"Laaaadies and gentlemen," he announced without giving me a moment's preparation. "Our youngest star, a veteran of many stages"—copious laughter; Drop dead, I thought—"the original, the inimitable Magda Dénes reciting the poetry of our times."

I bowed. In my very best former newspaper-reading voice, I began, "And when we were shot in Tarnopol . . ."

At my first sentence, a silence descended, the most total I had ever heard. ". . . our arms and legs strewn awry . . ." A woman started to cry. When I finished the third poem, all the Hungarians were weeping, and even many others who I assumed understood only the tone.

As the thunderous applause rose, I felt terrible. I wanted them to cry. I wanted them to remember and never to forget. This should be the time for the MC to look at me as if I were a creepy crawly. Instead he was pumping my arm and saying to the audience, "A major talent. My discovery. A major talent, ladies and gentlemen." Fortunately, I was followed by the cantor, everyone's most favorite.

The MC asked me to join the show as a regular. I jumped for joy. The experience ruined me for life. I kept thinking that if I pushed, pushed, pushed, I would get what I wanted, wanted, wanted, but it wasn't true. Not in the long run.

For the rest of our stay in Poking, however, I became a celebrity of sorts. I performed every Saturday, and people recognized me on the streets and said hello to me as I went about my business. The cantor became my mentor and friend. Once when I didn't show up for a performance because I was sick in bed, he came to visit and brought me a large Hershey bar as a token of his regard. Grandmother, who was the only one at home, was very impressed. So was I, although I faked nonchalance, which I regarded as a requirement of stardom.

Grandmother and I were alone most weekdays, because Babi and Éva were always out hanging around with people their own age. Rózsi and Mother had rented a room in Munich in the home of a former opera singer and her husband, and had gone back to bartering, this time in reverse. They took some of our food and cigarettes and traded them in Munich for cloth and pots and cologne and whatever else they could find. It wasn't that we had surplus food. In fact, we didn't have enough ever to eat our fill. But some of what we were given was so alien that only the threat of immediate starvation could induce us to eat it. Powdered eggs were one example. Peanut butter was another, but a special case. We were unaware that it had to be spread on bread, and so we tried to eat it by the spoonful. Consumed that way, peanut butter seals the mouth like dentist's wax and sticks in the gullet like glue. The sensation evoked our worst nightmares of death by asphyxiation, by drowning, by garroting, by choking on our own blood and vomit, as so many of our brethren had recently done.

Sometimes Mother and Rózsi stayed away for the weekend as well, so that we didn't see them for six, seven days running. I began to suspect that "bartering" was just an excuse to escape the dreariness of camp life, and the dull burden of Grandmother and me.

One morning, while they were in Munich, the school buzzed with excited, whispered news. The American soldiers who had occupied a small camp adjacent to ours had been transferred and had left overnight.

"What exactly are they saying?" I asked Tasha nervously. "What does it mean, 'they left'? Why would the Americans leave? Is there a new war? Will we be attacked? I must go home at once." I felt a heartbeat away from total panic.

Tasha laughed at me. "It's nothing like that," she said. "Don't worry. Whenever the Americans go, they leave things behind."

"What do you mean?"

"They leave furniture and dishes and stuff. Sometimes even canned food. Everyone gets excited because you're allowed to take whatever you find."

"I see." After several deep, embarrassed breaths, I calmed down enough to ask, "Will you go there?"

"No," Tasha said. "My parents decided we don't really need anything." She and her family had been in Poking for almost a year.

"Will the others go?"

"I don't know," Tasha said. "Probably their parents went this morning—those who wanted things."

"Can I go?"

"Sure. Anyone can go."

I was overcome with a sense of urgency. We needed so many things, and who knew what rapidly diminishing cornucopia lay just beyond the horizon? I raised my hand. When the teacher called on me, I motioned that I wanted to walk up to talk with him. He nodded. At his bench-desk, with my eyes fixed on the floor, I said, "I need to leave now."

"For the American camp?" he asked. I nodded, shame pricking my eyes. Leaving the house of learning to hunt for goods. What have I come to? "It's all right," he said, patting my head and smiling. "Go."

I turned to leave, then realized I didn't know where to go. He explained the route with great patience and kindness.

I set out over hills and through a lot of frozen brush, and reached the American barracks in half an hour. People wandered about carrying objects, walking in and out of buildings. Unlike the kids at school, they didn't seem excited. There was no smell of the hunt in the air, only tired gathering.

The first barrack I entered had been stripped bare. I guessed even exhausted gatherers could have the effect of locusts. In the second barrack, I found the task of my current life. In the middle of one of the rooms stood a table—intact, sturdy, well constructed. If I could lug it home, we could sit around it for dinner. I could do homework on it. Rózsi could play solitaire without cursing every five minutes because the cards flipped as she shifted her position on the bed.

I started pulling it. The treasure far outweighed me. I sat down on the floor to think. Words like "cantilever," "crossbar," "velocity," "flying buttress" swam around in my head, words that meant nothing to me. I never studied physics. I was just pretending to be a boy, mostly Ervin or Iván.

Pretending will get you nowhere, I said to myself. Pulling will. Could I push instead? I asked myself. Shut up and get on with it, I answered.

I pulled and pushed and yanked and groaned and cried and cursed. Like a lost worker ant, I was determined to reach the hill, regardless of the enormousness of my catch.

Every few feet I sat under the table and held on to its legs. Once, on getting up, I decided to knight it and name it Gulliver. I picked up a fallen stick, tapped its top three times, and said, "Rise, Sir Gulliver. You are possessor of all you see, in exchange for gallant service not yet rendered. Now fly." Nothing happened. Still, I no longer felt alone. The table and I were in partnership. I would give it a home and a life of purpose. Meanwhile, it spread itself over me, a sovereign, benign protector. Sir Gulliver.

We arrived home in about four hours. I banged on our door. "Grandmother, Grandmother!" I yelled. "Come outside. Look what I have brought!"

She stepped out with the black shawl Mendel had given her wrapped around her shoulders. "Where have you been?" she asked, weeping and wiping her eyes. "Where have you been? I have been so worried I didn't know what to do!"

"Oh, Grandmother, I'm sorry," I said, hugging her. Look what I have brought. It just took longer than I expected."

"A table," she said, with the widest grin I had ever seen on her. Her toothlessness, which I never noticed behind her pursed lips, now cut my heart. "A table," she repeated, nodding happily. "Now we can eat together like a family."

We placed the table in front of Grandmother's and Rózsi's beds and put the bench on the other side. That way, three of us could sit facing the other three. Not that lately there was all that much need for this cozy arrangement. Still, at least Grandmother and I could eat in comfort opposite each other.

When Mother and Rózsi returned home a day later, they, too, were delighted. "What an improvement," my mother said.

"Just wait," said Rózsi. "We brought things, too." Grandmother got a pair of new slippers, which she badly needed, and for which she was greatful. Babi and Éva each got a lipstick. They jumped up and down in delirous joy.

For me they brought a blue embroidered runner as long as my bed and four feet wide. We immediately tacked it to the wall above my bed. They also gave me brightly colored postcards of Passau, Munich, and Berchtesgaden, and little stuffed cloth figurines. Two were green-and-red skiers, the other two blond Gretchens about to dance. I tacked all seven items to the runner. The arrangement looked beautiful.

"So now you have a nursery, a child's room again," my mother said.

"Oh, yes. Thank you very much." What was I to say? That I didn't want German mementos because they were memento mori? They had hoped to make me happy, I knew, and the arrangement did look pretty. Where does right lie? And when do you lie about right?

The following Saturday, I perfomed as usual. All five of them came to hear me. I put all my feelings into the harrowing words I declaimed. The audience went wild.

On our way home, Anyu and I walked a little ahead of the rest. What I wanted to ask her was, "Now, now will you love me as much as you loved Iván? And will you stop escaping to Munich without me?" But of course I didn't. What I said was, "So what do you think?"

"You are a good performer," she replied. "You recite poetry very well. So did Ivánka. He was superb."

Gradually winter became spring. This change happened not in the slush at camp level, but at the upward far horizon among the trees. White turned black, then it turned green, until everything sang. Not us, though. Our recurrent silence-sickness had gotten hold of us again. This time a major contributor to its onset was the death of Bernát, the son of one of grandfather's murdered brothers.

Rózsi and Anyu had run into him in Munich. They dined together. "He looks wonderful," Rózsi said, "and he is very well off. He does business all over Germany and Austria."

"What kind of business?" Grandmother asked suspiciously. "Smuggling?"

That was a nasty accusation, because it implied the theft of medicine and other people's badly needed food.

"Not at all," my mother said, sounding offended. She regarded the Indigs, not my grandmother's family, as her people. "He trades American leather bomber jackets. Army boots. Watches and other such stuff. He buys them from a sergeant who imports them from America."

"He sent you his love," Rózsi said, "and he's going to come visit us in a few days."

At this Grandmother relented a little.

When he appeared, Bernát looked breathtakingly regal. Tall, majestically slim, with a chiseled nose and an easy smile. He wore breeches and riding boots, a tweed jacket, and a foulard instead of a tie. He was gloved and goggled to protect himself from the wind as he rode his metal-adorned mythic mount, an enormous motorcycle.

I couldn't believe he was related to us, or that he had spent two years in deportation camps, part of it with Dávid bacsi, who was his uncle also.

I didn't listen to the general conversation, because it would have interfered with my surreptitious, concentrated inspection of him. How did he do this? How did he avoid being reduced? Even his voice was elegant. Eventually I caught some sentences. "You don't need goods from me," he was saying. "You would just trade them at a loss. You need dollars." He produced an enormous wad from somewhere inside his jacket and started to peel off bills, making two piles.

Both Mother and Rózsi looked stunned. Before he was finished, Mother said, "Don't do this, Bernát. You need cash for your business. Besides, you are one of the cousins with whom we are hardly acquainted."

Bernát laughed. "I know," he said. "I never needed anything. That doesn't mean I don't know how in peacetime Zsiga bacsi helped all my brothers. You are his daughters. It's my turn now." He kept peeling and stacking, as we watched with shocked, rounded eyes.

"That's it," he said. "This is all I can afford today. But I will be back in two weeks."

He was not back in two weeks, or in three. Grandmother

started to mutter. "A true Indig," she said. "Munificent in promise, short on delivery." The three of us shook our heads in dissent, but we were unable to contradict the evidence.

A few days later, Mendel, who was Bernát's second cousin, but nothing like him, knocked on our door with the news. The week before, Bernat's motorcycle had left the road and, like Pegasus, taken to the air. For a long distance, they soared beautifully toward the sky, until Bernát became dizzied by the heights. Then mount and rider plummeted to earth, their parts inseparably mingled forever.

As with Iván and Ervin, there was no funeral, no remains to visit. His anonymous partners and the authorities took charge. Who cared, anyway? He was dead, wasn't he? Dead is dead. Facts can't be polished.

Bernát's death acted as the unraveler of our Poking life. I fell ill with feverish tonsilitis, a disease I had frequently suffered from as a child, but had not had since the October day in 1944 when we fled Teleki Tér. I resigned from performing, and I withdrew from school—forced to by illness, I told the teacher.

The opera singer in Munich sent a note to Mother and Rózsi saying that her brother had returned and that their room would hereafter no longer be available. Babi and Éva were summoned to Munich by UNRRA, the United Nations Relief and Rehabilitation Administration, which issued them visas to Amerika, petitioned by their aunt and uncle. "I am so sorry, Margit néni," Babi said tearfully, hugging my mother. "It should have been you and Magda who went first."

"We have no uncles in Amerika," Anyu said bitterly. My father had not answered the three letters she had written him.

Poking was emptying. There were *aliyahs* to Palestine, passports with working permits to Honduras, and myrrh-filled slave boats to Byzantium. The world was ready to make room for its migrants. Our family sat tight. "Amerika or bust," we would have said, if we had known the slogan.

In time, affidavits for us arrived from our Cuban cousin Kató, with separate letters to Rózsi and Mother. After the long, bleak wait, we changed our minds and welcomed our chance to go to Cuba. To Rózsi, Kató wrote, "Welcome. I can't wait for your arrival, and Emma néni's." Enclosed in the letter was an American twenty-dollar bill. To Mother, she wrote, "Although I am sending you and Magda an affidavit, I cannot imagine your need for it. After all, Gyula the Mr. Editor, who snubbed me for a lifetime, could bring you to Amerika. Certainly he's as well off as we are, and could supply you with money. Consequently . . ."

Over and over, my father's past arrogance became a liability for us. But at base and in truth, it also became something else for me, having nothing to do with the reality of him. I learned through these rebuffs that I had to grow my fate from my spread palms.

On the train to Paris, where UNRRA sent us to wait for our visas, we all wished Mother happy birthday. She had turned forty-three. I gave her a pencil drawing of flowers I had made in school. I wanted to draw tulips in a bowl, but the result was not very aesthetically satisfying. To compensate, I wrote under it, in my neatest hand, "To a very good Anyu happy birthday from your loving daughter Magda. P.S. When I make money, I will buy you a beautiful gift." She cried a little when she looked at it, and kissed me.

WE SEEMED TO arrive everywhere in the stealth of night, with furtive urgency and whispered instructions. Paris was no exception. I suppose the habits of a long war died hard, even among our organizers. When we got off the train at the Gare de l'Est, Zionist guides waited for our group. Our family's was called Shlomo, and he was French. Of course there are French Jews, I realized. I just never thought of it. It did seem a little strange. French was French. But then again, I used to think that Hungarian was Hungarian, until I learned better. I supposed French Jews had been taught the same lesson.

"Shlomo, Shlomo," my grandmother grumbled, after introductions. "All these newfangled names and customs. I bet you his mother named him Shlajme."

Shlajme / Shlomo explained in a combination of Yiddish and pantomime that we were going to a regular hotel, paid for by the Zionists. We were to stay there until someone arrived to fetch us. Probably tomorrow, possibly the next day. He ushered us into his car. We traveled through dark streets of intact houses. There was no rubble anywhere. No obscene bombed-out gaps gaped. Amazing. Still, this was not the Paris of my books. I saw no city of light, no teeming life. No pulsating energy took hold of my soul. Paris. Yet one more thing falsified in literature, and overrated.

The Hotel Gambetta, where Shlomo deposited us, was a small, third-rate establishment that to me appeared palatial. In the lobby, we sat on upholstered couches. It felt alien to sink into furniture again. Although I knew better, I bounced up and down a little for old times' sake. Shlomo handed Mother some French money and our temporary ration cards. He assured her again that someone would contact us before either ran out. We all shook hands, waved *au revoir*, and watched our lifeline recede through the door.

"So," Rózsi said. "We are in the dream city. And it's not worth a pile of dog shit."

A porter showed us to our rooms on the third floor. Surprisingly, he spoke Yiddish. Rózsi and Grandmother got one room, Mother and I another. Each room had a private bath. Everything was clean, and one of the bathroom spigots spouted warm water. I had last bathed in a tub in Munich, over four months before. Mother and Rózsi had taken me to a house that consisted entirely of bathrooms. For a fee, each of us had rented one, with two towels, and a washcloth. We brought our own soap. Ushered in and left alone by an unfriendly, blistering Brunhilde, I had been too scared to enjoy bathing. I rushed through it top speed, and then had to cool my heels outside the doors of Rózsi and Mother, who took their sweet time.

I opened the window to look out over the Place Gambetta. I could smell the spring odor of the gently swaying leaves on the chestnut trees that ringed the plaza. Behind them stood a circle of houses with lit-up windows. I couldn't see into any apartment, but I knew that families were in there, preparing dinner on a stove, exchanging news, sitting down on their familiar chairs. I was, on the other hand, an officially designated Displaced Person, in transit. I had a grossly reduced family, my possessions fit in a half-filled rucksack, my wherewithal was doled out by anonymous charity. There was no street in this city where I could walk and be recognized. All my connections were next door, and they consisted of three hurt old women as exiled as I.

By the time mother returned, I had the window closed and the shade lowered; I didn't want her to catch a glimpse of what I saw. She seemed very excited. "This hotel was a French underground safe house during the war," she said. "It is still run by the Zionists. The desk clerk speaks Yiddish, too. He

told Grandmother there is a restaurant around the corner
where we can eat. It is inexpensive. Hurry up. Rózsi and
Grandmother are waiting for us in the lobby."

Outside, we made two rights and came upon the restaurant
at the corner. Three steps led down to the entrance. The
maître d' greeted us and showed us to a table covered with a
red-and-white-checkered tablecloth. He handed each of us a
menu. None of us spoke. I heard quiet conversation at other
tables, and the occasional clink of a glass. I tried surreptitiously
to observe the diners. They all seemed to be enjoying themselves, couples and families and groups. On most tables, there
was a carafe of wine. My mind was not agile enough to cope
with the discrepancy. This time travel within a block and a half,
from war to peace, from extremis to normalcy, from outcast
dog to restaurant patron, was too much to absorb. I wanted
to climb on the table and yell at all of them, "How dare you
have a life, when ours was taken?" Hold on a moment, my
other self said. France was occupied by the Nazis. They suffered. They are entitled. Well, perhaps.

"So let's order," Rózsi said, "except I don't understand a
word of the menu."

"Never mind," my mother said. "It doesn't matter what the
dish is. We have to order the cheapest thing. It will require the
fewest tickets." Rózsi nodded.

When the waitress came, my mother pointed among the
entrées to the description opposite the smallest numbers, and
held up four fingers. The waitress nodded, then asked a question. "No, no," my mother said, meaning she didn't speak
French.

"*Oui, oui,*" the waitress said, getting irritated. Then she
added a long string of other words. We stared up at her,

uncomprehending. She tried again, with no better results.
Now she was angry.

The maître d' came over, and they talked to each other at
length. I wondered whether they were strategizing our ejec-
tion. I wouldn't have minded it, I realized. At least the world
would have reacquired its consistency.

But then the maître d' suddenly tapped his forehead, walked
away, and returned with some ration cards. He pointed to
them and made a give-me gesture. Ah, yes, we had those.

The surprise dish that arrived was tongue in raisin sauce. It
was excellent. So was the water and the long crusty bread,
which cost extra money and extra tickets. During the two
weeks we stayed at the Hotel Gambetta, we ate tongue six
times in reckless extravagance. To my added confusion, after
the second time we went to the restaurant, we were recognized and treated as regulars, allowed to surrender our ration
tickets at the end of the meal.

Two days after our arrival, Shlomo showed up early in the
morning to take us by metro to the Joint Distribution Committee's headquarters. We were to register and receive ID
papers, money, and ration cards. Mine had the designation J-
3, for children, which meant that I was entitled to a quarter
of a liter of milk every week, and some fresh fruit. We were
also to receive meal tickets for the Joint-run kitchen, tickets
for used clothing at the Joint warehouse, police registration
numbers, and God knows what other bureaucratic paper req-
uisites to attest to our existence and to ensure our continued
future.

The large hall where all this took place teemed with sweaty,
screaming, hysterical petitioners and sweaty, screaming, exasperated officials, French and American. We had to stand in

long disorderly lines for each separate registration item. It was forbidden for families to separate and stand in different lines simultaneously, because part of being ID'd was visual; the exact number of people who claimed to compose a family had to be there.

The procedure was endless. At nightfall, we were only about half done. A man jumped on a table and yelled in half a dozen languages, none Hungarian, that everyone was to return in the morning. Unaccompanied, we managed to reverse our metro ride and go straight to our restaurant. Never has a cow's tongue offered greater comfort or been more blessed.

Over demeaning long days of waiting and noise and frustration, life eventually got sorted. No one directly insulted us. Still, help of this sort and humiliation were inextricably intertwined. I watched the officials and marveled with envy at how easily they could be picked out even when they stood at the roiling center of the crowd. What made them so different, so unmistakably non-DP? Their clothes, yes, but that was the lesser factor. Some of the DPs were already wearing American used clothes and were, therefore, not all that differently attired. What then? The lack of despair on their faces. Their carriage. The knowledge they emanated that they belonged in the world. DPs, in contrast, were furtive as mice, wary as beaten dogs, watchful and savage as hungry wolves, sly as foxes. Yes, that was the difference. DPs had been hammered and diminished to an in-between species of the kingdom. They didn't even speak a common language other than tears.

We labored under the misapprehension that affidavits metamorphosed into visas with the inevitability of caterpillars turning into buttterflies. Consequently, when we no longer had to stand in line, we behaved like legitimate tourists. We figured we had two or at the most three weeks to see Paris before we left it. We rushed from sight to sight with gawking abandon. We marveled at the Tour Eiffel, Notre Dame, Sacre Coeur. We strolled at the side of the Seine, on the Left Bank, on the Champs Elysées. We visited the Louvre and the Arc de Triomphe. We sat in warm ticklish weather with little teasing breezes in the Jardin de Tuileries and the Cimetière du Père Lachaise, which was within walking distance from the Hotel Gambetta. Paris was beautiful, but only to my eyes, not to my soul. I didn't respond to it with the joy beauty usually evoked in me. These structures, these edifices, these wide, tree-lined avenues, were too grand for my sore, somber, shrunken heart. Paris flaunted its arrogant beauty; to resonate with Paris, you, too, had to be, or at least to feel, elegant and beautiful. Otherwise, the city was a taunt, a jeering reminder of all your lacks.

On an inspection visit to the Joint during this tourist season, we were informed of two unpleasant facts. First, that the waiting time for visas was unpredictable. They could arrive in a few months, a year, or whenever they arrived. Second, that the Hotel Gambetta was an interim shelter, from which we would have to move when our allotted two weeks were up. We were given a list of recommended hotels and told that we would receive a fixed sum every month to take care of our needs. It followed logically that the more one spent on lodging, the less one would have for food and other necessities.

We went to the first hotel on the list, on the Boulevard Magenta, chosen partly because it was on the same familiar metro line as the Hotel Gambetta station, and we felt proprietary.

The hotel was a big, rambling building which had clearly seen much better days. The rooms we were shown were large, but had no private baths. The Frenchman taking us around was the owner himself, the *patron*. He explained that he was a member of the Resistance, and all the rooms in the hotel were occupied by émigrés. Some from before the war, others more recent. He was a big man, who managed to be simultaneously affable in his gestures and surly in his speech. The last room we saw was quite large and very light. Rózsi decided to take it for her and Grandmother. Anyu opted to continue looking, because she deemed the price too steep. Rózsi had Kató's support to supplement the Joint's stipend; we didn't.

"There is no point in going by the list," Mother said when we reached the street. "We'll spend our days together in this place anyway. Let's just look for a small hotel nearby."

We got off the avenue and started looking for places on the side streets. We found several, but none seemed reputable. Finally, about three blocks away, we saw a small, neat-looking hotel with boxes of blooming geraniums at the windows. Inside, a woman concierge sat knitting in a tiny glass-enclosed space. We explained that we wanted a room. She looked disgusted. Two to a room, she pantomimed. Mother nodded and pointed to me and herself. With utter reluctance, the woman took us to a small, dark room on the ground floor, with a bathroom down the hall, shared by seven people. The price was about half that of the Magenta rooms. We took it. My heart shrank one more unit.

"It's only for sleeping and washing in the morning," Mother said. "We'll spend no time here, and everything is very clean, isn't it?"

I nodded. It was very clean. Dreary, depressing, and clean.

In a few days at Boulevard Magenta, we settled down to a livable routine. The *patron* had stored in his basement a great deal of assorted furniture, lamps, and odds and ends, to which he allowed his guests free access. As a result, we were able to furnish Rózsi and Grandmother's room in a cozy and very comfortable way. We placed their beds catty-corner to form a couchlike arrangement. From the basement we brought a dining table and several chairs and standing lamps. Although the lamps were flaky and somewhat crooked, with battered shades, they provided us in the evenings with sweetly diffused light.

We acquired two electric hot plates and an iron. Pots and pans attached themselves to us as if we were magnets. The Joint handed them out, and the *patron* had some in the basement. Cutlery and plates followed. Grandmother started to cook, and in a wink we were normalized, in a manner of speaking.

Shortly after we settled at Magenta, Pista Almási and Éva Váradi showed up, the young couple we had met in Poking. They still looked glamorous, and very right for Paris. Especially Éva. When I started going to the movies with them, I realized that Éva strikingly resembled Susan Hayward, and Pista looked a little like Cornell Wilde.

Pista got a job manufacturing handbags, a trade he had learned at Lederer in Budapest. For this we all looked down on him a little. It was perfectly acceptable to do any work at all as an émigré. But to have chosen a trade as opposed to a profession for one's life work we regarded as slightly *déclassé*. Only his involvement with Éva and his looks redeemed him.

Since Pista worked and Éva didn't, she spent her days with us. She came in the morning and stayed until Pista arrived to have supper, for which they contributed their share of ration cards and money.

One morning on the metro, headed toward Magenta, Éva

ran into a friend of hers and Pista's from Poking, whom we didn't know. His name was Tibor Szaltzer, Tibi for short. She invited him along to meet us. Tibi was a shy, gangly young man with an exceptionally long, thin neck that made his head appear to bob as if he were an amusement park trophy. His most prominent characteristic was an enormous Adam's apple that seemed to lead him forward. He had a sense of humor, but blushed too easily at his own jokes. Idle and magnetized like the pots and pans, he too joined our daytime household. But perhaps for him the true magnet was Éva. He looked madly in love with her, a fact I noticed but everyone else seemed to ignore utterly.

Tibi aimed to become an orchestra conductor. From time to time, picking up a wooden cooking spoon baton, he conducted, with exceptional vigor and devotion, the steam rising from grandmother's soup simmering on the electric burner. He hummed symphonic pieces as he did this, and we all listened in sad, respectful silence.

The last people to join our household in mid-July were Olga and her husband, coincidentally also named Pista. Rózsi and Mother ran into them at the Joint. Pista's mother had owned a stall in the Teleki Tér market where she sold live geese. Not exactly people my father would have taken to the Jappán, but the strip-mining of lives makes for unusual companions.

Pista was enormously charming despite his lack of polish. Rózsi told us later that he was rumored to be dishonest, a crook who would sell his mother for a profit. The latter aspersion was blatantly untrue, since he talked of his mother often, nostagically and with much love.

His wife, Olga, was a pretty, very simple-minded woman

much too nice to be called stupid, and five months pregnant.
Pista wheeled and dealed, bought and sold all day in the city,
while Olga spent her time with us.

One afternoon, while we were all just sitting around, Olga
asked my mother what she did before the war. Prompted by
some instantaneous bizarre inspiration, Anyu replied, "Oh,
you didn't know? I worked in the circus."

When we heard this, our eyes became fixed at middle distance, and none of us smiled. "You didn't," Olga said.

"But I did," my mother replied. "I don't understand how
you didn't know it. I was quite famous."

Olga was near fainting with wonderment. "What did you
do?"

"Well," my mother said, "I used to work the trapeze, but
then I had a small accident, a broken ankle, and after that, to
my great sorrow, I had to give it up."

Olga didn't quite know whether to believe her or not, so
she turned to the rest of us. "Did Margit néni really work in
the circus?"

"Yes," Rózsi said. "I don't understand how you never heard
her name."

Éva said, "Oh, I thought you knew."

I said, "My mother, she was the best."

Poor Olga had no options left. She believed, and said,
"Margit néni, please tell me. Tell me about the circus."

My mother started in, and for weeks she spun fabulous
yarns about circus life. I'm not sure where she got her mate-
rial, but the stories became beautifully elaborate fairy tales that
included gypsies who steal children, but then the children are
recovered, and tigers who escape their cages but then are
caught. She told of roaring crowds, a mysterious lion tamer, a

bearded lady who wrote novels under a pseudonym, and other breathtaking imaginings. She became Olga's daylight Scheherazade.

Although we were in the know, we, too, got caught up in the stories and enjoyed them tremendously. Sometimes I wondered, Is this cruel to Olga? Lying in general is cruel. It makes a fool of you. It undermines one of your most precious possessions—your hold on reality. It shakes your sense of yourself, until the knowledge your bones whisper becomes uncertain and suspect.

To be lied to is to be diminished, but also challenged to a dare. To meet the dare, one has to risk sanity, and declare, "I don't care what you say. I know what I know from within, although I cannot prove it."

On the other hand, to be lied to with one's consent is a thrill. It is the basis of many forms of entertainment. The difference is control. One is free at any time to unsuspend disbelief.

Olga believed and believed, and kept begging for more. To my guilty delight, mother obliged.

One day Olga said, "You never told me—what exactly did you do once your ankle broke and you couldn't work the trapeze?"

Without missing a beat, my mother replied, "I was the number carrier."

"What's that?" Olga asked.

"You know, in the circus, there are these big, round white boards with large black numbers painted on them. The first act is number one, the second act is number two, and so on. I was the one who carried that board around to show everyone which act was to come next."

Olga's eyes widened in wonder. "Really? And what did you wear?"

"A bathing suit," said my mother, "and high heels."

"And your hair?"

"Oh, it came down to my shoulders, and I would just fling my head back and my hair would fly and everyone would applaud."

Olga became daring. "Margit néni, would you show me how you did it?"

There was a moment's silence in the room. It was very hard not to laugh. "Well, of course, Olga," my mother said. "Gladly."

She got up, pretended to be holding a big board in front of her, and with graceful, semidancing steps, she walked all around the room, showing the number. When she finished with a flourish, put down the imaginary placard, and bowed, Olga burst into applause, as did we—and into belly-shaking laughter, because finally it was possible without alerting Olga to the hoax.

August came, and with it, on the second day, my twelfth birthday. I don't know how she managed it, because they were still very expensive, but mother surprised me with a wristwatch. As I opened the box, my heart sank with the sudden incontrovertible certainly that what I had most coveted at age nine in Budapest had totally lost all its meaning now at twelve in Paris. Who was there left to admire it? Who to tease me for my slavish pride in its ownership? Nobody.

Mother bought the watch from a young Hungarian black marketeer. He carried his stock strapped in rows on his arms, like a looting Russian soldier. I was given no choice before my birthday, because mother wanted to surprise me, but afterward she said, "Let's go look at his arms. Perhaps there is another one you would prefer."

"This one is fine, Anyu," I said. "It is perfect."

I was also acutely aware that I couldn't let my mother know of my indifference. She had saved and scrimped and sacrificed. It was not her fault that this watch measured a different time. It was God's fault.

So I overdid it. I thanked her three times a day for a week. I kissed her, I kissed the watch, I cuddled it, I showed it off. I said I was the happiest child in the world. Unasked, I told people what time it was. I made a show so large that, in retrospect, I don't understand how she didn't catch on. But then again, by that time, my skill at lying was directly proportional to my disapproval of it.

In September, the month of Iván's birthday, Mother registered me in a school that was walking distance from the Magenta. They assigned me to fourth grade, a major insult. I was unfamiliar with the customs, I didn't know a soul, I didn't speak French. Still, I was clearly expected, even by my acquired family members, to make good.

The first day was hell. So was the second. And so were all the days of my attendance. I was hopelessly lost, isolated, ignored. I, the winner of Hungarian prizes, the Poking star, was now the dummy. I didn't take to it well, and I didn't know what to do about it.

I also realized that I would never, ever learn to speak French. The reason was so secret that I could not have said it even to Iván, if he were there. The language, or rather the way you have to speak it, was too sexy for me. There was no matter-of-fact French for females. You had to purse your lips and catch your breath and tilt your head and make little gestures with your hands and shoulders. Regardless of what was said, there was always an undertone of "look at me, look at me." I was ugly and bloated and long-nosed and poor. I didn't want anyone to look at me.

I had to bring my lunch to school. Although I had never done this before, it represented no great culture shock. In Hungarian grade school, we used to bring our elevenses, which we ate at ten o'clock. The shock came when the girl seated next to me, who introduced herself as Yvette, gave me a sip of her drink. It was red wine mixed with water. For a panicky instant, I thought that she might be tubercular, and the drink a French version of my medicinal Tokaji. But she looked healthy. Also, I saw others drinking similarly colored liquids. I cottoned to the custom at once.

At home, as I expected, my report was met with total disbelief. "Wine in school?" Anyu asked, right eyebrow rising. "Do you think I am an idiot?"

"There is something wrong with this child," Grandmother said. "She's becoming inventive."

"Magduska, you shouldn't," Rózsi added, shaking her head. Olga and Éva looked at their shoes.

To aggravate matters, thinking of watch and wine, I burst into hysterical laughter. These people couldn't tell when I was telling the truth and when I was lying. My belly ached, and I had to gasp for air. In a senseless contagion, they all laughed with me. Finally, when the tears and hiccups around the room stopped, Mother said, "We laughed, fine. But lying is not funny."

"I am not lying," I said. "Really. You know milk is scarce. The water is not so good. They cut it with wine. It tastes better. We should all do that. Anyway, I will not go to school without it, and look different."

No one responded. In time, of course, I got my way.

In school, I could do nothing but math, at which I excelled because I was two years ahead of the class. But even with that subject I hit a snag. Evidently, the world added, subtracted, and multiplied by universal symbols, but division was another matter. I understood the problem, I did it, I presented the correct results, but I did not render it in its French form.

"*Mais non,*" Mademoiselle said. I thought one of us had to die by my hands. My wine-Yvette couldn't even do the first three operations. She kept getting *mais nons,* which I could tell depressed her. I offered to help. At first, her trust in me was minimal. But then her math performance improved, except in division. We got friendly. We strolled the schoolyard arm in arm. She taught me rudimentary French, Berlitz fashion. Table, chair, teacher, you, me. She tasted *körözött.* I tried sliced *lapin.* Had I known it was rabbit, and had I spoken French, I could have told her that in autumn, Irma used to cook rabbit stew every Thursday.

At the hotel, we ate no *lapin* or *cochon sauvage* or *cheval,* but Grandmother cooked fabulous Hungarian meals on the two little electric burners. She also gave enthusiastic cooking lessons to Éva, who was a near-perfect pupil. In the beginning, they occasionally clashed, when Éva in youthful recklessness suggested improvements on tradition. Grandmother was insulted and withdrew. Éva, not having lived with her, didn't yet know that dealing with Grandmother was like trying to caress a porcupine. But she learned, and managed with exemplary finesse, which I tried to learn.

Now that we had acquired auxiliary family members, I very much liked being home at the Magenta. Grandmother washed Rózsi's and her clothes in the sink, and Mother washed mine and hers, drying the clothes on a line strung from one wall to the other. This practice had several consequences. The climate of the room became tropical in all seasons, particularly when the evaporating moisture combined with the steam of cooking. The windows misted, our skins turned damp. As the clothes dried, the line rose a little, giving the impression of a curtain about to go up. One could imagine the promise of a performance, which, for a while, my circus mother fulfilled.

Rózsi, Éva, and the two Pistas chain-smoked. The smell of their cigarettes, combined with the smell of *gulyás,* filled the room with yet another set of atmospheric stimulants. The air we lived in was diverse and very busy.

So were we. Anyu, Rózsi, and Éva found work hemming skirts by hand for a French-Jewish clothing factory. Paid by the piece, they raced each other madly for fun, for profit, for triumph. At leisure Rózsi played solitaire. She considered the outcome of each game to be the answer to a question. The question was always the same: Will we get visas to Amerika? If the solitaire worked out, the answer was yes; if it got stuck, the answer was no. She played so seriously that each answer visibly altered her mood and her conviction regarding our prospects. As Grandmother and Éva cooked, Éva, to my delight, hummed or sang Hungarian pop songs, some written by my father. Olga massaged her belly, and begged mother to tell more circus stories. Mother knitted and sometimes obliged. Tibi gazed at Éva with such concentrated yearning that sometimes I imagined I could hear his heart cracking with the sickening sound of breaking bone.

It was into this milieu that I, in a state of inexplicable inattentiveness, invited Yvette. She was a game girl; as I threw the door open, her eyes widened, but otherwise she remained calm. *"Ici,"* I said. *"Asseyez-vous ici. Toi.* Sit here, however you say it."

She nodded. We started on math homework. In a little while, Grandmother brought a plate of Hungarian cookies and a cup of black coffee for each of us. Yvette refused the coffee, but ate several cookies. When the homework was done, she said, *"Merci,"* and shook my hand formally. *"Merci, Magda. Au revoir."*

At the door she bowed and said, *"Au revoir, merci."*

Everyone waved at her. *"Au revoir."*

We never revoired. Next day she was busy at recess, and the day after that, forever. In a few days, without my Yvette stories, my mother asked me, "What happened to your friend?"

"She had a heart attack," I replied, so fiercely that everyone stared at me and Mother dropped the subject.

Returning to school became more unbearable each day. The Yvette fiasco cast me again into the wilderness of isolation. Since I would never have another friend, there was no point to wondering, but I still worried what she had told the other girls. That I lived in a gypsy camp? That I was of the underworld? That Displaced Persons are parasitic, invisible, despicable termites?

If only I had known about them, how much solace I would have found in Erich Maria Remarque's *Arch of Triumph,* or *Down and Out in Paris and London* by George Orwell, or the movie *Casablanca.* Perspective is everything. Had I been able to see émigré life as in any way romantic, and the loss of status as independent of the loss of self, I would have been immeasurably cheered and bolstered. As it was, I compared my life to the imagined life of Yvette and of our classmates. I judged mine irreparably derailed and broken.

I suppose the adults noticed my dark despondency, because they instituted a number of restorative measures. Almost overnight, Mother knitted me a sweater in my favorite hue of red, with dark blue flowers across the front, and a big blue J-3 on my right arm. Wearing it, I walked the streets proudly, pretending to be French. The French responded. They smiled and pointed at my arm. J-3, eh? *Charmant. Oui,* J-3, I said, walking away swiftly, before the illusion of belonging shattered on the shoals of language.

Éva and Pista decided to take me to the movies every Sunday—sometimes to two movies. We ate *pommes frittes* by the expensive bagful as we waited in line. After the show, I insisted on telling them the plot, as if they had not been with me. "We just saw the same movie," Éva would tell me gently.

"I know, I know," I replied, my words pressured and urgent, "but listen to what happened next. . . ." They listened and teased me a little. None of us understood what I was doing or why. But they were not spooked, so I didn't panic. After a few weeks, the compulsion subsided. By then, I suppose, I could take in strange, continuous information and believe it without checking. Perhaps.

After one particularly oppressive school day, as I sat down for my coffee and cookies, Rózsi approached me. "Let's play girlfriends," she said.

I laughed. "What will that be? I will teach you math?"

"No," she said. "Adult girlfriends. The kind that insult each other under the guise of best intentions. You know what I mean. Like Mrs. Szabó and us, or your mother and me."

"Oh, sure," I said, envisioning at once immense possibilities and acres of supremacy. "You start," I said.

"Well, my dear," Rózsi said, "I think you ought to tie up your chin with a kerchief because its sudden fall could jolt the earth out of its orbit."

"I get it," I said, laughing. "But how will we score?"

"By satisfaction," Rózsi said, and I laughed again.

We played the game a lot, with fierce devotion. It was like the steam hole in a pressure cooker, helping me not to explode. Rózsi knew this, and she provided me with a venue.

"Dear Miss Dénes, have you been ill? You must have aged a year in the past week."

"Not at all, my dear Rózsi. It's your eyesight. Are the cataracts blinding you again?"

Once, while traveling on the metro, I started in without warning. "Those cigarettes, you know, I don't think you should continue to smoke them. Your voice is sort of—oh, I don't know. By now it can be mistaken for a trombone."

"A trombone, my dear? I have always had the voice of a flute, and I still do. Only recently the Philharmonic approached me when one of their flutes broke."

We laughed and descended to nastier depths. After many months of playing, we were by now most expert.

When the Frenchwoman sitting across from us stood to depart, she said, in Hungarian, "I have never heard such a vicious conversation between two people, particularly a child and an adult. I think it is deplorable. I think you both ought to be ashamed."

Red-faced, she left. We sat flabbergasted and laughed weakly. We never played girlfriends again.

One morning I woke with a sharp pain in my belly. I could barely stand. Anyu let me stay home, and after she helped me limp to the Magenta, I had a marvelous pampered day in Rózsi's bed. The next two days I went to school, physically fine. On the fourth day, I vomited, and was sent home. As soon as I arrived, I threw up again. "We have to call a doctor," Mother said, "but how?"

"Let's phone the Joint," Éva suggested. "They must have arrangements for emergencies."

"I don't know how to use the French phones," Mother said, close to tears.

"I do," Éva said.

In a few hours, I was in the office of a doctor who diagnosed appendicitis, not acute; time enough to go to the hospital tomorrow.

We arrived the next day in the late afternoon. The ward to which we were ushered was long, very clean, and murmurously quiet, with twenty beds, ten on each side. One was empty. A tall, perky, black-haired, green-eyed nurse met us at the door and pointed to it. *"Pour toi,"* she said, and smiled, flashing movie-bright teeth.

"What is she?" I asked.

But Rózsi and Mother shushed me. "Don't start," Rózsi said. "You need her."

A young, pale woman to the left of us sat up in her bed. "Actually, that is a very good question," she said in Hungarian. "I have been trying to figure out the answer for the past two weeks."

My heart leapt. A smart Hungarian next to me! What crazy luck. Thank you, God.

"Oh, you are Hungarian!" Mother said. No, she's a Hungarian-speaking Hottentot, I wanted to say, but kept quiet. I needed all of them.

"Yes," said the woman, leaning back on her pillows and closing her eyes. She was a person after my own heart.

Mother and Rózsi handed me my overnight bag, kissed me,

and left me in the woman's absent charge. "Be brave," Mother said.

"There is nothing to be brave about," Rózsi said, and made a funny face. I waved.

As soon as they were gone, I cleared my throat. The woman opened her eyes and sat up again.

"What's your name?" she asked.

"I am Magda Dènes," I said, standing up.

"Oh, sit down, for heaven's sake. You probably went to school at the English Ladies', right?"

"No. I would have, but I couldn't because of the government, and because we no longer had the money." I stopped, astonished at myself. It was the most true information I had given anyone in at least five years.

"An old story," she said. "Are you scared now?"

I swallowed a few times. "No, I am not scared," I said firmly. Then I added, "Yes, I am."

"What have you got?"

"Appendicitis."

"It's a breeze. I'm going to sleep now."

"Good night."

Just then, our nurse reappeared. She gave my new mate's face a few light slaps. *"Pas dormer,"* she said. "I told you not in the afternoon. Then there will be no begging for sleeping pills at night, which I won't give you anyway." I got this in translation. To me, again translated, the nurse said, "Undress. Get into your pajamas. The sheets from the laundry will be up soon, and I will make your bed."

Many hours later, when my bed was finally made and I got into it, the sheets were damp. This was a nightmare threat of my Szani childhood: The next level of punishment after eating your own vomit was to be wrapped in wet sheets overnight. One or the other, but certainly the two combined, was thought to improve character unfailingly and thereafter turn the culprit into a compliant and contributory citizen.

I cleared my throat. My mate sat up. "What is it now?" she asked.

"I beg your pardon. What is your name?"

"Call me Kati."

"Kati," I said, "my sheets are wet, and I haven't done anything." I burst into tears.

Kati rang for the nurse. Five minutes later, she rang again. In five more minutes, we both rang. At last our angel of mercy arrived. "It will dry as you lie in it," Kati said she said. There was a further exchange. "She says the ones folded in the cabinet are probably wetter still than yours, so there is nothing she can do."

"What should I do?"

"Ignore it," Kati said. "Pretend the sheets are dry." I did just that, and never forgave myself. One should adjust to the unalterable, yes. But with regard to the bad alterable, one should always make a fuss, a scene. Object. Create chaos. Rain anarchy. Reign.

Next morning I was walked to surgery by a different nurse. She told me to strip, and after I did, told me she couldn't find a dry robe, and shoved me into the OR stark naked. Instinctively, I stood like a celebrated ancient *Venus pudica*, my right arm covering my breasts, my left hand over my pubis, stunned by this sudden, intrusive brutality. I didn't cry, because I knew that weakness begets further punishment, but I could not stop myself from shaking.

"Qu'elle est belle!" someone said. *"Mais elle est très jolie et si jeune et si épouvantée. C'est très douce."*

I closed my eyes. I was in hell alone. Not even the devil for company. That's what I had gotten wrong. I always thought hell would be a dialogue with the devil. Could I wake up or fly away?

Someone took me by the shoulders, a man in a mask. "Not be afraid," he said in broken Hungarian. "I Magyar. I take care. Bad sin, no robe. I put blanket. I doctor to sleep."

"Thank you," I said.

"Lie down," he said.

I climbed on the table. To my immense gratitude, he immediately covered me. "Better?" he asked. I nodded. "Not be afraid," he said again. "I mask, you breathe. I look out. You all right. I promise."

I nodded. "*Köszönöm. Merci.*"

Lying on a large green leaf, I am twirling around and around in a lily pond. Five lilies with bobbing heads and huge insect eyes look down on me. They are speaking to each other in melodic, melancholy gibberish. Finally I catch a word. *Kész.* "*Kész?*" I repeat. "*Oui,*" someone says, "*kész. Fini.*"

It took hours until I knew who and where I was. Back in my bed, I fell asleep again, and didn't know that Mother and Rózsi visited. When I woke, I wept.

"What now?" Kati said, sounding most exasperated.

My mother," I said. "My mother. She never even came."

"Of course she came. Your aunt, too. They didn't want to wake you. They left you some candy. Look at your night table."

Oh yes, candy. Left by my aunt and mother, willing to break any rules except those regarding hospital visiting hours. Why couldn't they have waited until I woke up?

"Please take some," I said to Kati, offering her the bag. "Please take some as a favor."

She took several and smiled. "You are a weird kid," she said. "I'm going to sleep now. If our angel of mercy comes to slap me, kick her first."

"Oh, absolutely," I said. "I will, I will." And I would have, absolutely, except that in a few minutes I felt something warm and sticky spreading around my thighs. "Kati," I stage-whispered, "I think my wound has opened and I'm bleeding to death."

"Oh, God," Kati said, propping herself on an elbow. "Did I say you were cute? No? Good, because you're not. What makes you think your wound has opened? Have you looked? Are the bandages red?"

"I'm afraid to look alone," I said, hating myself for sounding pathetic.

Kati got up and pulled back my covers. "You got your period," she said. "Otherwise you're fine. You are not bleeding to death."

"I got my what?"

"You are menstruating."

"Oh. What do I do?"

"Call the nurse."

When she arrived, mercy-nurse went insane with pleasure. "*Ah, qu'elle est belle, qu'elle est bonne, qu'elle est extraordinaire. On my watch, a woman emerged.*" She kissed me on both cheeks and brought me a lot of cotton to put between my legs.

"What does this mean?" I asked Kati.

"Not much," she said. "When you have to walk around, you put cotton in your panties, and that will absorb the blood. When the cotton is saturated, you throw it away and put in new cotton."

"For how long?"

"Three days, five days—it depends."

"And you bleed all the time?"

"Well, pretty much."

"And you don't die of it?"

"No. Not anyone so far."

I was discharged in three weeks, long after I'd recovered. Back at the Magenta, I milked the drama of my surgery to the hilt. I complained of phantom pains, and when I walked, I pressed a little pillow against my belly, claiming that without it, I would faint and my insides would extrude.

They put up with me for a week. Then Mother said, "Enough!"

I knew it was enough. This was not a defensible position. So I changed tactics. I went on strike. At one late-morning breakfast, when everyone was present, except the two Pistas, I announced, "I am not going back to school. No matter what. I just can't. I learn nothing there. I do nothing. I sit all day in nothingness, alone."

"You think you're so smart you no longer need schooling?" Mother asked with dripping sarcasm.

Éva interrupted. "I don't think that's what Magda said. I am sorry to interfere. But I think Magda is a very conscientious student. This school just doesn't suit her."

"That's what I said," I promptly agreed.

"Doesn't suit her?" Mother repeated. "What else is there? In France, you go to a French school."

"Not necessarily," said Olga, speaking up for the first time since I had known her. "Pista told me there is a Hungarian school in Paris. He said if we got stuck here, we would send our child there when the time came."

We all turned to her. "What school? Where is it?" Anyu asked.

"We'd better wait for Pista," Olga said. "Sometimes I get things a little mixed up."

When he arrived in the evening, we pounced on Pista. "What do you know about the Hungarian school? Where is it? What does it take to get in?" We questioned him at machine-gun speed.

"Just a minute," he said, holding us back with his palms held forward and high. "I don't know that much about it. I know it starts in the afternoon, and the instruction is in Hungarian. That's it. That's all the fellow told me."

The Hungarian school was several metro stops away. It started in the afternoon, after the French schools let out. My classmates, born in France, were the progeny of working-class immigrants whose Hungarian patriotism propelled them to coop up their girls an additional three hours every weekday to learn the heritage of their parents and perfect their language. They were all good Catholics, and many of them wore large crosses around their necks. The faculty were of the same ilk.

Within three afternoons, all the dams of my enraged spirit broke, and I began a wild rampage. Obviously, in this school, I was the queen of language. No one spoke Hungarian as well as I did, not even many of the teachers. I spoke out of turn, I interfered, corrected, baited, pounced, argued, and mocked with insolent, relentless abandon. Pity the child who innocently asked whether I had done my homework. Instead of stooping to answer, I would correct her grammar and explain that I didn't need to do the type of homework we were given at this school, because I knew the answers by heart. I made it known that I was better educated than the others, and that I could with rage, but with minimal effort, flatten anyone in any subject. My knowledge was a snare, my tongue a sword. I drew blood with it, and the taste sent me into the feeding frenzy of a crocodile. I was a hungry menace. I wanted to chew to pieces the whole Hungarian world, throw it up in vomit, spread it over the country, until nothing grew there, until there wasn't a single young man left. That is what I wanted. Then, instead of calling it Hungary, we would call it Iván-Ervin Land, this desert, this nothing. Let the Hungarians partake of the legacy they left me.

I had no doubt that my behavior was inexcusably bad and unfair. These particular people had done nothing. Still, I made at least one of them cry almost every day. I didn't cry. I felt light-headed, sick at heart, and disgusted with myself. To say that I couldn't stop was not exactly true. I didn't try. I wanted to be God's whip, wreaking havoc on the enemy.

One day Mademoiselle Rosé took me aside. She, too, wore a cross, but I knew, through years of trained watchfulness, that her name until not too long ago must have been Rosenbaum or Rosenbloom. Also, she had given herself away to me by trying to protect me, softening my transgressions in front of the others. I hoped against hope that she bore news of my expulsion. "My dear," she said in Hungarian, "you are so smart, so well educated. Why do you provoke the entire school to hate you? You must stop the meanness and the sarcasm. Don't you want to get along? Don't you want to be liked?"

I looked at her as if she were insane. "No, Mademoiselle Rosé," I said. "I don't want to be liked, and I definitely don't want to get along. You know what I want? I want to give them good reasons to hate me. I don't want to be shunned because

I am a Jew. I want to be despised because I am beating the hell out of them. And one more thing: I want to be feared instead of fearing. Mademoiselle Rosé, I think you too would be better off . . ." I stopped abruptly. The last sentence had slipped out in the heat of my declaration. "I am sorry," I said. "I speak only for myself. The rest is none of my business. I apologize."

Mademoiselle nodded, but said nothing. She looked sad, and slightly flushed.

"May I please go now?" I asked. Wordlessly, she nodded again.

At home I told no one of the incident. Still, during the evening both Anyu and Rózsi asked me at different times, "Did something happen at school, or on the metro?"

"No, nothing. Nothing happened anywhere."

Very soon, my predicament as guilt-assailed avenger was resolved. The UNRRA notified the Joint, which sent a messenger with the news. Our Cuban visas had been granted. We were to leave Paris in three days and go by train to Bilbao, from where we would sail to Havana.

Being a wandering Jew had its advantages. Just as things got too tight for me, we moved. The only music I had to face was internal. But then again, my musicians took no rest. They knew no seasons, no moon from sun. They just kept playing, on and on.

The car on the Bilbao train was a normal third-class carriage. It was not designed for Displaced Persons, and it had no guides from the Joint. For the first time in over eighteen months, we were traveling as ordinary civilians, indistinguishable from the rest of the population. It was May. I felt ungratefully glad to leave Paris behind.

"So," I asked Rózsi, "did your solitaire games foretell this trip? In total, did you get more yeses than nos?"

"I don't know," Rózsi replied ruefully. "I should have kept a record."

"Yes, what a pity," I said. "With two effortless columns of checkmarks, we could have gathered evidence. If the answer was yes, we could have become fortune-tellers.

"We could lie about it," Rózsi said.

"Don't say such things to the child," my mother said primly, wakened from her dozing. Rózsi and I laughed. My mother somehow never caught on that Rózsi and I had conversations as a game. Nothing we said was meant, or referred to anything outside the dialogue. It was a poor child's entertainment, requiring no props. It was also our gentler version of girl-friends, which, after the metro incident, we continued not to play in unspoken consent.

Spain was many degrees warmer than France, we realized as soon as we stepped off the train in Bilbao. A salty, exciting smell of the sea floated in the air. I was very eager to remeet the ocean, which I had not seen since I was three and which I didn't remember.

We searched for our guide, who was not there. Gripped and curious, we walked away from the station, planning to return shortly. Almost immediately, we came upon the edge of a market.

We didn't quite dare to venture in, but at its outskirts we saw a grocery stall, with oranges piled high outside. We had not seen oranges in years. Mother, who imagined that through some blessed chosenness I spoke every language on earth, said, "Here is some Spanish money I got from the Joint. Go in and buy four oranges, one for each of us."

I went in, and with my incredible language skills, I pointed to the oranges, held up four fingers, and showed them my money. The shopkeeper twirled a newspaper into a cone, dropped in four oranges, took my money, and gave me change. I walked out, yet again proving to my mother my extraterrestrial endowment in communication.

She counted the change and said, "Go back, they gave you too much."

My mouth fell open. Rózsi looked at her and said, "Have you gone insane?"

"No," my mother said, adamant and irate. "No. We are starting a new life. The old habits of war must end now. They must end. We can no longer live like savages. This is where we begin again. I think she got too much change."

"How can you even know that?" Rózsi asked.

"I am going by the French-Spanish exchange rate," Mother said. To me, she said, "Go back. Tell them."

Yeah, tell them. I went back, showed them the oranges, and pointed to the money. They didn't get the picture. I said, *"Très beaucoup, thès beaucoup,"* in French. They looked at me blankly. I said, *"Sehr viel, sehr viel,"* in German. They shrugged. I said, *"Túl sok, túl sok,"* in Hungarian.

Someone from the back of the store answered in Hungarian, "Not at all. In fact, this store is greatly overpriced." It was a young man standing on a ladder in the back, arranging merchandise.

I started to laugh. "You are Hungarian," I said.

He said, "I don't know how you were able to guess. They overcharged you. Go away."

I put away the money and left. I didn't inform Mother of the exchange. I simply said, "No, they charged it right." I didn't want to disappoint her. A new world, new habits, a return to honesty, a return to normalcy. What naiveté, and what dog shit.

As we walked farther into the marketplace, our Zionist guide ran after us. "Hey, hey," he yelled in Yiddish. "Are you the four I am supposed to meet? Sorry I am late." We said it was all right. He said, "You want to walk around in the market? I can wait here at the edge. Go ahead." He lit a cigarette and leaned against a stall. We were glad of the conferred freedom.

As we walked on, we could see that whereas the four oranges had cost me thirty centavos, here for five centavos you could get a dozen oranges. Rózsi pointed it out to Mother. "Margit. New leaf? New honesty? New standards? Five cents for a dozen. Get it?"

My mother shrugged. "I think we should change anyway. Go back to normal."

"Yeah," said Rózsi, "I agree. But can you make the world go back to normal? Or for that matter, was it ever normal?" Mother shrugged again. We walked on.

The colors of the market were unbelievably beautiful. Yellow bananas, and yellow lemons tinged with green, and greener limes, and deep green spinach, and lettuce in rainbow greens. Red tomatoes, purple eggplants, pale gray mushrooms. The palette of God was more various and cheering than any painter's work. And so it should be, if He existed. Oh God. One of these days I would really make Him mad. Sir, the previous "Oh God" was a matter of habitual exclamation, not an address. Please. Thank you. Where did I stand on this issue anyway? Did I have to resolve this in a Spanish market, after a long journey?

We wanted to buy everything, but of course we bought nothing. What would be the use? We were going to a hotel, and everything would rot. Rózsi the profligate said, "Come on, Margit. Let's buy a dozen oranges for five centavos. We'll have sixteen. So what? We can squeeze them into our bath-water."

"Go ahead," Mother said.

"Yes, go ahead," I said. Even Grandmother said yes.

The market had no ration cards, and everything was available at almost no cost. Perhaps I'm dreaming, I thought. But then I thought, How could I, *I,* have such an expansive dream? From the corner of my eye, I spotted something. What was that? Grapes? Grapes. I turned to my mother. "That's grapes, right? Is that its name?"

Anyu sighed. "You want some?"

"Oh, no, no," I said. "No, I didn't mean that. I just forgot the name."

The guide whistled for us. We trooped back. "We have to go," he said. He drove us to our hotel, a better hotel than any we had stayed in since we left Budapest. We got two rooms adjoining, and private bathrooms, as in the Hotel Gambetta. I asked no questions; I waited for no permission. I ran the tub and stepped into it. After me, the deluge. When I was done, ah, there were towels. Half a dozen large, soft, fuzzy towels. I used three. What a fabulous day. Also, a day of surprise. I mostly thought that talking, reading, and writing were the important things of the world, especially talking, if you had the proper person to talk with. My remaining family were not terrific at it, but Éva and hospital Kati were. Iván, of course, was the best. Talking keeps at bay many savage demons. But today I had seen something new, something no one had taught me. Smells and colors and the texture of things are also bulwarks against the encroaching dark.

Scrubbed clean and smelling fine from real soap, we sat around waiting for the dinner that we were told would be served in our room. Within minutes, a knock sounded at the door. A waiter appeared, gliding a table set with a heavy white tablecloth, linen napkins, porcelain plates, crystal glasses, and silverware. Oh, my, I thought. What a good thing it is to emigrate to Cuba!

Next he brought a very large basket filled with various kinds of hot rolls and breads, and a plate with a large slab of butter. At the center of the table he placed a tray filled with salami, ham, sausages, various cheeses, olives, tomatoes, pickles, and green peppers, all beautifully arranged. As he left, he said something we didn't understand. Probably *bon appétit.* Motionless, we stared. The table was a work of art. We ate well, carefully, with delight, fair to each other, until the last morsel was gone. We drank the soda water supplied with the meal. We had a very good time. "I am full. Are you full?" I asked Anyu.

"Yes," she said.

"So am I," said Rózsi.

"Me, I am more than full," said Grandmother.

Based on the look of the market, we had expected more, it is true. But in fact what we had had was enough. A little less than plentiful, but quite sufficient.

Someone knocked on the door. It was the waiter. He took everything away, but left the door open. He wheeled in a little cart with a soup tureen and four soup plates. He set the plates before us, and served the soup. He also brought us another basket of bread. When he left, we burst into laughter. Stupid

Spaniards! We laughed very hard. Stupid, dumb Spaniards. They serve soup after they serve dinner!

"I wonder if it's really the custom," Rózsi said.

"No," I said, "he probably just forgot. He forgot to serve the soup, and then he figured instead of wasting it or getting reprimanded, he'd serve it as an afterthought."

"All right, let's try it," my mother said.

We all tasted a bit. Actually, it was very good—a kind of bean soup, not Hungarian, but good.

"Ah, what the hell, let's eat it," Rózsi said. "Our stomachs won't know the reverse order."

We ate in high humor, laughing indulgently at these strange customs or this foolish waiter's error.

The knock sounded again. The waiter retrieved the plates, and the soup tureen. We wanted to tease him about his error, but of course we didn't speak Spanish. Again he left the door open, and reappeared with a large tray of roasted chickens, home-fried potatoes, tomato salad, and spinach on the side. He gave us fresh plates and fresh knives and forks and left.

We looked at each other. Rózsi was the first one to burst into tears. "Oh, my God," she said. "This was a four-course dinner. The first tray was the appetizer. There was no mistake. We made the mistake. Now it's too late. I'm too full to eat the chicken. I'm too full to eat anything. The cold cuts and the cheeses we could have kept for tomorrow. We could have started with the soup, and we could have eaten the chicken. And the potatoes and the spinach and the salad. As it is, we can't keep them and we can't eat them."

Grandmother sounded teary, too. "Why didn't they tell us?" she asked.

I got angry. "Don't they know where we come from?" I said. "Why didn't someone warn us?"

There was nothing to do. We couldn't eat any more, although Mother cut the chicken and we each tasted it. It was excellent, but it stayed on the tray. We tasted a little spinach, too. It was wonderful, but it stayed in the bowl. Everything was good, and we couldn't eat another morsel.

Why this event occasioned the despair it did, since our bellies were full, I didn't quite understand. But we were despairing. Somehow, the cumulative burden of our many hungers was subsumed into the metaphor of this one meal. I was crying, too, not because of what I had just missed, but for the meals uneaten by Iván and Ervin, which they would never be able to make up. Never again would they have a four-course dinner. From the looks of this one, I would have many. That's why I cried. I wasn't sure why the rest of them cried. We didn't share information, only the handkerchief, which we passed around because we only had one.

Dessert also came, rich, elaborate profiteroles in chocolate sauce, beautiful but anticlimactic. We already knew Spain was choking with food. No longer curious, we tasted it as spoilers. It was incomprehensible that just four train-ride hours away, people were on ration cards, that eight hours away, they stood in line for slop at communal kitchens. Who was the architect of this order, this disorder?

In the morning, the Joint guide gave us some more money, and told us we were free until five in the evening, at which time he would take us to our ship, the *Magellan*. I had hoped it would be the *Niña*, the *Pinta*, or the *Santa María*. I voiced this to the adults, who looked at me blankly. Where the hell was my brother?

We left Grandmother in the room to rest while the three of us strolled around Bilbao, a shimmering port city of colors and smells and noisy, vibrant life on the streets. For the first time in long years, we saw shops filled with merchandise. Mostly cheap goods, but after the deprivations of war, the ecstatic joy of sheer quantity far outshone quality considerations.

I wanted to return to the market, but I was embarrassed to say so. They would never understand that I wanted to say goodbye again to Teleki Tér, if only in its shinier, approximate effigy.

We stopped at a store that had a tray of sunglasses outside its windows. I looked at them covetously. "You may pick one," Mother told me.

"No thank you," I said. They probably cost too much. I didn't want her to spend our money, although ever since I started going to the movies with Éva and Pista, sunglasses had become one of the three items in the world I most wanted to own. The other two were a macintosh and a fedora.

"Go ahead," Rózsi said. "Half of it is my gift."

Delighted, I nodded and kissed them both. Picking was hard. I liked a pair with big white frames. On the other hand, white would never go with misty macintosh autumn afternoons. Still, we were headed toward sunshine. What to do? Perhaps choicelessness is not as bad a state as I had always thought. It saves you from conflict. Or perhaps all states and choices cost something.

"Come on!" Mother interrupted my musings. "We can't stand here all day."

"I don't know," I said. "Which pair would you take?"

"It's your decision," Mother said, withdrawing.

"I would pick the first one I fell in love with," Rózsi said.

The white frames covered half my face, which I regarded as a bonus.

At five, as agreed, our guide arrived at the hotel. We and three other people, a Romanian couple and a Polish man, waited for him in the lobby. To the sea, to the sea, he said, swaying slightly. Grandmother translated tersely: "He is drunk."

We rode through increasingly neglected streets, until at last we reached the edge of the sea. As we got out of the car, the guide pointed to a structure twice the length of Teleki Tér 5, and a little taller. "This is your boat," he said.

The behemoth obscured the ocean entirely. All I saw of water was little waves tossing debris at its side below dock level. Men carried various-sized crates up the gangplank, hoisting them onto their backs. They grunted and yelled at each other as they struggled. Some of them had long lit cigars stuck in the corners of their mouths. Some wore shirts without sleeves, and even from a distance I could see large drops of sweat on their shoulders. A big metal machine with a huge oscillating forked tongue also loaded between boat and quay, merchandise too heavy for humans to budge. The machine screeched, men shouted, the behemoth emitted loud rumbling sounds and occasional shrill whistles. People rushed around carrying their luggage, or looking for it. Some greeted each other with shrieks of delight, while others said goodbye tearfully.

The chaos of the scene stirred a small, slow tremor in my heart that gained momentum with the force of an avalanche, until I started to shake violently and my teeth locked.

"What's the matter with you?" Mother asked, looking terrified. "What's wrong?"

"I don't know," I whispered through my teeth. "I can't stop."

Grandmother looked at me and half screamed. "*Shema Yis-rael!* The child has St. Vitus' dance!"

"What are you doing?" Rózsi asked sharply, fear as usual turning to anger in her.

"I don't know," I whispered again, but even as I said it, I began to catch a glimmer. I had shaken like this in the dirty men's toilet in Teleki Tér when the Nyilas were looking for us. Perhaps the chaos on the quay propelled me back to those times. Or to that first day of chaos after the liberation when we ventured to the streets. How strange. I reacted without remembering.

As I was thinking this, I gradually calmed down, until I could open my mouth and say, "I'm all right. I don't know what happened. It must have been something I ate, or perhaps the sun." I felt like crying.

By now the ship was almost fully loaded, and the passengers became visibly more restless. There was more pacing, more looking at watches; more passing officials were stopped with questions.

Some people, however, had been allowed to board as soon as they arrived. They all seemed to be well dressed, and to have a great deal of baggage. They stepped out of their cars or taxis, porters grabbed their belongings, and one official or another helped them go up the stairs that led to the ship's uppermost deck.

"Who are they?" I asked my mother.

"First-class passengers," she said. "They have the most expensive tickets. They have private cabins with windows, and private baths."

"Where will we travel?"

"At the darkest bottom," mother replied bitterly. "In steerage. Same level as the cargo."

"Will we ever see light?" I asked, getting nervous.

"Probably. We can't go three weeks without fresh air."

After the second-class passengers had also boarded, our group was finally called. We ascended the stairs, each of us carrying our single piece of permitted luggage. Except for Grandmother, whose suitcase Rózsi carried, while Anyu and I helped her walk.

Stepping on deck, we were asked again to show our tickets and passports. The officer in charge looked up sharply as Rózsi presented her UNRRA-issued little pink parody of a passport, wherein she was officially identified as a Displaced Person. He said something fast to a sailor, who carried the message to the captain, seated in a high deck chair several yards away. He, too, looked at us, but I was unable to see behind his face.

As we waited in line to be greeted by him, Mother whispered urgently into my ear, "Magduska, it's up to you."

"What is?"

"I just remembered that not only will we travel at the bottom, we will also be put in the same dormitory with all these people," she said.

This was shocking, very unpleasant news indeed. "No separate quarters for families?" I asked.

"No. You must beg the captain."

"What do you mean?" I asked, but I knew. Here came a task again, the end result of which I, too, desperately wanted. But I knew the execution was beyond my power. I was too young, too small, too resourceless. This should not be my burden.

"You must beg him," Anyu repeated heatedly. "Only you can do it."

"You are crazy," Rózsi whispered to Mother.

"No, I am not," Mother said. "She can do it."

I was next in line, and I stepped forward to be blessed. As far as I could see, that was all the captain had been doing so far. As each steerage passenger reached him, he raised his right arm in a combination gesture of salute, benediction, and dismissal. The passengers nodded and proceeded toward a door that swallowed them.

I stopped. "Señor," I said, looking straight into his eyes. "Señor Captain."

He looked back at me, astonished. "Capitán," he said, correcting me automatically.

"*Sí—Capitán. Señor Capitán, gracias,*" I said, mixing up the words I learned at the market for "please" and "thank you."

"Por qué?" he asked.

"*Capitán,*" I said, "*s'il vous plaît—un chambre pour le quatre. Por mon famille.*"

"*No hablo francés,*" he said, smiling. Then, pointing toward the others, he said, "*Su familia.*"

"*Sí, Señor Capitán.*" He started to laugh. Encouraged, I began again. "*Bitte schön, eine zimmer.*" I held up my forefinger. "*Eine—zum die vier.*" I held up four fingers and pointed toward my relatives; then I pointed downward.

He laughed. "*No hablo alemán,*" he said.

I was near tears. He saw it and called over the passport checker. "*Was wollen Sie?*" the man asked me.

"*Ein zimmer, bitte schön. Zum die vier. Meine Grossmutti ist sehr krank und alt. Sie musst eine zimmer haben, ohne l'étranger.*" I was mixing things up again, so I stopped in utter defeat.

The man translated, and he and the captain exchanged some words. "*Sí, bien,*" the captain said. To me he said, "*Sí. Puede*

tener su cuarto, señorita. "He laughed. *"Qué muchacha."*
Mother, who had understood the outcome, whispered,
"Kiss his hand."

"No."

She insisted, her breath hot on my ear. "Kiss his hand."
I offered my hand. He shook it. Against my entire nature,
all my better judgment, and with burning rancor until the
grave, I grabbed his hand and kissed it.

"Ay, señorita!" he said. *"No, no, no. No es necesario. Por
favor! Ay, por Dios."* He felt almost as bad as I did. He understood me. He knew, I hope he knew, he must have known,
that kissing hands was not my way. I was forced.

For the rest of the evening, I refused to speak to my mother.

After walking down steep stairs for more minutes than it
took at Teleki Tér to reach from fifth floor to street level, we
arrived at our cabin. It was a room with four bunks for eight
people. Probably for the sailors, because it doubled as the storage room for linen. There was a basin large enough to wash
ourselves in careful segments from head to toe, eliminating
our need for the communal shower.

Towels we had by the hundreds, and a tight little toilet
behind a door. It was an entirely livable arrangement, win-
dowless but airy, at sea level but spacious. No one said thank
you to me.

The next morning at breakfast, we discovered that the captain had also arranged a separate table for us.

By eleven a.m., we had docked at San Sebastián. "We have
traveled backward overnight," Mother said. "In the opposite
direction to where we are going. I wonder why. Magduska, go
find out."

I looked at her with my father's eyes. I shook my head very

slowly, once in each direction. I didn't take my eyes off her. I had seen my father do this, and imitating him, I understood the rage and power the gesture conveyed. Could he have been right sometimes? I felt faint with the treachery of the question.

Mother jumped up. "I will go ask," she said, all bustle and light. When she returned, she said, "It's just a little detour to pick up cargo. By tomorrow, we'll be in Vigo, which is on our way. Let's go see the city."

San Sebastián looked like a debonair English lord. It was tight-lipped, haughty, and elegant. I wondered why they didn't stop DPs at its entrance gate. The waiter at the café where we ate lunch looked so disgusted with us that his contempt dripped onto my food and made it inedible. An expensive city, far more than Bilbao. To make matters worse, we passed a girls' school as it was letting out. Their skirts were at mid-calf; mine, in Parisian chic, was above my knee. They pointed and whinnied and commented to each other behind hand-hidden mouths. Mother stopped. "How rude!" she said.

"Let's just walk on," I said, donning my sunglasses.

When we got back to the ship, Mother said, "We have three more stops—two in Spain, one in Portugal. If you want me to, I could let your skirt down. Just in case."

I stayed silent. She had a point. Did she think it was a point, or did she just want to make up? I didn't know.

After a while she turned to Rózsi. "So what do you think?" she asked.

Rózsi shrugged. "It's not a matter of skirt length," she said. I hoped she would add something, but she didn't.

"No," I said, making up my mind. "Don't bother. I've put up with worse. Thank you anyway." We didn't kiss or hug.

Whatever it was, gambit or goodwill, it did not appease me.

Vigo was a comfortable fisherman's town, where I wanted to take off my shoes and socks to walk in the sand by the sea, as I saw the local children doing. Mother wouldn't let me. I protested, but secretly I agreed. Penniless and unprotected, you can't take chances in a strange land—or anywhere else.

The following morning we docked in Lisbon, city of my heart. I fell in love, love as unreasonable, as inexplicable, as that emotion always is. Why white Lisbon? I don't know. I just felt I had been there before. Perhaps a very long time ago, before souls had memory.

We walked around, we gawked and gaped. Lisbon was too civilized to take notice of us. I promised myself to return someday in the cloak of empress.

Cádiz next, a port city across from Africa, dirty and dangerous. As we bargained in the market for a thin blue enamel bracelet for me, a man sneaked up behind me and pulled at my braids until my head snapped back. I screamed in astonished pain. Rózsi, hearing me, hit him with her pocketbook, hard enough to make him run away. Enraged, she took off after him. We ran after Rózsi in panic, yelling, "Stop! Stop! He may have a knife!"

Two more nights and days, and we were sailing the open sea. This was not an event that needed announcing. We began to vomit with baroque extravagance. We threw up in chamber arrangements of quartets, trios, duos, and solos. The toilet was never empty, and it was never clean. This produced vomit on vomit in rich design, which induced further vomiting.

Once, in the bathroom, Rózsi said to me, "You know, I'd rather be dead than go through this. It's too awful."

"Not me," I said. "This is not the time. I'll recognize when the time to be dead comes. If you want me to, I'll tell you, because I will know."

"Please don't start with your philosophical conversations," she said. "I have a pounding headache. Please shut up."

"Well, fine. I was just offering."

"Please," she said. We both vomited again.

Finally, one morning, pale and shaken, ill and tremorous, we dared breakfast. It tasted good, and it stayed down. We went on deck—the lowest deck, to be sure, but with the same air and the same horizon that existed above.

I didn't like life on the ship. It reminded me of the Szani, except, of course, I wasn't alone, and there was no tormenting Dóra neni. But the spirit of the two places was the same. I felt trapped, claustrophobic, headachy. There was nothing to do and nowhere to go. I took ridiculous little constitutionals from one end of the boat to the other. I counted my steps, and deliberately angered myself by coming out with a different sum in the two directions. I sat in a deck chair and watched the view, which, although in perpetual motion, was as boring as a mountain. Hour after hour it was the same, changing only by degrees of light. Nature is fine, but I was a city child. A boulevard café was not boring. Lonely, yes, often; sometimes discomfiting in its grandness, but never boring.

I also hated communal living. The recurrence of the same unwanted faces day after day drove me crazy. To shut them out, I tried to wear my sunglasses indoors, but Mother forbade it. She said I looked peculiar, God forbid.

We all hid behind our Hungarian, which no one else spoke. We stayed away from the other steerage passengers by pretending not to understand them when they spoke to us. We fooled no one. After a while, we acquired a shield around us, composed of their collective reproachful glances.

The only one who made a friend was Grandmother. One day as she sat on deck, an old Spanish lady dressed in black lace sat down next to her. At first, and for a long time, they both stared out to sea. Eventually they began to talk, and arranged to meet in the afternoons. Grandmother reported to us every night. The lady was widowed. She had four children, two sons and two daughters, and fourteen grandchildren, although one daughter had only one child, which was a cause of pain for the lady.

"How do you talk to each other?" Rózsi asked.

"I don't know," Grandmother said. "I really don't know. But I told her about your father, and about Iván and Ervin and hiding in the basement. And she told me that she comes from the country, and the war wasn't very bad, although the Germans, I think it was the Germans, anyway somebody took away their cows, and some of their pigs, but they hid the chickens. She had a hard time."

"Do you know how old she is?" Rozsi asked.

"Yes, she's seventy."

"How do you know?"

"She showed me a seven and a zero."

"Do you know her name?"

"Of course. Her name is María. She knows my name, too. Emma."

The friendship proceeded beautifully. Occasionally they cried together a little, and patted each other's shoulders. When the lady disembarked in New York, Grandmother was truly sad. She aged a lot on that trip. She looked bent and permanently startled.

One morning when I woke, I realized that the boat's forward motion had stopped. We were rocking in place from side to side. I heard the loud whine of machinery, heavy banging, and men shouting in yet another strange language. We must be in New York! The thought made me sit upright in my berth. I am in Amerika! I felt like weeping at the enormity of this fact. Amerika, the fabled, the mythic, the coveted. At last, Amerika. The knowledge that we had no visas, and therefore would not be allowed to set foot on land, dampened my enthusiasm only a little.

The four of us dressed like demons, skipped breakfast, and rushed topside. Today even steerage passengers were allowed to go to the highest deck. Amerika lay across a river, and it was . . . tall. These were not towers like the Eiffel; these were regular buildings, blocks long, turned upright. The tops of some of them were obscured by clouds.

"Is it a trick of light?" I asked my mother breathlessly. "Is it a mirage?"

"No," she laughed. "They are called skyscrapers. They are so tall they touch the sky." I had heard the word before, but I thought it was an allegorical expression. I had never actually visualized what the word might mean.

"Are there streets between them where you can walk and look up?"

"There must be," my mother said, annoyed, as she always was when she didn't know the answer to my question.

I stuck to the railing for hours. Why would any American write *The Wizard of Oz?* I wondered. This was Oz. But better, because it was real. If it was real.

"I think I'll go down to step on Amerikan soil," I said to Mother and Rózsi.

"You can't," Rózsi said.

Mother gasped. "They will stop you. Maybe they will even arrest you."

"Have I not lived for years with false papers? Am I not a trained prestidigitator?" I asked. "Here is the red, there is the red; now you see it, now you don't? I know how to get away with things. Just don't interfere."

I seemed to have touched in them some store of uncharacteristic mischief. They started to laugh. "Try it," Rózsi said.

"Don't wander far," my mother added.

They kept on laughing with a vitality I had not heard from them in years.

I walked to the gangplank, two stories below, and put a hand on the pile of luggage a stevedore was carrying. Step by step, I followed him out. No one stopped me. On the ground, I walked this way and that, not looking up. Hey, Amerika, forbidden or not, I'm standing on you. I am here, I am me, I am Magda, Magda in Amerika! Hey!

Around a corner, I noticed, to my horror, a sign which said "Exit," a word I knew. It meant I could walk out of there. Just like that. Free in Amerika, alone in New York. Oh my God! I backed away and rushed to the landing in front of the boat. To save face, I started shouting in Hungarian, "Anyu, Anyu, where should I go now?"

As I expected, I was converged upon by various serious-looking men in tight little hats. "Up, up, dammit!" is what I thought they said. Their annoyance and angry gestures transcended language.

"Well," said Rózsi, when I reached them at last, "you almost became an Amerikan citizen."

"Definitely," I said. "I just didn't want to abandon you."

Next day was visiting day. Friends and relatives with previously cleared identification were allowed to board ship and bring gifts. Laci and Pali arrived with their wives, Rozi and

Gretel. The men were the children of my grandmother's brother Herman. He was a sculptor and an atheist who lived in Havana, not on speaking terms with his sons.

"Oh, Margit," Laci said, embracing my mother. "Oh, Margit, I am so happy that you survived. I have always loved you."

"I know, Laci, me too," Mother said, falling into his arms. The rest of us, love-starved, looked on with envy.

"Emma néni," said Pali, "I am very glad to see you."

"You still have the same beautiful eyes, Pali," my grandmother said. "Just like when you were a child. You had no face, only eyes. And no one could resist you. You got whatever you wanted."

"Within limits," said Pali.

"I am not talking about your mother," Grandmother said.

"Enough," Rózsi said loudly. "Anyuka, you will not bring up the past."

"No, no, I didn't mean to," Grandmother said. "I was just remembering how Pali was always my favorite."

"Thanks," Laci said, then laughed falsely.

"Well," said Gretel, "let's unpack what we brought you." What they brought us was lengths of salami and sausage, two roast ducks, hard-boiled eggs, cheeses, *lecsó*, *gulyás*, and strudel of three different flavors: cheese, poppyseed, and cherry.

"I want to make sure that you understand that Géza and Sándor, who will be here soon, also contributed equally," Gretel said.

In a little while, Géza and his wife, Elsie, arrived with Sándor and his wife, Margie. The men were sons of my grandmother's sister Róza, who had died young. Her husband had remarried and his new wife had raised these boys. In consequence, they didn't seem like family. Throughout my life I had heard the lives of these people told as bedtime stories. Mr. Memory Laci. Ask him anything from 600 B.C. to now. The answer will pop out like a telephone token you buy from a machine. Pali was a bed-wetting whiner as a child, and Géza stuttered because his stepmother scared him. This was not what I saw. I saw guilt-ridden, compassionate, middle-aged men, trying to set something right, something they barely grasped and which, in any case, no amount of goodwill could fix, ever.

"I don't suppose you would want to tell us what happened there," Laci said.

"You are right," my mother replied, setting her face to iron. "You know the important things, anyway. My father, Zsiga bácsi, died. My son was murdered. So was Rózsi's son. That is it."

They hung their heads.

"Tell us about life in Amerika," Rózsi said to ease matters. They tried, but they didn't want to reveal themselves either.

Out of nowhere, my grandmother asked, "Are you rich?" General embarrassed laughter followed.

"No, not rich," Pali said, "but not poor. Not if you remember what poor was when I was growing up."

"Remember? I am that poor now," my grandmother said.

"Mother, please," Rózsi said.

"Well, it's true. At their poorest, they had more than we have now. See these shoes?" She pointed to her feet. "They are my only pair. See this dress?" She shook her collar for emphasis and let go with a snap. "I have one other."

"Anyuka, stop," my mother said.

Géza cleared his throat. "I am sorry," he said. "Actually, if you need a few dollars, I could—I mean I will—I want to."

"What are dollars? I don't even know what that means," Grandmother said, lying imperiously.

This conversation was not about goods or money. It was about the loss of her husband and grandsons, her long years of fear and confinement and hunger. It was about her dark resentment at the luck of these relatives who had escaped all that. I could feel us and the Americans lining up on opposing sides of the Ping-Pong net of fortune. We were outnumbered. I thought we'd better let it go.

In the middle of this harmonious, merry celebration, my father appeared at the cabin door. He was as tall as Iván, but much broader, and not nearly as handsome as my mother had said he was. He held in one hand a bunch of wilted white carnations. Laci noticed him first. "Oh, hello, Gyula," he said. "I didn't think we'd see you here. When I called you, you said you might not come."

"Don't be your usual idiotic self," my father said. "I just wanted to get rid of you. You offered to drive me to Brooklyn. You come from Queens. I live on Central Park South. I couldn't figure how you figured that lift, you softbrain."

My father turned to me. "You must be Magda," he said. "These are for you." As I took the flowers, I ordered them: Shed your petals now, not in half an hour. Fly about like flakes of ash in the wake of devastating fire. Do it.

"*Szervusz,* Gyula," my mother said.

"Um, Margit," said my father, "how are you? Do you think I could take Magda to some other place?"

"There is the deck. There are lounges, too. The boat is half empty," my mother said, looking pale and shaken.

"Come with me," my father said, stepping into the corridor. I stood still.

"Go," my mother said. I shook my head. "Go," my mother said again. "He is your father."

As we sat down, my father patted my cheek. "You have grown, Magduska," my father said.

"Eight years have passed," I said.

"You know what happened to me coming here?" he asked.

I shook my head. You got arrested by the Gestapo? The Nyilas made you kneel on the steps of the Danube? The unbribed Hungarian KGB were after you at the border? What happened, dear Father? Let me hear and suffer with you.

"Well, you see, I live in a neighborhood almost like Személynök Utca. This is the waterfront. A wild nowhere. I had to get out of two taxis before one agreed to bring me. At the offer of a good tip. And then, and then we nearly got hit by a big Cadillac. That's a car mostly owned by gangsters. You know, it is really lucky for you that you are not going to live here. You can't imagine the barbarism, the gangsterism that goes on in this city. Someone gets mugged or shot every five minutes. People get run down by buses. Knives are put to their throats. This is a jungle. No one is safe. New York is like a penal colony."

I was astonished to realize that this man really thought that he was brighter than I. He had not set eyes on me since I was five years old, and now he was regarding me as some snot-nosed moron he could scare and manipulate. When he stopped running down New York, I said, most politely, "That bad, huh? Sorry to hear that. It sounds awful. Can't you manage to escape? To some nice place, like a tropical island? Perhaps Kató and her husband could send you an affidavit. I mean, I don't know them, but . . ."

My manner was apologetic, and I kept my voice soft and

bland as pudding. He glanced at me sharply, then looked away. I could see him struggle. He didn't know. Was he dealing with sarcasm, or total dimness? He couldn't make up his mind, and started to boil. I was tempted to give the show away by saying what I really felt about him, but I figured that would open up the playing field and allow him a chance to rebut. I remained silent.

"So how are you doing in school?" he asked.

"School," I repeated. "Well, you see, that's hard to say. Schools closed when the bombing got too frequent and too vigorous. Anyway, I couldn't have attended. I was hiding in a basement. To save my life. After I hid in the attic," I added helpfully. Then, in an obviously courteous attempt to keep the conversation going, I asked, "I don't suppose the gangsters closed down the schools in New York. Or did they?"

By now he had caught on, and he was very angry. He was angry! He had exposed me to mortal danger, to suicidal despair, to irreparable loss, to unending sorrow, and he was angry.

"You are a bright child," he said caustically, "but not very pleasant." The monster creep obviously expected me to come apart at his disapproval.

"I know," I said, without altering my demeanor. "Starving for prolonged periods of time while simultaneously being fed on by packs of lice tends to corrode one's pleasanter side."

He was nonplussed, speechless. Round one was mine. I'd be damned if I'd sit for round two. I stood up. "It's been nice to meet you," I said, bowing. "However, I have other guests on board, and I must not neglect them."

"I am your father," he yelled, rage distorting his face. "You stupid rag! You are out of your mind."

"Quite possibly," I said, holding to my pudding mode. "Lengthy intense suffering does that at times."

I took the long way around the deck to reach my family and relatives. Yes, I had won. Sometimes there is no more tragic defeat.

THE SHIP WAS scheduled to reach Havana in three days. We sailed on bluer, gentler seas. The sun shone more brightly than before. The crew was happy because they had shore leave and Havana was evidently a very hot town for sailors. I was informed of this in pantomime by our waiter.

Anyu was not in a good mood. She seemed jumpy and listless, and picked on me often. I overheard her say to Rózsi, "What do you think will happen to us? What is our fate?"

"Margit, we have always managed," Rózsi replied.

"Yes, but it is different now. Also different for you and me. You have some money; I don't. Kató will help you and Mother. I am not so sure about us. I'll be forty-four in a few days. I don't speak Spanish. I have no salable skills. I have to support a twelve-year-old, and there is no more Joint, no more Zionists, no more official help. I can't imagine how we will live."

I couldn't either. When you join a world, everyone already occupies a place in it. How can you force people to move over and make room for you? Fear, like a creeping vine, wound itself around my heart and squeezed it until I barely breathed.

That night, I had a terrible dream. Iván and I were walking in the Kerepesi Cemetery. It was autumn, perhaps October. I had a tubercular fever.

"Let's play hide and seek," I said.

"No," said Iván, looking sad. "We can't play. From now on, you are on your own."

"Are you leaving me?" I asked, terrified and started to cry.

"I will never leave you," Iván said. "But you are on your own."

"Is that a riddle?" I asked.

"No, it is the truth you know," he said and stepped behind a tombstone.

The Bible has to have it wrong, I thought when I awoke. It says, "The race is not to the swift, nor the battle to the strong." Not always, but often it is. To the very swift, and to the very strong. That is what I must become. An arrow and an anchor.

From this lump? Iván could have done it. But you? Yes, I. For both of us.

The next morning, Mother combed my hair into braids and gave me my sailor dress to wear, made in Paris for the occasion by Margit and Éva, *couturières par excellence*. We crowded onto the railing with everyone else.

Gradually the city, Habana, came into view. It was light, bright, gleaming. It looked like a fairy-tale city. Nothing like Europe, nothing at all. In the distance, under the blazing sun, Morro Castle emerged. I imagined it to be on fire, twirling on the foot of a duck.